# THE EMPIRE OF MIN

# The Empire of Min

*by*

## Edward H. Schafer

*Associate Professor of Oriental Languages*
*University of California*

PUBLISHED FOR THE HARVARD-YENCHING INSTITUTE

## CHARLES E. TUTTLE COMPANY

RUTLAND VERMONT · 1954 · TOKYO JAPAN

Published by the Charles E. Tuttle Company
28 South Main Street, Rutland, Vermont, U.S.A.
1, 1-chome, Kasuga-cho, Bunkyo-ku, Tokyo, Japan

First edition, September, 1954

Printed in Japan by
Kasai Publishing & Printing Co.
Tokyo

# CONTENTS

INTRODUCTION *page* vii

I.   LANDSCAPE 3

II.   COURT 13

III.   HISTORY 31

     THE PREFECT 31

     THE PRINCE 33

     THE KING 35

     THE EMPEROR HUI TSUNG 37

     THE EMPEROR K'ANG TSUNG 42

     THE EMPEROR CHING TSUNG 46

     THE TYRANT (CHU WEN-CHIN) 53

     THE TRIMMER (LI JEN-TA) 57

     THE WARLORD (LIU TS'UNG-HSIAO) 61

IV.   ECONOMY 63

     PRODUCE AND TRIBUTE 63

     COURT EXPENDITURES AND TAXATION 70

     CURRENCY 74

     FOREIGN TRADE 75

     POPULATION CHANGES 78

V.   ARTS                                                     *page* 80

   ARCHITECTURE                                                  80

   MISCELLANEOUS ARTS                                            85

   LITERATURE                                                    87


VI.   RELIGION                                                   90

   GENERAL                                                       90

   BUDDHISM                                                      91

   TAOISM                                                        96

   OFFICIAL CULT                                                100

   MANICHAEISM                                                  102

   FOLKLORE AND POPULAR RELIGION                                102


   APPENDICES                                                   111

      MAP OF MIN                                                113

      TABLE A.   THE WANG DYNASTY OF MIN                        114

      TABLE B.   ORTHODOX AND MIN REIGN TITLES                  115


   BASIC SOURCES                                                117


   INDEX                                                        123

# INTRODUCTION

THE tenth century has been one of the most neglected eras in Chinese history. In particular, that part of it known to traditional historiography as the "Five Dynasties" has received scant treatment by Chinese and non-Chinese scholars alike. The poverty of accessible material in European languages on this complex and important field for historical and cultural investigations is readily appreciated after a glance at such bibliographical sources as the catalogue of the library of the Harvard-Yenching Institute, Henri Cordier's *Bibliotheca Sinica*, or especially at those sections in any general history of China which purport to cover the period. The neglect of this era is partly explained by the greater attraction the study of dynasties ruling over a unified China offers, and partly by the relative scarcity of source materials in Chinese. But the tenth century deserves the attention of historians of civilization in the Far East for the purpose of revealing the continuous development of events and institutions from the late T'ang period into the early Sung. The heavy black line which divides T'ang from Liang on our chronological charts is a more imaginary line than the equator. A case in point: such offices as that of *Chieh-tu-shih* 節度使, which I translate "Legate,"[1] or of *Shu-mi-shih* 樞密使, for which I prefer "Chancellor,"[2] had obscure origins in the T'ang dynasty, and yet

---

[1] See *T'ang shu* 50.3752a (all page references are to the K'ai-ming edition of the *Twenty-five Histories*) for a sketch of the evolution of this title. By the beginning of the tenth century, to hold the legateship meant to hold the supreme military and civil authority in a province.

[2] I use Wittfogel's translation. Originally a eunuch empowered to transmit petitions to the Emperor, the *Shu-mi-shih* became the highest administrative office in many of the tenth-century states, and was no longer restricted to eunuchs. The significance of the title may best be appreciated by a study of the biographies of its incumbents in this period. But see also *Wu Tai shih* 24.4416d, and especially *Wen-hsien t'ung-k'ao* (Commercial Press edition of Wang Yün-wu, Shanghai, 1935) 58.523.

the holders of these dignities became, in a majority of cases, the real potentates of China before the close of that dynasty, and they were of central importance in the Five Dynasties' era. The student of political institutions in the Far East will understand very little indeed if he watches the development of these offices up to the year 907, and ignores them after that. Or looking ahead into history, some important elements of the plastic and literary arts of the Sung period, which we are inclined to think of vaguely as springing full-fledged from the inhumanly brilliant minds of eleventh-century geniuses, were in fact initiated and given their significant forms in the Five Dynasties. An example of this is the rectilinear "architectural" style of painting, *chieh-hua* 界畫, well-known from the hands of Sung and later painters, but which was created in the Five Dynasties' period by Kuo Chung-shu 郭忠恕.[3]

A conscientious search of source materials in western languages will turn up a few articles on the Wu Tai period. Most of these are brief. The only complete historical sketch of the period which I have seen is by Ch. Piton in *China Review* 10(1881-82).240-259, under the title, "A Page in the History of China, a Sketch of the period commonly called the 'Five Dynasties.'" This gives a conventional picture of political events and episodes in the lives of the members of ruling families based on such compilations as the *T'ung-chien kang-mu*—but even this much is unknown to most students of China.

In recent years, fortunately, this gap in our knowledge has been partially filled by the labors of Wolfram Eberhard, whose contributions to the sociology and political economy of North China during the tenth century deserve high commendation. I mention only two of his titles: "The composition of the leading political group during the 'Five Dynasties,'" in *Asiatische Studien* 1/2(1947).19-28, and "Some sociological remarks on the system of provincial administration during the period of the Five Dynasties," in *Studia Serica* 7(1948).1-18. Equally important are his studies of the non-Chinese peoples of the north in this period, particularly the Sha-t'o Turks.

Yet the concept of the orthodox transmission of the Mandate of Heaven has made the study of the Northern Dynasties appear comparatively thoroughgoing when compared with the almost total neglect of the very real kingdoms of Central and South China, whose claims of legitimacy have not been recognized by the official historiographers of the later empire. It is to one of these practically unknown states, often passed over without a word or mentioned in a brief paragraph, in standard histories, that I have

---

[3]   See Osvald Siren, *A History of Early Chinese Painting* (London, 1933) 1.132.

devoted the present study.   But before proceeding to matters directly concerned with the empire of Min, I wish to pay my respects to those scholars
who have preceded me off the beaten track into the colorful realms which
almost disappeared from the view of history under the heel of the Sung
conqueror.   I may have missed some, and to them I apologize.   I have
noted the work of E. H. Bowra, whose article, "The Liu Family, or Canton
during the Period of the Five Dynasties" in *China Review* (1873).316-322,
gives a sketch of the history of the dynasty which for fifty-five years enjoyed
a virtual monopoly of the opulent trade of Southern Asia and its surround-
ing waters.   Of much greater scholarly import is the fine study by Edouard
Chavannes, "Le royaume de Wou et de Yue" in *T'oung Pao*, Volume 17.
Finally, the archaeologists and historians who have presented us with the
tomb of Wang Chien 王建, sovereign of the kingdom of Shu in Ssu-
ch'uan, a refuge of artists and poets in the tenth century, deserve our
homage for a magnificent discovery.[4]   Space does not permit that I mention
here all of the scholars in China itself who have been interested in piecing
together a picture of these so-called Ten Kingdoms out of the refuse of
history.   I must, however, honor my predecessor in the study of tenth
century Fukien, Wei Ying-ch'i 魏應麒, who began a detailed investigation
of the civilization of that province under the rule of the Wang family,
which he published in the *Weekly* of the National Sun Yat-sen University
Philological and Historical Research Center under the title *Wu Tai Min
shih k'ao chih i* 五代閩史稿之一.[5] This introductory paper is wholly concerned with religion and mythology in the Min empire, the greater part
of it being devoted to a catalogue of religious structures in Fukien, with
the dates of their erection and other pertinent facts.   Less bulky, but not
less important, is the same author's analysis of the traditions current at the
beginning of the tenth century, concerned with the inevitability of the
imperial rule of the Wang clan, and the general metaphysics underlying
this belief.   Some of this material I shall have occasion to quote in my own
study of Min history, but I shall not hope to rival Mr. Wei in completeness
—due in part to the inaccessibility to me of some sources which were available
to that scholar.   I have the courage to continue an undertaking already
so well begun, only because I do not know that Mr. Wei has continued his
draft history, and because a study of the same subject in the English language
is desirable.

As for primary sources, the single reference which should provide,

---

[4]   Reports will be found in *HJAS* 8 (1944-45).235-240 and *Archives of the Chinese
Art Society of America* 2 (1947).11-20.
[5]   *Kuo-li Chung-shan Ta-hsueh yü-yen li-shih-hsüeh yen-chiu-so chou-k'an* 國立中山大學語
言歷史學研究所週刊, several issues in 1929.

and in the case of many studies of Chinese history has in fact furnished most of the useful subject matter to the investigator is, of course, the standard set of dynastic histories. This becomes, in the case of the Ten Kingdoms of the tenth century, a reference of secondary value. There is an important exception to this generalization: personages whose lives were closely interwoven with the fortunes of the last rulers of the T'ang dynasty or of the founder of the Sung dynasty receive adequate biographical treatment, though more often in the *T'ang shu* or *Sung shih* than in the *Wu Tai shih*. But although the rulers of the orthodox empires of the Yellow River basin are rather fully treated in the two *Histories of the Five Dynasties*, along with the men historically fortunate enough to have lived in the north at this time, the Emperors of the southern states (as many of these rulers styled themselves) are given only the sketchiest treatment, and much contempt. Of the two, the *Hsin Wu Tai shih* of Ou-yang Hsiu is the more adequate when it comes to these secessionist kingdoms, whatever may be the other failings of that work *vis-a-vis* its rival compendium. Yet even this book has been criticized for its inadequate treatment of these states by the early Ch'ing author of the *Springs and Autumns of the Ten Kingdoms* (十國春秋), Wu Jen-ch'en 吳任臣. It contains several glaring errors of fact, as when Ou-yang Hsiu writes of a certain Prince, Wang Chi-kung, as son of the second Emperor of Min, although abundant evidence shows that he was in fact his younger brother.

The *Chiu Wu Tai shih* of Hsüeh Chü-cheng emphasizes the illegitimacy of these states, whose administrative and noble titles are regularly prefaced by the term *wei* 偽 "counterfeit." Moreover the editor disdains to employ the chronologies adopted in those lands, using the reign titles of the Emperors of the Five Dynasties as temporal reference points. While Ou-yang Hsiu gives a separate chapter to each of the Ten Kingdoms (*chüan* 61-70), and also a synoptic chronological table (*chüan* 71), Hsüeh Chü-cheng compresses his accounts of the sovereigns of these kingdoms into a chapter devoted to "Hereditary Lines" (世襲列傳 2, *chüan* 133), and three chapters concerned with "Usurpers" (僭偽列傳 1-3, *chüan* 134-136). It should be emphasized that neither of the two official histories of this period contains monographic material (志) on the institutions of the Ten Kingdoms. It is relatively easy to write a superficial political history, compared with the immense difficulty of gleaning random bits of information from a multitude of sources to produce a partial picture of the social, economic and cultural life of these areas, which at best must be full of lacunae and uncertainties.

But far outweighing either of the two dynastic histories in the mass of information provided about the kingdoms of the south in the tenth

century is that eminently readable compilation, the *Tzu-chih t'ung-chien*
of Ssu-ma Kuang. A contemporary of Ou-yang Hsiu, Ssu-ma Kuang far
outdid the former in the impartiality with which he treated the various
places and personalities of China in this era. His monumental work is
crowded with detail about events in every subdivision of the empire, making
it possible to survey orthodox and unorthodox states alike with great
objectivity. The *Tzu-chih t'ung-chien* has been the important single source
for my own examination of the history of Fukien in the tenth century,
especially in the field of political and diplomatic history.

For the rest, there is little except data set down as miscellany in various
small books—anecdotes about the foibles of eminent men, much of it clearly
intended to reveal the frivolity or immorality of sovereigns who presumed
to challenge the universal authority of the rulers of the north. Nonetheless,
such sources provide considerable material on court festivals, the arts,
religious life, dialect words for common objects, country customs, folklore
and many other things perhaps more deserving of study than the deeds
of murderous courtiers and virtuous advisers. In addition to this body
of data, there is the epigraphic material. This is not too abundant, and
for the most part not observable at first hand, being preserved in the
transcriptions of scholars who lived between the tenth and twentieth centuries, but it cannot be neglected, especially for supplementary facts about
the titles and activities of important statesmen. The virtual absence of
contemporary histories of the tenth-century states written by their own his-
toriographic bureaus has been in part explained by Ma Ling in his own
preface to his *Book of Southern T'ang*. He states that the governments
of the Ten Kingdoms did in fact have their official historians, and cites as
an example of their common fate, the situation in Southern T'ang, where,
under the moral pressure of the new Sung empire, and presumably for
more practical reasons too, the high-minded historians burned their own
drafts.

The easiest way to write a cultural and political history of the empire
of Min for readers of English would be simply to make a translation of
part of the *Shih-kuo ch'un-ch'iu* of Wu Jen-ch'en (A.D. 1628-89?). This
work, by the learned mathematician who did the calendrical section of the
*Ming shih*, is in 114 chapters, supplemented by two chapters of new material
compiled by Chou Ang  周昂. Wu Jen-ch'en cites, in his preface, as
precedent for his labors the earlier composition of such historical supple-
ments as the *Springs and Autumns of the Sixteen Kingdoms*. These claim
to supply the deficiencies of contemporary standard histories with regard
to the autonomous "barbarian" states holding the north of China after the
initial disintegration of the Chin  晉 empire. Valuable as Wu Jen-ch'en's

work is, there remains the difficulty of checking his sources, an important point since he wrote six centuries after the events he describes. Therefore, although the *Shih-kuo ch'un-ch'iu* is frequently cited by recent writers as a primary and infallible source, I hesitate to use material from it, however attractive, unless it can be checked elsewhere.

The present study does not pretend to exhaust every detail of the civilization of tenth-century Fukien. It is a preliminary investigation, doubtless full of faults. But it is hoped that it will serve to indicate what can be done in future studies of a whole culture.

# THE EMPIRE OF MIN

# I

# LANDSCAPE

T HE climatically intermediate position of Fukien, tropical or semitropical for the most part, merging with temperate regions in the north and northwest, permits it to support a mixed flora and fauna, sharing some types with the north, some with the south. By way of sketching the physical background for the events described in this study, I record here the plants and animals of that province specifically mentioned in the writings of contemporaries, particularly by the poets of the Min empire. These are the things which impressed their imaginations:[6] in settled places were such handsome trees as the plum (梅 and 李), the red plum (紅梅), the peach (桃),[7] the cassia (桂), the banana (蕉), the lichee (荔枝)[8] and the apricot (杏). In the uplands, or about temples, were numerous conifers of various genera (collectively 松柏). The poets mention the pagoda tree (槐, *Sophora japonica*), the weeping willow (柳, *Salix babylonica*), the catalpa (梓, *Catalpa ovata*), the paulownia (桐, *Paulownia tomentosa*) and the sandalwood (檀, *Santalum album*). Flowers were abundant everywhere: the peony (牡丹, *Paeonia moutan*),[9] the herbaceous peony (芍藥, *Paeonia albiflora*), many kinds of roses (玫瑰 and

---

⁶ See *ChWTS*, chapters on Min, *passim*. For good accounts of the physical and human geography of Fukien, see especially G. B. Cressey, *China's Geographic Foundations* (New York and London, 1934) pp. 10, 12, 34, 71, 121, 334-6, 339-41, 346-7 and Floy Hurlbut, *The Fukienese, A Study in Human Geography* (Ph. D. Dissertation, University of Nebraska, May 1930. Privately published in 1939).

⁷ The poet Han Wo 韓偓 dwelt at a village called "Peach Forest," on a creek of the same name (桃林溪). *ChWTS* 75.1139. This was near Ch'üan Prefecture.

⁸ Both Han Wo and Hsü Yin 徐寅 wrote poems in praise of the lichee, the glory of the province. Han Wo has a set of three which he wrote in 906, the year of his arrival in Fu, praising the beauty of the trees in extravagant language. *ChWTS* 78.1180-1.

⁹ Very frequent in the poems of Hsü Yin.

薔薇),[10] orchids (蘭), hibiscus ([木] 槿花, *Hibiscus syriacus,* and 木芙蓉 *Hibiscus mutabilis*), chrysanthemums (菊),[11] "cockscombs" (雞冠, *Celosia cristata*),[12] water lilies and lotuses (荷 and 蓮).

Better known, however, to the general reader than the writings of the tenth-century poets of Min are those of Chiang Yen 江淹 of the sixth century, who has left a set of *Fifteen Panegyrics* on the flora of Min (閩中草木頌十五首).[13]  Among the fifteen plants which he celebrates as particularly worthy of remembrance is the camphor tree (豫章, *Cinnamomum camphorum*), one of the most important forest trees of Fukien.  The *Sou-shen chi* 搜神記[14] mentions the great camphor trees at Chien-an in the Three Kingdoms period, and the botanist Li Shih-chen 李時珍 gives Chang Prefecture as a major source of camphor, adding that the substance resembles "dragon-brain" (龍腦).  This raises the question of whether or not the *lung-nao* sent to the north as tribute by the rulers of Min was the genuine imported article (*Dryobalanops*) or merely local camphor.[15]  Other local flora which dominated the Min landscape and were lauded by Chiang Yen were the coir palm (栟櫚, *Chamaerops excelsa*); the Cunninghamia (the so-called "Foochow Fir"), chief source of timber in modern times (杉, *Cunninghamia sinensis*); the tamarisk (檉, *Tamarix chinensis*); the wax myrtle (楊梅, *Myrica rubra*); the magnolia (木蓮, *Magnolia obovata*); the sweet flag (石菖蒲, *Acorus sp.*); the yam (薯蕷, *Dioscorea batatas*).  Two other trees certain to attract literary notice in ancient as in modern Fukien are the honey locust (皂莢, *Gleditschia japonica*), reported in a tenth-century courtyard at Ch'üan Prefecture,[16] and the red-flowered crab apple (海棠, *Pyrus spectabilis*).[17]

The fauna of the region receives less attention from the poets, but monkeys are fairly frequent,[18] and bears have been mentioned.  There is also evidence of elephants in Fukien in the tenth century: this animal was still abundant in Eastern Kuang-tung in the ninth century—herds were

[10]  Han Wo has a poem, written at Sha District in 909, entitled "Viewing the roses in the rain at Sha District on Cold-food Day." It reads, "Everywhere I encounter roses . . ." *ChWTS* 75.1146.

[11]  This plant does better in the north.

[12]  Originally from India. Used as a garden flower in China.  See G. A. Stuart, *Chinese Materia Medica* (Shanghai, 1911) 101.

[13]  *Chiang Wen-t'ung chi* 江文通集 (*SPPY*) 3.21b-23a.

[14]  18.120 (*TSCC*).

[15]  See Chapter on Economy, below.

[16]  Hsü Hsüan 徐鉉, *Chi-shen lu* 稽神錄 (*TSCC*) 5.46.

[17]  Ch'en Ssu 陳思, *Hai-t'ang p'u* 海棠譜 (*TSCC*) a.4.  A thirteenth-century writer citing an early reference.

[18]  See for instance the poem of Hsü Yin which refers to the monkeys of the Wu-i Mountains, *ChWTS* 82.1240.

seen at the Prefecture of Ch'ao 潮, then located on the Fukien border.[19]
Even in the twelfth century, in 1171, several hundred of the beasts trampled
autumn crops there.[20]  Elephants were also frequently seen in the Yangtze
basin in the tenth century.[21]  It is almost beyond question, then, that these
animals existed in the uplands of Fukien during the Min dynasty, but the
Fukienese did not recruit them into their army, as was done by the sovereigns
of Southern Han.[22]  Among other large mammals known in tenth century
Fukien, the most notable was the tiger.  The Ming dynasty *Tiger Compendium* (虎薈) reports tigers at Chang Prefecture in the reign of Sung
Jen Tsung (1023-56), and at Fu Prefecture in the late eighth century.[23]
These dates straddle our period—certainly the carnivore occupied Fukien
continuously as it is still there.  More than one kind of deer made Min its
habitat.  The doubtful *ching* 麞 will be observed below, under Economy.
To this, if not an error in the text, must be added two other genera.  Chan
Tun-jen 詹敦仁, who lived during Later Chou, in his *Essay on the founding
of An-ch'i District in Ch'üan Prefecture*,[24] when describing the bounties of
nature in that region, writes that the 麞 and the 麈 are native to it.  The
*chang* is a variety of musk-deer, specifically *Moschus chinloo*.  *Chu* is
another name for *mi* 麋.[25]  The latter word is now generally used for the
elk or moose, but formerly designated the rare genus *Elaphurus,* a native of
South China, adapted to living in marshy ground.  Indeed the dictionary
*Tz'u-hai* quotes *Chu-yeh-t'ing tsa-chi* 竹葉亭雜記 to the effect that *"chu is
the modern ssu-pu-hsiang,"* the latter being identified by a modern zoological
dictionary as *Elaphurus.*  As for the most abundant of the large native
fauna, the humans of Fukien were regarded by outsiders as "stubborn,
contentious, and difficult to manage."[26]

The actual appearance of the capital of the Emperors of Min can be
reconstructed only partially and with considerable difficulty.  One reason for
this has been stated in the *Yü-ti chi-sheng*: "When the Ch'ien clan
capitulated (內附),[27] they [i.e., the architectural monuments of the Min

[19]  Liu Hsün 劉恂, *Ling-piao lu-i* 嶺表錄異 1.8a.

[20]  *Wen-hsien t'ung-k'ao* 311.2438.

[21]  E.g., *SS* 1.4498a, c, and *Wen-hsien t'ung-k'ao* 311.2438.

[22]  See *SS* 481.5699b.

[23]  Ch'en Chi-ju 陳繼儒, *Hu hui* (*TSCC*) 4.47 and 4.55.

[24]  泉州初建安溪縣記, reproduced in *T'u-shu chi-ch'eng* 圖書集成 " Chih-fang tien " 職
方典 1051.

[25]  *Shuo wen.*

[26]  Ch'en Shih-tao 陳師道, *Hou-shan t'an-ts'ung* 後山談叢 (*TSCC*) 4.33.  An eleventh-
century work which includes anecdotal material on the Five Dynasties period.

[27]  I.e., when the rulers of Wu-yüeh, who held Fu-chou from 947, turned their
territory over to the Sung government.

rulers] were razed without exception; only the remains of one pavilion facing the yamen have still survived down to the present."[28]   Therefore the Sung topographers had little to go on, and modern students have even less.   Nonetheless it is possible to outline some of the features of the capital, even though their relative positions often remain obscure.

The city, as it increased in size during various dynasties, had built newer and more extensive walls, each enclosing the remains of the others.   The oldest was the so-called *tzu-ch'eng* ("minor wall" 子城), originally built in the third century[29] and improved during the T'ang dynasty.[30]   In A.D. 901, Wang Shen-chih built an outer wall, called the *lo-ch'eng* ("enveloping(?) wall" 羅城), which became the city's major rampart.   A few years later, sections of *chia-ch'eng* ("hemming walls" 夾城) were constructed south and north of this.   These were also called *yüeh-ch'eng* ("lunar walls" 月城).[31] Of the gates frequently mentioned in contemporary texts, it is not always possible to tell which of the various walls they stood in, but the most important were probably in the Enveloping Wall.   There were gates opening to the four cardinal directions, and others in between.[32]   In three directions the wall faced affluents of the Min River.   Only the North Gate almost certainly opened on the countryside.

Of the four chief gates, the most important strategically was the West Gate, and it was against this that attackers of the city hurled most of their troops.   When Wang Yen-ping came from Chien Prefecture to join Yen-chün in an attack on Yen-han (January 927), he attacked the West Gate, and finally entered the city by scaling the wall.[33]   Again when Yen-ping brought his fleet from Chien in 931, this time against his half brother Yen-

---

[28]   *YTCS* 128.14a.

[29]   See map in Wang Ying-shan 王應山, *Min tu chi* 閩都記, written 1612, reprint of 1831.

[30]   *FCTC2* 6.1b.

[31]   *FCTC2* 6.1b gives the date of construction as 909, but *Min tu chi* has 907 on its map of this wall.

[32]   According to *FCTC2* 62.1b, the names of the gates in the original *tzu-che'ng* were K'ang-ta'i 康泰, I-hsing 宜興, Feng-lo 豐樂, An-ting 安定, Ch'ing-t'ai 清泰 and Hu-chieh 虎節; those in the *lo-ch'eng* were Yung-an 永安, Li-she 利涉, Hai-yen 海晏, An-shan 安善, T'ung-chin 通津 and Ch'ing-yüan 清遠. According to *FCTC1* 17.4b, the K'ang-t'ai (on the east) and An-ting (here given as Ting-an, on the southeast) were constructed by Wang Shen-chih.   Yung-an was north, Li-she was south, Hai-yen was east, An-shan was northwest, T'ung-chin was southeast, Ch'ing-yüan was southwest.   The same source adds a Yen-yüan 延遠 Gate on the northeast, but gives none for the west.

[33]   *TCTC* 275.13a.   These personages will be identified, and these events more fully described later, under Court and History.   The main city gates are referred to by directional terms like "East" or "West" in *TCTC*, rather than by the designations preserved in the gazetteers.

chün, he directed his main assault against the West Gate, while sending his son, Chi-hsiung, against the East Gate.[34]   On this occasion, Chi-hsiung was opposed by Wang Jen-ta 王仁達, Commander of Galleons (樓船指揮使), so that we must assume water flowing close to the East Gate as well as the West.[35]   One version of this battle states that Yen-ping himself was killed in his ship on the Nan-t'ai River 南臺江,[36] which was a part of the Min River flowing south of the city.[37]   Later, in 940, Yen-hsi built another wall west of Fu Prefecture as added protection against Yen-cheng.[38]   When the latter's deputy attacked the city in May 943, we are told that he "penetrated its western rampart," which was doubtless this outer wall, but was finally defeated and driven away.[39]   Still later, in September 946, the Southern T'ang forces, after capturing Chien Prefecture from Yen-cheng, attacked Fu, and succeeded in taking the "outer wall." This too may refer to the wall of Yen-hsi west of the city.[40]   Finally the soldiers of T'ang were led by a traitor, via the Mountain of the Horse-herds (馬牧山),[41] to the bridge leading to the Shan-hua Gate 善化門, which seems to have been the special name of one of the western gates of the capital.[42]

We have seen that Wang Chi-hsiung was opposed at the East Gate by a fleet of warships, and thus may infer that it too must have been accessible from the Min River. Such a belief is borne out by the events of 945, when Yen-cheng directed one of his naval attacks against the East

[34]   There is some discrepancy in the texts on this.   *TCTC* has "East Gate," but *WTS* says Chi-hsiung attacked the South Gate.

[35]   *TCTC* 277.12a-b.   The map of the city reproduced in *Min tu chi* shows a stream around the city wall on all sides except the north, connecting with the West and East Lakes.   It must also have been directly connected with the Min River.

[36]   *WKKS* b.6b.   The standard version of Yen-ping's death relates that he was captured by soldiers as he was borne away from the conflict in a grain measure and was later decapitated.   *TCTC* 277.12-13a.

[37]   See *FCTC1* 9.23b.   The full course of the Nan-t'ai is described in Ch'i Chao-nan 齊召南, *Min-chiang chu-shui pien* 閩江諸水編 (edit. of *Hsiao-fang-hu-chai yü-ti ts'ung-ch'ao* 小方壺齋輿地叢鈔) 3a.   It is told that a former King of Yüeh once caught a white dragon fishing in this river.   See *YTCS* 128.13b and *T'ai-p'ing huan-yü chi* 太平寰宇記 100.4a.   For this reason it was also once called the Tiao-lung River 釣龍江. *Min-hsien hsiang-t'u chih* 閩縣鄉土志 305a.

[38]   *TCTC* 282.12a.

[39]   *TCTC* 283.11a.

[40]   *TCTC* 285.5b.   *FCTC2* 6.1b states that the "Hemming (or Lunar) Walls" were extended east and west by Wu-yüeh, but this took place later.

[41]   A western spur of the Mountains of the King of Yüeh (越王山), themselves north of the city.   See *FCTC1* 5.2a.

[42]   *TCTC* 285.9b.   It is strange that no gate by this name is given in the catalogues of *FCTC1* and *FCTC2*.   See n. 32.

Gate.[43]   This gate, or one near it, bore the name Tung-wu, "Eastern
Military" (東武門), for when the army of Wu-yüeh coming by way of the
Estuary of Fishnets (罾浦), entered the prefecture in December 946 on the
invitation of Li Jen-ta, to support him against the threat of Southern T'ang,
their progress was barred by the T'ang soldiery, who had obtained the
occupation of the East Gate.[44]

Of the South Gate we hear less, and historical records do not mention
its special name.   However, a second fleet from Wu-yüeh, arrived at Fu in
April 947, beached at the Estuary of White Shrimps (白蝦浦), attacking
the T'ang army in conjunction with a sortie from the capital itself, and
crushed the T'ang forces "south of the city."   It would appear that although
the South Gate could be approached by water, there was some difficult
terrain to cover between the river and the city wall.   The Wu-yüeh marines
had trouble disembarking in the mud, even though covered by bamboo
mats, in the face of the T'ang archery stationed between them and the city.[45]

I have only two references to the North Gate, one for the summer of
945 when the armies defending Fu against Yen-cheng encamped by the
North and West Gates,[46] and again for 939, when Wang Chi-p'eng and
his family fled from the capital through the North Gate to find refuge in
the Sterculia Range (梧桐嶺).[47]   In the latter case, since the texts make
no reference to the royal family's making a voyage in boats, it may be
presumed that they traveled overland, and that then, as now, the prefectural
city of Fu was not completely surrounded by water.

Within the city proper were other gateways.   The names of six were
known in Sung times:   Tzu-ch'en 紫宸, Ch'i-sheng 啓聖, Ying-t'ien 應天,
Tung-ch'ing 東青, An-t'ai 安泰 and Chin-te 金德.[48]   These were the
entrances to the imperial enclosure itself, a city within a city.   The Tzu-ch'en
Gate was named in imitation of a gate by the same name in Ch'ang-an
under the T'ang Emperors.   It was outside this gate that the luckless Yen-
han concluded his reign under the executioner's sword.[49]   The Ch'i-sheng
Gate was the scene of the attack on the palace by the partisans of Li Fang
in 935.[50]   At this time it and the Ying-t'ien Gate were burned by the rebels.

43   TCTC 284.16b.

44   TCTC 285.12a.

45   TCTC 286.13b.

46   TCTC 284.16a-b.

47   TCTC 282.5a-b, 6a-b, and CFWC.   The range was in Hou-kuan District 侯官縣.
See FCTC1 5.18a.   Fu Prefecture was divided into a number of districts, two of which
comprised the prefectural city, Hou-kuan on the west and Min on the east.

48   YTCS 128.14a.   " Metal Virtue " refers to the westerly principle.

49   TCTC 275.13a, and commentary of Hu San-hsing.

50   TCTC 278.16a-b, 279.21a-b, and WTS describe this and other incidents at this gate.

The map of the city in *Min tu chi* shows the Tzu-ch'en Gate as the main entrance to the imperial city, flanked by the Ch'i-sheng and Ying-t'ien Gates. The An-t'ai and Chin-te Gates are shown isolated from any wall, standing inside the east and west entrances through the city wall. *Min tu chi* also states that the Chen-Min Terrace 鎮閩臺 in the center of the city was erected by the Min dynasty, but I have not seen it mentioned in contemporary sources.[51] I am unable to locate the position of the Tung-ch'ing Gate, though it must have been somewhere in the east judging from its name.

The great marketplace of the city was called "The Market of Wu-chu" (無諸市), so named after the famous king of this land who lost his realm to the omnipotent forces of Ch'in Shih Huang-ti. Here the decapitated head of Yen-ping was exposed by his vindictive brother, the future Emperor Hui Tsung.[52]

The chief port of the city is called simply "The Sea Gate" (海門) in the single reference I have to it. This was the place of disembarkation of the ambassadors from T'ang in 933, and Hu San-hsing places it south of the city on the coast, near Fu-ch'ing District 福清縣.[53] Closer to the capital was a harbor constructed in the last years of the T'ang dynasty by Wang Shen-chih. This was at the former Yellow Point (黃崎) in the District of Min, a barrier to shipping because of its dangerous rocks and heavy breakers. The obstruction is said to have been destroyed in a great storm, after which the place was converted into an artificial harbor by Shen-chih, and named "Sweet Pear Harbor" (甘棠港).[54]

Several water parks owe their origin, or at least their redecoration, to the Min rulers. One such was the "Stream of Mulberries of Lustration" (禊桑溪),[55] beautified by Wang Yen-chün for the delectation of his lady, Golden Phoenix.[56] Also reconstructed by Yen-chün, though in existence in the Chin dynasty, was the West Lake, located about two *li* west of the district seat of Min.[57] This too was a favorite pleasure haunt of his beautiful

---

[51] *Min tu chi* 3.1a. According to *FCTC*1 17.5a, it was built in 953. The Terrace played the role of a symbolic sacred mountain guarding Min.

[52] *WKKS* b.6b. *TCTC* 277.13a has Yen-ping executed in the marketplace, but *WKKS*, as already noted, makes him meet his death in his flagship. See *Han shu* 95.0604d for King Wu-chu.

[53] *TCTC* 278.5a.

[54] *WTS* and *YTCS* 128.10a. Strangely, the *Ming i-t'ung chih* 明一統志 78.36a has moved the harbor to the remote northeastern part of the province, later Fu-ning-fu 福寧府.

[55] 禊 was originally a ceremony of exorcism by aspersing, carried out on a river bank, but already in the Han dynasty was tending to become a formal holiday without special religious meaning. See *Shih chi* 49.0166b.

[56] *CFWC.*

[57] *YTCS* 128.8a-b, *Min tu chi* 15-1a.

concubine, who, in one of her songs, describes it as being red with lotuses.[58] On the occasion of the summer festival of Tuan-yang 端陽 (fifth of the fifth month), Yen-chün placed in this lake dozens of "festooned catamarans" (綵舫), each manned by twenty or thirty palace girls. The verses of Golden Phoenix tell us that there was also a South Lake, the scene of contests among these pleasure boats. Both lakes had a central island of which the lady wrote: "Green rushes and purple water-peppers cover their central islets."[59] Further from the city proper was "Dipped Moon Pond" (蘸月池), at the side of "Snowy Peak" (雪峰). Here an old cunninghamia,[60] said to have been planted by Shen-chih himself, still survived in the Sung dynasty.[61]

Less information about the Prefecture of Chien is available for this period. We know, however, that the city was surrounded by a wall, which faced water on at least two sides. When Yen-hsi sent troops to attack Yen-cheng there in 940, the soldiers west and south of the city wall found themselves cut off from their objective by water, and turned to burning the houses of the people who were so unfortunate as to dwell outside the wall.[62] The situation north of the city is obscure, but apparently there was no river there. In the war mentioned above, part of Yen-hsi's host was defeated at "Tea Mountain" (茶山) north of Chien, doubtless by a sortie from the city itself.[63] The final victory followed another sally, whose success depended on the sense of security felt by the invaders across the river. Yen-cheng sent out daredevils by night to ford the stream and invade the camp of the besiegers.[64] Although saved from his brother on this occasion Yen-cheng took measures to increase his security against future attacks, and in 941, the following year, built another wall, twenty *li* in circumference,[65] around the prefectural city.

It is worth noting that although the Min River is hardly navigable for large vessels, it served to carry the fleets of Chien Prefecture to the mouth of the river on several occasions. Thus, when Yen-ping came to Fu Prefecture to join his adopted brother in an attack on King Yen-han, "having gone with the current, he arrived first."[66] The point is that Yen-chün's

---

[58] *CFWC.* Her poems appear in *ChWTS* 87.1329.

[59] *CFWC.*

[60] 杉, a term commonly applied to the cryptomeria, but in Fukien more usually used for the forest tree, cunninghamia. See Stuart, *op. cit.* 134.

[61] *YTCS* 128.12b. The text has "Cloudy Peak" (雲峰), but I believe this to be an error for "Snowy Peak."

[62] *TCTC* 282.9a-b.

[63] *Ibid.* This was a famous tea growing area; see *YTCS* 129.6b.

[64] *TCTC* 292.9b.

[65] *TCTC* 282.14a.

[66] *TCTC* 275.12b-13a. Hu San-hsing comments on this passage thus: "Following

ships had to come by sea from Ch'üan Prefecture. Yen-ping later attacked Yen-chün himself, sending a naval force down the river.[67] It is also clear that warships were sent upstream, for we read that in 942 Yen-cheng prepared a fleet to repulse the troops sent against him from Fu Prefecture.[68] It is possible that this involved an amphibious operation, but it seems more likely that a ship-to-ship action was envisaged by Yen-cheng. The latter, for his part, sent a thousand battleships against Fu in January 945.[69] It is not possible to determine the size of these "battleships," but they probably were not large, in view of the hazards of the journey between Chien and Fu.

Ch'üan Prefecture, although already quite populous, was at this time of minor importance compared with Fu and Chien, and contemporary accounts say little of its physical makeup. A wall (*tzu-ch'eng* 子城) was built by Shen-chih early in the tenth century, with gates named Hsing-ch'un 行春, Ch'ung-yang 崇陽, Su-ch'ing 肅清 and Ch'üan-shan 泉山, in the east, south, west and north respectively. Walls enclosing more space were constructed by Liu Ts'ung-hsiao, who succeeded to the hegemony of Southern Fukien after the collapse of the Wang family.[70] Indeed, most tenth-century construction work in Ch'üan was the work of the warlord Liu,[71] although some buildings preserve the memory of members of the Wang tribe, for instance, the Fa-yün Temple (法雲寺) built by Wang Yen-pin, a prefect.[72]

It would be fruitless to enumerate all the mountains of Fukien, and it is a task deserving a special monograph to attempt to discover what names were current for them in the tenth century. A few are intimately connected with the names of the Min rulers and hence deserve mention. From the capital city a peak, situated in the District of Hou-kuan, was visible which under the summer moon gave a strong impression of being snow-covered. It

the current from Chien Stream 建溪 and descending eastward to Fu Prefecture, the river takes a winding course for several hundred *li*, and the current is very swift. A light boat starting at dawn will arrive in the evening. [The statement in the] *Chiu-yü chih* 九域志 that it is 520 *li* from Chien Prefecture southeast to Fu Prefecture presumably refers to the land route."

[67] *TCTC* 277.12a-b.

[68] *TCTC* 283.4a-b.

[69] *TCTC* 284.8b.

[70] *FCTC2* 6.1b.

[71] See *Ch'üan-chou-fu chih* 泉州府志, *passim*.

[72] Not to be confused with Yen-ping. *Ch'üan-chou-fu chih* 16.29b. The text has 廷 for 延. The temple bore a gateway inscription, "Roost in Seclusion" (樓隱). Cf. the phrase *chu yin* 居隱 in Yang Hsüan-chih 楊衒之, *Lo-yang ch'ieh-lan chi* 洛陽伽藍記 (*Hsüeh-hsin t'ao-yüan* edition) 2.4a, used of a monk who "resided in seclusion" on a certain mountain.

was named by the founder of the dynasty, Shen-chih, who said of it, "This should be called Snowy Peak."[73]   The mountain is also remembered as the site of the Buddhist temple whose abbot, Cho Yen-ming, enjoyed a brief rule as Emperor of Min in 945, the puppet of Li Jen-ta.[74]  Also in the Prefecture of Fu, in the District of Min, was "Phoenix Pond Mountain" (鳳池山), the site of a Buddhist temple of the same name, said to be the burial place of Shen-chih and of his wife, the Lady *née* Jen 任.[75]   On another mountain, southwest of the Prefecture of Fu, an unnamed member of the dynasty built a Manjusri terrace (文殊臺), surrounded by four other terraces arranged according to the cardinal points.   Hence the mountain came to be known as the "Mountain of the Five Terraces" (五臺山).[76] Near the Prefecture of Chien was an "Iron Lion Range" (鐵獅嶺), where the magical purple fungus (紫芝) is said to have suddenly appeared on the day of the occupation of Min by the Wang clan.[77]  This is clearly the same as the "Iron Lion Summit" (鐵獅頂), three *li* south of the prefectural city, named for a small shrine on its top containing images of Manjusri and a lion cast in iron.[78]  In the Prefecture of T'ing was a mountain remembered also for its associations with the imperial family, but with a religion other than Buddhism.  This was the "Mountain of the Jade Maiden" (玉女山), fifteen *li* south of Ch'ang-t'ing 長汀 District, so-named because it was there that a daughter of one of the Min Emperors trained herself as a Taoist adept.[79]

[73]  *YTCS* 128.7b.   The mountain 180 *li* from Fu-chou city.  *FCTC*1 5.18a.

[74]  *TCTC* 284.14a-b.

[75]  *YTCS* 128.11b.  *FCTC*1 39.16b places Shen-chih's grave under "Lotus Flower Peak" (蓮華峯), but elsewhere states that this was only the last of several places where his body reposed.  "Phoenix Pond Mt." was placed under the jurisdiction of the District of Hou-kuan early in the Sung dynasty.  *FCTC*1 5.21b-22a.

[76]  *YTCS* 128.12b.

[77]  *YTCS* 129.7a; *FCTC*1 11.5b.

[78]  *YTCS* 129.9a.  We do not know, however, that these images date from the tenth-century.

[79]  *YTCS* 132.6a.

# II

# COURT[80]

THE brothers Wang 王, founders of the Min state in Fukien during the late ninth century, were the sons of a farmer of the town of Ku-shih 固始, attached to the Prefecture of Kuang 光 in modern Honan.[80a] From these rude beginnings, via the route of successful banditry, or in nicer language, as free-lance condottieri, they were able to make the rich lands and seaports of Min the freeholds of their numerous sons and grandsons. Many years later, in the spring of 945, Li Jen-ta 李仁達, a sharp-witted trimmer who briefly inherited their estate, characterized the career of the brothers in these words: "Long ago Wang Ch'ao 王潮 and his younger brothers were just nobodies of Kuang-shan 光山, yet they took Fukien like [i.e. as easily as] turning a palm."[81]

The brothers' names were Ch'ao, Shen-kuei 審邽[82] and Shen-chih 審知. During their military career, before they settled permanently in Fukien, they were known collectively to their comrades-in-arms as "The Three Dragons" (三龍).[83]

Of Shen-kuei little is known, except for his liberal education and

[80] In this Chapter I have arranged such anecdotal, biographical and social data about eminent personages of Min as do not fit readily into other chapters devoted to such restricted matters as political history and economics.

[80a] *WTS*. The old man's name was Wang Jen 恁, and his wife was a woman of the Tung 董 family.

[81] *TCTC* 284.14a-b.

[82] He appears as Shen-pang 審邦 in the record of an inscription, but the historians agree on Shen-kuei. He is called simply Kuei 圭 in *WKKS*. His grave is placed at Chin-chiang District 晋江. *FCTC*1 42.9a.

[83] *WKKS* b.5a. A local gazetteer, *Ch'ang-lo hsien chih* 長樂縣志 10.2a states that a certain Wang Hsiang 王想 was a younger brother of Shen-chih, and came with him from Ku-shih to Fukien. He held office in the admistration of Ch'ang-lo. I have not seen him mentioned elsewhere.

patronage of refugee scholars.[84]

Ch'ao, styled Hsin-ch'en 信臣, the eldest brother, has left a more complete record in history, but that is little enough except for the important fact that he was the first member of the Wang family to hold a legally authorized post in Fukien—that of Prefect of Ch'üan 泉州刺史. He had begun his official career as District Recorder (縣史)[85] at Ku-shih. To him also belongs the credit for the conquest of the Five Prefectures of Min ( 泉, 漳, 汀, 福, 建). His army is said to have been well-disciplined—not an unruly mob.[86] He never attained princely rank, however, an honor reserved for the youngest of the brothers, Shen-chih, the true founder of the Min dynasty. Ch'ao was posthumously entitled *Ssu-k'ung* 司空, and was buried under "Coiling Dragon Mountain" (盤龍山) in the District of Nan-an, Ch'üan Prefecture.[87] A memorial inscription was written for him by the eminent poet Huang T'ao 黃滔, and the Ming dynasty ordered annual sacrifices at his grave.[88]

Shen-chih bore the style Hsin-t'ung 信通,[89] but was known to his fellow soldiers as "Third Gentleman of the White Horse" (白馬三郎) because he habitually rode a white steed.[90] He is said to have been manly and heroic in aspect, with the square mouth and high-bridged nose traditionally associated with such qualities.[91] He was seven-and-a-half feet tall.[92] Nothing is known of his life before he embarked upon a career as an adventurer.[93] During his brother Ch'ao's lifetime, he served him

[84]  *TS* 190.4075c.  His style was Tz'u-tu 次都.

[85]  Some sources have 縣佐 (*TCTC* 254 and *CWTS*).

[86]  *TS* 190.4975b-c.

[87]  *TS* 190.4075c.

[88]  *FCTC*1 42.24b.  *FCTC*2 15.6b notes the existence of the "Temple of the Great Prince West of the River" (水西大王廟), erected to Ch'ao's spirit by his brother Shen-chih.  The same text tells of the "Shrine of the Prefect Wang" (王刺史祠) erected by the natives of Ch'üan Prefecture to their former lord.  This was rebuilt during Sung.  *FCTC*2 15.19b.

[89]  *WTS*.

[90]  *WTS*.  "Third Master" since he was the third brother in age.  *FCTC*2 3.2b states that "the Third Gentleman of the White Horse" shot eels (鱔) in the Eastern Mountains in a certain stream, which was therefore named "Eel Stream" (鱔溪).

[91]  *WTS*.  *Ts'e-fu yüan-kuei* 册府元龜 220.4a adds the words "purple-colored" before "square mouth."

[92]  *Ts'e-fu yüan-kuei* 220.4a.

[93]  *NTS* 28 states that he had been a farmer but the text of this work is virtually identical with that of *WTS*, which has the word "Jen" (Shen-chih's father) here, making it appear that the name was omitted in *NTS*.  Nonetheless Shen-chih may well have worked his father's land.

faithfully, and even suffered beatings for his sins without showing resentment.[94] After his rise to absolute power he never forsook the plain manner
of living which he had followed in the camp. His frugality was proverbial.
As Prince of Min he continued to wear hempen sandals, and conducted his
private and public affairs in rude buildings which he never repaired.[95] It
was characteristic of him that on one occasion when his pongee skirt was
torn, he patched it with a piece of cloth from a bag used for straining
wine.[96] Despite his former career as a brigand, he was not cruel; indeed
he was "indulgent in punishment,"[97] showing a marked devotion to polite
manners and cherishing the company of polished scholars.[98] His virtue
was honored in later generations, and he attracted the attention of the T'ang
court, which ordered the erection of a tablet in his honor at the family temple
in Hou-kuan District.[99] The prime reason for this honor and others which
followed[100] must have been his unswerving allegiance to the T'ang dynasty
during its last years when he might readily have maintained himself in
unassailable and independent dignity. He died full of glory in 925. His
body was moved several times in later years, but its final resting place is
said to have been at "Lotus Flower Peak" in Hou-kuan District.[101] There
is a tradition that the Prince's grave was opened by robbers in 1429, and a
gold bracelet, a jade girdle, a glass bowl and a portrait of Shen-chih himself
removed.[102]

Some of Shen-chih's comrades-in-arms are known only from the
location of their graves,[103] but something is known of several of his followers.
An orphaned nephew of the Prince, brought up as his own son, seems to

---

[94] *TCTC* 261.8b.

[95] *TCTC* 267.9a.

[96] *WKKS* b.5b.

[97] *TCTC* 267.9a.

[98] *WTS. Ts'e-fu yuan-kuei, loc. cit.,* has a characterization of his rags-to-riches career.

[99] *FCTC*1 39.26b. This was the "Tablet for Virtuous Government" (德政碑)
erected in 905 near the Ch'ing-ch'eng Temple (慶城寺). The text was composed by
Yü Ching 于兢, Vice-President of the Board of Rites. A photograph of the tablet will
be found among the plates in Tokiwa Daijō 常盤大定, *Shina Bukkyō no Kenkyū* 支那佛
教の研究 vol. 2 (Tōkyō, 1941).

[100] E. g., a tablet entitled *Lang-yeh-chun-wang Wang Shen-chih shen-tao pei* 瑯琊郡王王
審知神道碑 was erected at his grave. *FCTC*1 39.27a.

[101] *FCTC*1 39.26b.

[102] *Min tu chi* 25.3b-4a. It is also reported that near the royal grave was a mound,
deep red in color, popularly named "Rouge Mountain" (胭脂山), where a daughter of
Shen-chih was buried. The ground was colored by her washed-off makeup. For other
traditions and tales connected with this site see *ibid.* 4b-5a.

[103] For instance, that of a soldier, Yü Hsiung 虞雄, who died in battle in Shen-chih's
service, and was buried at Su-t'ien Village 蘇田里 in Fu-ch'ing District. *FCTC*1 40.10a.

have devoted the early part of his career to attempting to make Shen-chih even more virtuous than he was. The youth's name was Wang Yen-ssu 延嗣, an avid reader and an orthodox Confucianist. He tried to persuade Shen-chih not to accept office from "rebellious" Liang, and even proposed a union of southern states for the purpose of restoring the T'ang dynasty. He censured Shen-chih for wasting the people's substance in sending tribute by sea to the Liang court, especially since much of it was lost in marine disasters. He was as unsuccessful in these recommendations as he was in attempting to turn his foster father from his support of the Buddhist religion, but at least he seems to have had something to do with Shen-chih's decision to avoid the usurpation of imperial dignities. After the accession of Wang Yen-han 延翰, he lived in retirement in the mountains near Yen-p'ing, having changed his surname to T'ang 唐 in honor of the late dynasty. He became a teacher of classics after the conquest of the northwestern part of the Min empire by Southern T'ang, and finally held office under Sung.[104]

Another member of the Wang clan who, although not important to political history, deserves remembrance for his encouragement of foreign shipping at Ch'üan Prefecture, is Yen-pin 延彬, son of Shen-kuei, who inherited his father's post at the southern port. He is remembered chiefly for his extravagant living and for his patronage of letters. When suffering from the aftereffects of too much wine, he would pour several vessels of borneol (*lùng-nao*) over himself, after which he would sleep until noon. Whether this expensive antidote cured him, or whether it was simply the extra sleep, is not definitely known. He was remembered by posterity as *Yün-t'ai shih-chung* 雲臺侍中, since he was buried at "Cloudy Terrace Mountain."[105]

Wang Yen-han, the first of his clan to openly seek royal status, was the eldest son of Shen-chih, and was styled Tzu-i 子逸. He is described as a tall man, "radiantly handsome as jade."[106] It would seem that his manners were not as pleasant as his appearance, for he is also described as "arrogant, licentious, cruel and violent,"[107] and there is certainly evidence for the arrogance and licentiousness. He treated his brothers with contempt, especially Yen-chün 延鈞, Prefect of Ch'üan,[108] later Emperor of Min, and Yen-ping 延稟, Prefect of Chien. His estrangement from the latter was due to his demand that Yen-ping act as his procurer in obtaining beautiful

---

[104] The biography of Yen-ssu is preserved in *FCTC*1 171.1b-3b.

[105] *WKKS* b.910-10a. *FCTC*1 42.19a locates his grave at Ch'ing-ko Village 清歌里 in Nan-an District. Doubtless the two places are the same.

[106] *WTS*.

[107] *TCTC* 275.11a.

[108] The succession of Prefects of Ch'üan was Ch'ao, Shen-kuei, Yen-pin, Yen-chün.

women for his harem.[109]   This request was in line with his policy of "taking
freely of the daughters of his subjects."[110]   Yen-han's predilection for lovely
young girls meant misfortune for those of his choice.  His wife, *née* Ts'ui
崔, said to have been ugly and lecherous—certainly she was cruel—was
jealous of her husband, who left her after the death of Shen-chih.  It is
recorded that she made a practice of confining her most beautiful rivals in
special rooms, where she kept them in fetters, beat their cheeks with pieces
of wood carved in the form of human hands and stabbed them with iron
awls.  Some she is said to have flogged until the silken bonds which tied
them were soaked with blood.  We are told that eighty-four ladies died
within a single year as a result of these barbarities.[111]   It is even alleged
that this harridan brought about the death of Shen-chih by poisoning.[112]
There are two different stories of her demise, both consonant with the
principle of poetic justice.  One relates that she was killed by a stroke of
lightning from a clear summer sky,[113] another that she was felled by an
evil spirit.[114]

Yen-han himself, abandoning the simple life of his father, established
a formal court, entitled himself King (國王), and adopted all the manners
and institutions proper for a true Son of Heaven.  He was addressed by
his inferiors, however, simply as "Your Highness" (殿下).[115]   After a
brief and inglorious reign he was put to death by his brothers, and buried
at the "Mountain of Grand Tranquillity" (太平山), southwest of the
capital, the site of the graves of many other eminent men of that age.[116]

Yen-chün, posthumously the Emperor Hui Tsung 惠宗 of Min, was
ambitious, extravagant and, at least in his last years, insane.  He is frequently
contrasted by the historians with his father Shen-chih, especially in view
of the huge expenditures he made on construction.[117]   His court was in all
respects that of an Emperor, and his treasury held the ceremonial regalia
appropriate to that office.[118]   He seems, however, to have shown a glim-
mering of modesty in that he created only five ancestral temples after his
accession, although the Chou dynasty tradition allowed seven for a Son of

[109]  *WTS, TCTC* 275.12b.
[110]  *Ibid.*
[111]  *WTS, WKKS* b.5b.
[112]  *WKKS* b.5b, *TCTC* 275.13a.
[113]  *WKKS* b.5b.
[114]  *WTS.*
[115]  *TCTC* 275.11a-b.
[116]  *FCTC1* 39.17a.
[117]  *TCTC* 278.6b.
[118]  *TCTC* 278.5a.

Heaven, five being the number alloted to a feudal lord.[119]  He canonized his father and grandfather posthumously, as was proper, yet an anecdote tells that the parsimonious and loyal Shen-chih reproved him in a dream for wearing imperial robes in Shen-chih's temple.[120]  It is also said that at first Yen-chün proposed to adopt the abbreviated title of "Augustus of Min" (閩國皇), but that he was dissuaded from this mediocre course by the Hanlin Scholar Chou Wei-yüeh 周維岳, who said that it would be equally appropriate for himself to use the title *Han-lin hsüeh* 翰林學 (minus *shih* 士).[121]  If this was modesty, it was consistent with Yen-chün's policy of respect for neighboring states, in view of the smallness and remoteness of his empire—a policy which left his domain in peace during his own lifetime.[122]  Yen-chün seems to have had some affection for his mother, *née* Huang黃 , a consort of Shen-chih.[123]  The tradition is that he bestowed the name of "Brocade Village" (錦里) on her native place on the occasion of a visit to her.  This village was at the Ling-hsiu Mountain (靈秀山) in Nan-an District, and the dowager was buried there.[124]

Yen-ping, the adopted brother of the Emperor, with whom he was on uneasy terms after his accession, has left little record of his personality.  It is said that he had lost an eye, and was known by the epithet of "Single-eyed Dragon" (獨眼龍).[125]  He was worshiped posthumously at the "Temple of the Noble and Devoted Prince" (英烈王廟) erected to his genius at Shun-ch'ang 順昌 Village in Chien Prefecture.[126]

One of the more important personages at the court of the new sovereign was Hsüeh Wen-chieh 薛文傑, who won Yen-chün's favor by his ingenious

---

[119] *TCTC* 278.5a.  See *Li chi* (*SPPY*) 12.8a for the prescriptions on ancestral temples.  The correct number of these temples was a matter of debate early in the T'ang dynasty.  See *T'ung tien* (Comm. Press, 1935) 47.269c-270a.  Seven seems to have been generally recognized as correct, however, if there were sufficient known male ancestors.  Possibly Yen-chün was not so much modest, as ignorant of the names of his early forbears.

[120] *WKKS* b.5b.

[121] *WKKS* b.6a.  I follow my source in giving this tale here, but I strongly suspect an anachronism.  When Wang Yen-hsi took the imperial throne in August 941, he styled himself Augustus of Great Min.  Moreover Chou Wei-yüeh was a favorite courtier of this monarch, and is not elsewhere alluded to in connection with Yen-chün.

[122] *TCTC* 278.5a.  The exception to this statement was the siege of Chien Prefecture by troops of Wu (Huainan), acting without official orders, in 934.

[123] The lady had not been Shen-chih's chief wife.  She was the daughter of Huang Na-yü 訥裕, an official under Shen-chih.

[124] *FCTC1* 42.23b, 25a.  On the same occasion he named the local post station "Brocade Field" 錦田, and the stream "Brocade Stream" 錦溪.

[125] *WKKS* b.6a.

[126] *FCTC2* 15.23b.  This was popularly "Secretary's Temple" (侍郎廟).

proposals for filling the court treasury. This man had formerly held the title of *Chung-chün-shih* 中軍使.[127] Now he became *Kuo-chi-shih* 國計使,[128] and came to exercise considerable power over the Emperor's mind. He was able to persuade his lord that the male members of the royal family had designs on the throne, and in consequence of the repressions visited upon them by the suspicious Yen-chün, one nephew, Wang Chi-t'u 繼圖, actually did plot a rebellion because of his indignation. He was discovered and put to death with over a thousand other persons.[129] Wen-chieh himself came to a bad end. The crafty financier had constructed a kind of wheeled cage (檻車) for the transportation and exposition of criminals, which had iron spikes through its floor and roof, so that the unfortunate culprit could not move without puncturing himself.[130] Wen-chieh was the first to suffer from this device, being punished in it to placate the angry mood of some rebellious troops.[131]

Yen-chün's suspicious disposition and his distrust of the young princes is further evidenced by his treatment of his nephew, Wang Jen-ta 王仁達. Jen-ta was an astute, well-read man who enjoyed some fame as a skillful lancer.[132] He was Commander of Galleons, and largely instrumental in the defeat of the hapless Yen-ping, thus making the elevation of Yen-chün possible. After this victory, Jen-ta became "Commander of the Household Division" (親從都指揮使), but his reputation, along with his uninhibited, extroverted personality, seem to have irritated the Emperor, who began to look for reasons to do away with him. On one occasion, he attempted to trap the young officer with a question about the regicide, Chao Kao 趙高 of the Ch'in dynasty: "Chao Kao indicated a deer to be a horse, to make Erh-shih 二世 [of Ch'in] appear muddle-headed—is such indeed the case?" Jen-ta replied, "Erh-shih of Ch'in *was* muddle-headed. Therefore when Kao indicated a deer to be a horse, it was not that Kao was able to make Erh-shih appear muddle-headed. Now Your Majesty is intelligent and enlightened. Your court officials number less than a hundred. Their risings and residings, their activities and passivities—Your Majesty is familiar with them all. If there is one who dares to assume your awful prerogatives, you

---

[127] *TCTC* 278.7b. In archaic times armies were divided into three sections, the over-all command being held by the commander of the "Central Army." See *Tso chuan* (Duke Huan 5).

[128] Literally, "Commissioner of National Accounts."

[129] *TCTC* 278.9b-10a. The text here describes Wen-chieh as "Inner Chancellor" (內樞密使). This is an error. That office was held by Wu Hsü 吳勗 at this time (see *TCTC* 278.5a).

[130] *WTS*.

[131] *TCTC* 278.16a-b. See Chapter on Economy for details.

[132] *CKC* 10.99-100 has his biography.

need only exterminate him and his clan." This politic reply convinced the Emperor of Jen-ta's devotion to the throne, and he bestowed rich gifts on him.[133]    However, his jealousy continued and on a later occasion he remarked to an attendant, "Jen-ta has a superfluity of wisdom, yet I am able to have my way with him. But he is not a [proper] servant for a young lord."[134]  This was meant to signify that Jen-ta might prove too powerful an influence over the Heir Apparent, and was a sly hint at possible usurpation by his nephew. Thus justified, Yen-chün brought false charges of conspiracy against Jen-ta and had him and his family put death.[135]

Yen-chün was much married. His first wife was the Ch'ing-yüan Princess 清遠公主, daughter of Liu Yen 劉巖, ruler of the Southern Han empire.[136] This lady died young, whereupon he took a woman, née Chin 金, as his wife. The latter was virtuous but unattractive to him.[137] Finally, being enamoured of a former maid-in-waiting (侍婢) of Shen-chih, née Ch'en 陳, he made her his consort, with the title Shu Fei 淑妃. This woman, the famous Golden Phoenix (金鳳), has been characterized as "vulgar and lewd."[138] But, like Yang Kuei-fei, she has captured the imaginations of both historians and romancers, and more has been written of her than of any other woman of Min. Like Kuei-fei, she brought about the advancement of her own family—her relatives Ch'en Shou-en 守恩 and Ch'en K'uang-sheng 匡勝 were both appointed Palace Commissioners (宮使)[139]—by the infatuated Emperor. In March 935, Yen-chün elevated

[133] *WTC*. A somewhat different version of the incident appears in *CKC*. See *Shih chi* 6.0026d for the original story, in which Chao tests the loyalty of the Ch'in offici-aldom to himself by counting those who agreed with him in calling the deer a horse. The phrase 起居動靜, which I have translated " risings and residings . . . activities and passivities," may deserve a more limited interpretation: " their activities and passivities at the [imperial] audiences." *Chi-chu* assumed the meaning of " complimentary interview with the Emperor [by the officialdom] " in this period. See *WTS* 54.4450d, which refers to the reign of Ming Tsung of Later T'ang.

[134] *TCTC* 278.15a ; cf. *WTS*.

[135] *TCTC* 278.15a.

[176] *TCTC* 279.16a-b.

[137] *WTS*.

[138] *TCTC* 279.16a-b. The titles Shu Fei, " Immaculate Consort," and Hsien Fei, " Estimable Consort " (賢妃), which appear frequently in texts referring to the wives of the Min Emperors follow the pattern of Sui and Early T'ang, when the four ladies next below the Empress were entitled Kuei Fei, " Noble Consort " (貴妃), " Immaculate Consort," Te Fei " Virtuous Consort " (德妃) and " Estimable Consort." These titles were abolished in mid-T'ang by Hsüan Tsung. See *TS* 47.3743c and *Chiu T'ang shu* 44.3250a.

[139] Hu San-hsing notes that this office was created by Min. See *TCTC* 279.16a-b. It was a common title among the various kingdoms of this era, and was generally held by eunuchs. Thus the all-powerful eunuch Kung Ch'eng-shu 龔澄樞 was " Commis-sioner of the Palace of Dragon Virtue " 龍德宮 and concurrently of the " Palace of Myriad Flowers " 萬華宮 at Canton in the Southern Han empire. See *Sung shih* 481.5699c.

Golden Phoenix to the rank of Empress.[140]  But the monarch's mind was failing, and his impatient or romantic Empress took two successive lovers from among the habitués of the court.  The first was Kuei Shou-ming 歸守明, a handsome personal attendant of the Emperor, generally known as Master Kuei 歸郎.[141]  This was in October 935.  Shou-ming in turn acted as pander for Li K'o-yin 李可殷, Commissioner of the Artisans Institute 百工院使.  The Empress's philandering was known to the public generally, but no one had the courage to bring it to the attention of the afflicted sovereign.[142]  K'o-yin was the artificer of the "Nine Dragon Tent," whose interior was more enjoyed by himself and Shou-ming than by their imperial patron.  A popular song about these meetings in a pavilion supposedly devoted to the marital pleasures of the Emperor ran, "Who speaks of the Nine Dragon Tent?  It stores only one Master Kuei."[143]  During Yen-chün's illness (July 935), the Heir Apparent had an affair with an inmate of the imperial harem (宮人), named Spring Swallow (春燕), surnamed Li 李.[144]  The Prince (and future Emperor) then obtained the maid from his father through Golden Phoenix.  Yen-chün gave her up reluctantly.[145] He was then suffering from hallucinations, and intoxicated at a great banquet for his troops held at the "Pavilion of the Great Bacchanal" 大酺殿, he imagined that he saw an apparition of Yen-ping, his foster brother. The assassin Li Fang 李倣, agent of Chi-p'eng 繼鵬 the Crown Prince, was now convinced of the Emperor's insanity, and had him killed along with Prince Chi-t'ao 繼韜, Golden Phoenix and the unregretted Master Kuei.  The palace girls must have had some affection for their lord, for when he lay tossing with pain from the stabs of the mutinous soldiers but not quite dead, the harem beauties "put an end to him, not being able to endure his suffering."[147]

[140] *Ibid.*

[141] The language of the sources makes it evident that Master Kuei had served the Emperor in the role of catamite.

[142] *TCTC* 279.19b.

[143] *WTS.* i. e. only the eight dragons embroidered on the tent were actually present. The ninth dragon, Yen-chün, was absent.

[144] *WTS* uses the expression 烝之, "had incestuous relations with her."  The girl, his father's handmaid, was strictly speaking taboo to him.

[145] *WTS*; *TCTC* 279.18a-b.

[146] *WTS.*

[147] This happened on November 17, 935.  The *Unofficial Biography of Ch'en Chin-feng* (陳金鳳外傳), whose authenticity has been questioned, gives many more details about the court of Yen-chün.  I have considered the possible value of this text below, on page 119. Here are some paraphrased and abbreviated excerpts from it:  Golden Phoenix was a native of the town of Wan-an 萬安 in Fu-ch'ing District.  After her elevation to the

Chi-p'eng, second Emperor of Min, was a wild, quick-tempered man,[148] and an arrogant libertine after he took the throne. His chief talent was his skill as an archer.[149] The story is told of him that he proposed an invasion of Southern T'ang, trained troops for the venture and asked for an omen of success. He set up a metal basin at the end of the archery range, at a distance of fifty or sixty paces, and said to the assembled company, "If I hit it in one shot, I shall reduce Chiang-nan!" He accomplished the feat but, although he sent his soldiers to the northwestern border, the invasion never took place.[150] The new Emperor's temperament is revealed in anecdotes which tell of his relations with his advisers. One of these, Yeh Ch'iao 葉翹, a kind of Seneca to this eastern Nero, left the court when he found that his advice was no longer heeded. Chi-p'eng reproached him

rank of empress, she and the Emperor led a riotous life in the "Palace of Enduring Spring" 長春宮 which he built for her. At these parties great couches were placed about, and the Emperor embraced Golden Phoenix, surrounded by the girls of his harem, all quite naked. In particular, the imperial couple was wont to make love behind the screen of crystal from Champa, which enclosed an area forty-two feet in circumference, while the palace girls were encouraged to watch them through the screen. Parties were also often held by the "Stream of the Mulberries of Lustration," where the odor of incense, the clash of jade ornaments, the light of torches, and the sound of musical instruments attracted great throngs of observers. On the fifth day of the fifth month, boat races were held on the West Lake. Each gaily decorated vessel held between twenty and thirty maidens clad in short tunics, who plied the oars. The Emperor himself watched the spectacle from his great "Dragon Boat," while Golden Phoenix sang ditties of her own composition. One such song goes: I. "The Dragon Boat is sculled along/East and further east./The lotus gathered on the lake/Are red and redder yet./ The ripples toss and toss.../The water swells and swells.../I am parted from the lotus flowers/By a road I cannot pass." II. "On West Lake and South Lake/They match the festooned boats./Green rushes and purple water-peppers/Cover the central islets./The ripples range and range.../The water spreads and spreads.../Afar I offer the Sovereign Lord/Ten thousand years of joy!" On such occasions elegantly dressed sightseers gathered in masses on the banks to watch the brilliant games. Golden Phoenix owed her introduction to the Emperor to Li Fang, but after her rise to favor she slighted him. The man took his revenge by presenting Spring Swallow, his younger sister, dressed in elaborate finery, to the susceptible monarch. Yen-chün instantly became enamoured of the pretty girl, who was then only fifteen, and made her "Excellent Consort." Henceforth he deserted the pleasures of the crystal screen. Later, however, he returned to Golden Phoenix at the urging of the Hanlin Scholar Han Wo, who improvised a poem to recall his former lover to the Emperor. The Heir Apparent then fell in love with Spring Swallow, seduced her, obtained her from his ailing father and after his accession made her his Empress.

[148] *WKKS* b.7a.

[149] See the story of his death in *TCTC* 282.5a-b, 6a-b.

[150] *WKKS* b.7a.

for his neglect and provoked this polite retort from the old man: "Your old servant's guidance and assistance were incompetent, with the result that since Your Majesty ascended the throne, there has not been a single good thing to praise. I wish to beg leave for my old bones [i.e. to retire]." The Emperor soothed this "National Patriarch" (國翁) with fine speeches and rich presents and prevailed on him to remain at court,[151] although there is no evidence that he ever took the sage's advice. Chi-p'eng was not so gentle with another of his ministers who presumed to find fault with him. The "Remonstrator" (諫議大夫), Huang Feng 黃諷, sincerely indignant at his lord's evil ways, took farewell of his wife and children, and fulfilled his duty by presenting himself at court with an admonition, prepared to die. The Emperor did not take kindly to the reproof and ordered Huang Feng beaten. Feng replied, "If I deceived my country or were disloyal, I would hold no resentment even for [the penalty of] death. But to be flogged for straight admonition is something I will not endure." This dignified resistance was more than Chi-p'eng could endure and he had his Remonstrator degraded to the status of commoner.[152] Huang Feng's grave was remembered in later generations on the sunny side of "Yellowbank Mountain" (黃岸山) in Hou-kuan.[153]

The Emperor's violent temper showed itself even more markedly at his all-night drinking bouts. In his drunkenness, overcome with suspicion or uncontrolable rage, he made no distinction between stranger and relative, or commoner and minister. His favorite sport was to compel his courtiers to intoxicate themselves with wine; his attendants were then to watch for breaches of ceremony committed under such circumstances. On one occasion he had his cousin Chi-lung 繼隆 decapitated, and frequently executed other relatives whom he suspected of disloyalty because of some fancied slight induced by overdrinking. His paternal uncle, Yen-hsi 延羲, who was to succeed him on the throne, was so alarmed at the precariousness of his position, that he feigned lunacy, as has been asserted of the Emperor Claudius in a similar case. Yen-hsi held the title of "Minister of State for the Left" (左僕射), but Chi-p'eng, apparently taken in by his assumed witlessness, sent him off to a mountain temple as a Taoist priest. Later, however, he recalled him and immured him in a private residence.[154]

Chi-p'eng's Empress, Spring Swallow, sinks into obscurity after the death of Yen-chün. The young Emperor gave her the title Shu Fei on his

151 *TCTC* 279.21a-b. This took place in December 935.
152 *TCTC* 281.17b.
153 *FCTC*1 39.14b.
154 *TCTC* 282.5a-b, 6a-b.

accession,[155] and later made her Empress. She is not mentioned again in
the histories until her violent death in her husband's company.

A member of Chi-p'eng's court, Liu I 劉乙, is noteworthy as having
finally managed to escape the flood of wine which deluged the imperial
gardens. This man, remembered in political history only for having been
chosen to entertain Lu Sun 盧損, the Ambassador from Chin, was a very
elegant personage,[156] but of rather sensitive disposition. On one occasion
he took part in a drunken brawl over a singing girl and when sober again
suffered extreme pangs of remorse. He went so far as to collect all available
documents on the evils of drink and from them compiled a *Canon of the
Hundred Repentances* (百悔經) as a warning to himself. It is alleged
that he never touched another drop.[157]

Chi-p'eng's downfall may be attributed directly to his mishandling of
his praetorians. Yen-chün, when he assumed the purple, had created two
divisions of guards from the old soldiers of his father Shen-chih. These he
named the Kung-ch'en 拱宸 and K'ung-ho 控鶴 Divisions (都).[158] His
son, however, preferred to have a body of men whose interests were linked
completely with his own; so he enlisted two thousand bravos, the scum of
the marketplace,[159] in a devoted band which he named the Ch'en-wei
Division (宸衞都). He awarded them especially rich donatives, which,
along with other signal honors, excited the resentment of the other guards,

---

[155] I follow *TCTC* 279.20a-b; *WTS* says Shu Fei. We have seen that *CFWC* made
her the Hsien Fei of Yen-chün. Possibly this is correct, and *TCTC* gives her this title
anachronistically, in which case she became "Immaculate Consort" of Chi-p'eng—this
was the higher title under T'ang at least.

[156] *WTS*.

[157] *CIL* a.18b-19a. Three poems by this worthy are preserved in *ChWTS* 87.

[158] The title of the first of these bands of imperial guards derives from the famous
passage in the second chapter (*wei cheng*) of the *Lun yü* where the virtuous ruler is compared to the polestar (辰), deferentially saluted (共) by the other circling stars. 拱宸
is 共宸, the graph 宸 being used for *ch'en* when the latter word applies metaphorically to
the imperial seat. The phrase "Bridled Crane," with its Taoist connotations, was not
uncommon in the T'ang dynasty. The Empress Tse-t'ien established a bureau for her
personal servants entitled the "Repository of the Bridled Crane" (控鶴府) (*TS*
76.3868a). The last T'ang Emperor, Chao Tsung, was served by military officials called
the "Officers of the Bridled Cranes and Paraded Horses" (控鶴排馬宮)(*TS* 50.3752d).
The title was known outside of Min in the tenth-century: the "Bridled Crane" Army
(軍) revolted against the Later T'ang dynasty at Pien 汴 Prefecture in 926 (*WTS*
6.4400a and *CWTS* 36.4247c). The term *tu* 都 was commonly applied to military
guard organizations in this period, and I think the translation "division" is suitable.
A division was commanded by a *chih-hui-shih* 指揮使, which I translate simply "commander," though more properly it might be "directing commissioner."

[159] *WKKS* b.7a-b.

especially the commanders of the two old divisions, Chu Wen-chin 朱文進 and Lien Chung-yü 連重遇. These men were even more embittered after the burning of the Northern Palace when the Emperor made Chung-yü and his troops sweep up the embers. Finally, on the night of August 29, 939, Chung-yü led his guards against the royal palace. The Emperor and his consort fled to the protection of the Ch'en-wei Division, but its headquarters were fired by the rebels on the following morning, and in the battle which ensued the Ch'en-wei Guards suffered a bloody defeat. The thousand or so remaining fled the city with the royal family. They were intercepted and, after the death of their sovereign, the remnant made its way north to safety in Wu-yüeh.[160]

It is said of Yen-hsi that, when he ascended the throne vacated by his suspicious nephew, he was afraid that the troops which came to escort him to the palace had been sent to arrest him by Chi-p'eng. Again he resembled the Roman Claudius. At any rate, he took refuge in a privy.[161] Despite such an inauspicious beginning he soon sent a pair of verses to the neighboring states announcing his accession: "The Six Armies leap for joy before the Gate! The Assembled Ministers shout for pleasure under the Sun!"[162] His enthronement was not universally welcomed. The Remonstrator Huang Chün 黃峻 is said to have remarked to an associate, "It is not fittingly 'Perpetual Eminence'[163]—indeed I fear that it is the first year of 'Great Benightedness' (大昏)."[164] Yen-hsi was the twenty-eighth son of Shen-chih,[165] so that, although we do not know the year of his birth, he may well have been as young as Chi-p'eng or even younger. The sources do not credit him with a more admirable character than his nephew for he is described as "arrogant, lascivious and cruel."[166] Moreover, he is said to have been "wilful, obstinate and difficult to manage"—the opinion of Chi-p'eng's minister Wang T'an 王倓, whom Yen-hsi had feared greatly.[167] Like his predecessor he was suspicious and jealous of the members of his family, perhaps with some justice, in view of raids made on his territory

---

[160] *TCTC* 282.5a-b, 6a-b.

[161] *WKKS* b.7b. The subject of privies as asylums deserves study. They are ghost-haunted places.

[162] *Ibid.*

[163] Alluding to the reign title Yung Lung (永隆) adopted by Yen-hsi. *WKKS* gives 曦 for the Emperor's new name. *K'ang-hsi tzu-tien* recognizes the latter character as a legitimate "abbreviation" of 曦.

[164] *CIL* a.6b.

[165] *WKKS* b.7b.

[166] *TCTC* 282.8b.

[167] *WTS*. See more about T'an below under Religion.

by his brother Yen-cheng 延政, Prefect of Chien and later a rival Emperor.
At any rate, he put many of his relatives to death.[168] In the summer of
941 he began the systematic extermination of his kinsmen and of meritorious
old courtiers. This provoked the above-mentioned Huang Chün to make
an appearance at court carrying his own coffin. He censured the Emperor
most severely but was not taken as seriously as he had anticipated. It is
recorded that Yen-hsi said, "The old fellow has gone mad!" and sent him
to Chang Prefecture in a minor official capacity.[169] Yen-hsi resembled
Chi-p'eng in another respect—his addiction to drinking, or at least to seeing
his courtiers drunk. He practiced the hallowed "ox-drink" with his
ministers, and set the penalty of death for anyone so bold as to secretly
get rid of his wine.[170] His nephew Chi-jou 繼柔 made this fatal mistake
at a party given in the Nine Dragon Pavilion late in September 942, and
was decapitated forthwith, along with his guests.[171] A similar incident
occurred in January 943, when the Minister Li Kuang-chun 李光準 was
so far gone in his cups as to resist an imperial whim. The Emperor ordered
him seized and publicly decapitated. The unlucky minister was taken to
the marketplace, where he lay befuddled with drink, calling for his favorite
slave girl, Spring Warbler (春鶯).[172] The executioners took pity on him,
carried him to a dungeon and left him in manacles. At the court session
on the following day Yen-hsi remembered him and restored him to his
post.[173] That same evening another great feast was held, and this time
it was the Hanlin Scholar Chou Wei-yüeh who suffered imperial displeasure,
and, accordingly, was seized and jailed. He was shown the utmost respect
by the prison guards who even dusted off his bench and released him when
sober, apparently accustomed to such incidents. This Wei-yüeh was a
famous winebibber, noted for his remarkable capacity. On one occasion
the whole company was disabled by intoxication with the exception of
Wei-yüeh. Yen-hsi asked an attendant how it was possible for the scholar
to hold so much wine in view of his small body. The lackey produced an
ingenious explanation: Wei-yüeh had a special entrail to accommodate the
wine. The Emperor proposed to have the toper sliced open in order that
he might inspect this marvelous bowel but was dissuaded by the attendant
—apparently a quick-witted fellow—who pointed out that Wei-yüeh's

[168] *WTS ; TCTC* 282.8b.

[169] *TCTC* 282.17a-b.

[170] *WTS.* The imperial wine cups were silver leaves, which because of their fragility
were commonly called "winter-melon slices." See *WKKS* b.7b.

[171] *TCTC* 283.5a.

[172] *WKKS* b.7b-8a. In this text he is styled simply Li Chun 李準.

[173] *TCTC* 283.6a-b.

inevitable demise as a result of such an operation would leave his master without a first-rate boon companion for his drinking games.[174]

In addition to his predilection for elegant brawls, Yen-hsi's most obvious failing was his subservience to women. His empress, the Lady *née* Li 李, daughter of the Titular Minister (同中書門下平章事) Li Chen 李眞, was, like himself, fond of drink but cursed with a sulky and petulant disposition. Yen-hsi was devoted to her at first, but in awe of her.[175] In April 943, however, he took a fancy to the Lady *née* Shang 尚, whom he entitled Hsien Fei. This girl is described as exceptionally beautiful, and the Emperor was so enamoured of her that, when in his cups, he would kill or pardon anyone at her suggestion.[176] The Empress, with some reason, was jealous of her rival and entertained the idea of removing her husband and enthroning her son Ya-ch'eng 亞澄.[177] Subsequently Yen-hsi's assassination occurred at her instigation.[178]

The brief rule of Commander Chu Wen-chin and his colleague Lien Chung-yü, following the murder of Yen-hsi, has left little record of court life. We know only that Wen-chin dismissed palace girls and halted architectural construction as a political move to highlight the extravagance of the assassinated Yen-hsi.[179] These moves were made necessary by the speech of Chung-yü in which he attempted to justify the regicide to the great lords of Min: "In former times, T'ai Tsu, the Warlike Emperor [i.e. Shen-chih], braved arrows and stones in person, becoming in consequence the founder and possessor of Min. But it came about that his progeny was lascivious and cruel, and not on the Way, and now Heaven abominates the Wang family. . ."[180]

Of the court of Li Jen-ta and his puppet priest we know nothing. The pseudo-Emperor Wen-chin had at least the grace to show his contempt for the turncoat Jen-ta when the latter was still a disgruntled officer of the guards.[181]

---

[174] *Ibid.*

[175] *TCTC* 283.1b; *WTS*. The title *T'ung chung-shu men-hsia p'ing-chang-shih* implied that although its bearer held no high office in the regular hierarchy, he was entitled to the prerogatives of a grand minister (*tsai-hsiang* 宰相), hence my translation.

[176] *TCTC* 283.11a; *WTS*.

[177] *WTS*.

[178] Yen-hsi had a reputation for being overfond of women. This made it possible for Yü T'ing-ying 餘廷英, Prefect of Ch'üan, a "greedy and lustful" man, to seize the daughters of the folk for his own uses, falsely claiming that they were for the imperial harem (*TCTC* 283.5b; *WTS*).

[179] *TCTC* 284.3a.

[180] *WTS*.

[181] *TCTC* 284.14a.

Wang Yen-cheng, Emperor first of Yin 殷, then of Min, seems to have resembled Shen-chih his father, at least superficially. This is obvious in the descriptions given of his simplicity and avoidance of ostentation in his conduct of public affairs: "Yen-cheng wore a brown robe when attending to business, and in headquarters' conferences and receptions of envoys from neighboring countries he continued to carry out the rites of a military garrison (藩鎮)." This refers to the year 943 in which Yen-cheng first restored the ancient dynastic title of Yin.[182] The former Emperor spent his final years as a subject of Southern T'ang, being entitled first "Independent Prince" (自在王), later "Prince of Kuang-shan" (光山王 i.e., of his old native village) and finally "Prince of Fan-yang'" (鄱陽王).[183] He was buried first at Shou-ning 壽寧 District in the Metropolitan Prefecture of Fu-ning 福寧, but his body was finally moved to "Lotus Flower Peak" in Hou-kuan District by his son Chi-hsün 繼勳. The latter was an official under the Sung Emperors, and wished his father's grave to be near that of Shen-chih. Hence the villagers came to style the site of the tombs of these two illustrious rulers, "The Mountain of Kings' Graves" (王墓山).[184]

The external politics of the empire of Yin were largely conditioned by the breach between Yen-cheng and Yen-hsi, though later the conflict with Southern T'ang dominated all aspects of national life. It is said that Yen-hsi's enmity towards his brother was due to the letters he received from the latter accusing him of various crimes and moral weaknesses.[185] However this may be, Yen-cheng seems to have made at least one effort to reach a reconciliation, for in the summer of 940 he sent an officer to Fu Prefecture with a written oath (presumably of allegiance), gifts of female slaves and a censer for aromatics.[186] However, this was before Yen-cheng took the imperial title for himself. Another source of disagreement was Yen-cheng's request that he be made Legate of the Wei-wu Army (威武軍), the original source of Shen-chih's power in Fukien. Apparently he felt that if his brother deserved to be King (國王), he himself deserved the great title of Legate, which still carried considerable weight in the eyes of the outside world. But Yen-hsi refused to honor Chien Prefecture with the martial

---

[182] *TCTC* 283.9a-b. *WKKS* b.9a-b makes him Emperor of Great Shang 大商. The substitution of this equivalent, which is nor repeated in any other source, is bewildering. I am tempted to postulate a taboo on the character 殷 by the anonymous author of *WKKS*, as appearing in the name of one of his ancestors, but this is pure fancy.

[183] *WKKS* b.9a-b; *WTS*.

[184] *FCTC*1 39.17a.

[185] *WTS*.

[186] *TCTC* 282.10b-11a.

title which had belonged to Fu Prefecture since the days of the conquering Shen-chih. He compromised by creating the title Chen-an Army (鎮安軍) and making Yen-cheng its Legate. This was far from satisfying the ambitious prince, who changed the name of his garrison to Chen-wu Army (鎮武軍), possibly regarding the title as more closely resembling that of Shen-chih's original corps, and also as more indicative of his own temperament.[187] In August 941, however, Yen-hsi made himself Emperor of Min, and thereafter the breach between the two brothers was permanent. This conflict was the occasion of one point of criticism made by P'an Ch'eng-yu 潘承祐 in his memorial to Yen-cheng; indeed, it was the first point of ten. Ch'eng-yu spoke of the fraternal battle as "injurious to divine principle."[188] Certainly, it was permanently injurious to the empire.

One of the more eminent of Yen-cheng's courtiers was Huang Jen-feng黃仁諷, first Commander of the Fei-chieh Division (飛捷[都]), and later, when Fu Prefecture fell into Yen-cheng's hands, Commissioner of Police (鎮遏使) at Fu.[189] Jen-feng had been a soldier from his youth, with an honorable career until he took change in Fu Prefecture after the death of Lien Chung-yü. Disgruntled with Yen-cheng's nephew Chi-ch'ang 繼昌, his nominal overlord in the new Southern Capital, he plotted with Li Jen-ta to remove the Wang family from power. In retaliation for this betrayal, Yen-cheng executed Jen-feng's wife and children in the marketplace of Chien. Jen-ta put Jen-feng in command of the troops to resist the punitive army of Yen-cheng and was able to bring about its defeat. But he afterwards repented his abandonment of his true lord and his leaving his family to its fate. Jen-ta did not like this weakness and had Jen-feng put to death.[190]

More fortunate was Hsü Wen-chen (許文稹), a native of Ch'üan Prefecture, who served all the rulers of Min, ending with Yen-cheng. He was magistrate in T'ing Prefecture under the latter, and was highly regarded as a man of strict principles, feared and loved by the people under his jurisdiction. He remained faithful to Yen-cheng and was confirmed as Prefect of T'ing after the conquest by Southern T'ang. Finally he was captured by Chou Shih Tsung and treated with great honor.[191]

---

[187] *WKKS* b.9a-b ; *TCTC* 282.14a. It was at this time that Yen-cheng received the title of Prince of Fu-sha 富沙 from Yen-hsi, i. e. February 941.

[188] *TCTC* 283.11a. Details of the memorial will appear in later sections.

[189] *TCTC* 284.12a. This office gave him full powers in Fu Prefecture on behalf of Yen-cheng, who, being preoccupied with the war against Southern T'ang, had to remain in Chien.

[190] *CKC* 10.98-99.

[191] *Ibid.* 10.99.

A third notable of Yin is the notorious Yang Ssu-kung 楊思恭, known as "The Flayer" (剝皮), who will be discussed below, under Economy. After the fall of the Min empire he was taken to Chin-ling 金陵, the T'ang capital, and executed in the Chien-k'ang Market 建康市.[192]

Such were the personalities whose fortunes caused the rise, the maintenance and the collapse of the only independent Fukienese state since the formation of the Chinese empire.

[192] *Ibid.* 10.100.

# III

# HISTORY

## 1. THE PREFECT

THE Wang family was one of the many clans which rose to power or fame from the disorder attendant on the insurrection of Huang Ch'ao 黃巢.[193] The founder of the house's fortunes was Wang Ch'ao although he held no title of nobility during his lifetime, and can be counted as a member of the dynasty of Min only by restrospective courtesy. The events leading to his hegemony in the province of Fukien follow.[194]

A certain Wang Hsü 王緒, at the head of a band of partisans, attacked and reduced the town of Ku-shih late in the ninth century. The Wang brothers, Ch'ao, Shen-chih and Shen-kuei, had a reputation for military talent in this town and were recruited into Hsü's host.[195] The Prefect of Ts'ai 蔡, Ch'in Tsung-ch'üan 秦宗權, was levying troops wherever he could, for the purpose of a strong attack on the great rebel Huang Ch'ao. Accordingly, he secured the appointment of Wang Hsü as Prefect of Kuang 光 in the hope of inducing him to join forces. Hsü showed no great haste in preparing to join the proposed operations, whereupon Tsung-ch'üan sent soldiers against him. Hsü immediately departed from Kuang Prefecture at the head of his men, now many thousand strong, and moved into the South, looting all the way. The bandit army, including the brothers Wang, penetrated Fukien and proceeded as far as Chang-p'u, the southernmost town of consequence in the province.

---

[193] Our history does not begin in Fukien. However, that province had suffered the ravages of Huang Ch'ao's troops, which looted the land in the fall of 878, and reduced Fu Prefecture in 879. See *TCTC* 253.8b-9a.

[194] I base this account on *WTS*.

[195] Ch'ao held the title of military aide (軍校) according to *WTS*, but *TCTC* 254 and *CWTS* make him drillmaster (軍正).

Unhappily for himself, Hsü was distrustful and envious of his more talented subordinates, many of whom he put to death on various imaginary charges. Ch'ao felt some alarm, and persuaded a fellow officer to join him in leading a mutiny against their leader. The dissidents ambushed Hsü from a clump of bamboos, seized him and imprisoned him. Eventually Hsü committed suicide. These events took place at Nan-an. By virtue of his foresight in "protecting" his comrades from the dangers of a mistrustful leader, Ch'ao was promoted to the chieftainship by popular acclaim. He injected some discipline into the horde and undertook the ambitious venture of occupying the great port of Ch'üan. The prefect of that place, Liao Yen-jo 廖彥若, an avaricious and violent man, managed to hold out in the city for over a year, despite his unpopularity. But the siege was finally successful and Ch'ao became the head of Ch'üan Prefecture. In 886, by petition of Ch'en Yen 陳巖, Observator of Fukien (福建觀察使),[196] Ch'ao received his appointment as Prefect of Ch'üan from the imperial court of T'ang.

The ambitions of the new Prefect were not yet satisfied however. When Ch'en Yen died in 892, leaving his son-in-law, Fan Hui 范暉, as Deputy (留後), Ch'ao dispatched his brother Shen-chih to capture Fu Prefecture.[197] Shen-chih found that a protracted siege was necessary and his casualties were very heavy. At one stage he asked permission to raise the siege and withdraw, but was refused. He requested more troops and Ch'ao's own presence. Then he heard that Ch'ao had remarked, "Soldiers and commanders are quite used up—I shall have to go myself." Shen-chih was somewhat alarmed at this, and intensified his siege operations. Fan Hui was seized and decapitated by his own men, and the prefecture was put into the hands of Shen-chih.[198]

Ch'ao was now in control of the whole province, in recognition of which, the T'ang Emperor Chao Tsung established the Wei-wu Army with headquarters at Fu Prefecture, and made Ch'ao its Legate.[199] This appointment was effected on October 12, 896.[200]

[196] I resurrect an obsolete word to express the precise meaning of *kuan-ch'a-shih*. M. des Rotours' renderings are impossible to handle.

[197] *CWTS* puts Yen's death in 890. The title of *liu-hou* " Deputy " was assumed by a nominee for the post of Legate or of Observator, pending formal confirmation by the court.

[198] This incident is not mentioned in *WTS*. I rely on *CWTS*.

[199] He held the concurrent civil title of Observator.

[200] *TCTC* 260.19b. *WTS* has Ch'ao only as Observator, and dates the creation of the Awesome and Martial Army from after his death, with Shen-chih as its first Legate. This statement is contradicted by four sources: *TCTC, CWTS, TS* 190.4075c and *Ts'e-fu yüan-kuei* 223.16a-b.

December 897 found the new Legate ill in bed, and Shen-chih acting in his name as military governor (知軍府事).[201] On January 2, 898 Ch'ao died,[202] leaving his younger brother as dictator of Fukien.


## 2.  THE PRINCE

On his brother's death, Shen-chih assumed the high command in Fukien but propriety urged that he cede the authority to his older brother Shen-kuei, who had become Prefect of Ch'üan when Ch'ao moved his headquarters to Fu.  Shen-kuei, however, preferred to remain where he was, "in view of the merits of Shen-chih."  Thereupon Shen-chih memorialized the T'ang court to the effect that he was now Deputy Observator and Legate.[203]  On April 14, 898, the court confirmed him in this role and on October 25 the Emperor appointed him Legate of the Wei-wu Army.[204]  Shen-chih also received court titles from the almost extinct T'ang empire, and now had outstripped his late brother by far.  These titles were "Titular Minister," and Prince of Lang-yeh 瑯邪王.[205]

New honors followed with the establishment of the dynasty of Liang in 907.  In that year Shen-chih was given the concurrent title of Keeper of the Seal (侍中),[205a] and two years later he became Prince of Min 閩 王, the highest level he was to attain.[206]

[201] Shen-chih had been Vice-Observator and Vice-Legate (副使) (*TCTC* 261.8b and *CWTS*).  *TCTC* notes specifically that in leaving the command to Shen-chih, Ch'ao passed over his own sons, Yen-hsing 延興, Yen-hung 延虹, Yen-feng 延豊 and Yen-hsiu 延休.  We hear no more of these worthies, creating the suspicion that Shen-chih may somehow have done away with them.

[202] *TCTC* 261.8b.

[203] *TS* 190.4075c.  For a modern study of Shen-chih's administration, see Kuo Yü-lin 郭毓麟, Wang Shen-chih chih Min chih cheng-chi 王審知治閩之政績 (*Fu-chien wen-hua* 福建文化 1.18.14-15).

[204] *TCTC* 261.10b, 13a.

[205] *WTS; TCTC* 262.1a.  For "Titular Minister" see note 175.

[205a] In full *Men-hsia shih-chung* 門下侍中, sometimes translated "Chancellor," but I have preferred to suggest his primary duty in the T'ang court.  In the tenth century, this and other court titles were purely nominal.

[206] *Wu Tai hui yao* 11.143; *WTS; TCTC* 266.7b, 267.3b.  *Ts'e-fu yuan-kuei* 196.13a has him made Prince of Min in the summer of 907.  I follow *TCTC*.  In 907 Ch'ien Liu 錢鏐 became Prince of Wu-yüeh 吳越, and in 909 Liu Yin 劉隱 (in Canton) became Prince of Nan-p'ing 南平.  *WTS* records (without date) that Shen-chih received the title of Secretary of State (中書令) from Liang.  The same source states that the Prefecture of Fu was elevated to the status of a Great Government-General 大都督府.  I do not find this data elsewhere.  The title of Prince of Min was bestowed by the scholar Weng Ch'eng-tsan 翁承贊, a native Fukienese in the service of Liang.  The patent was conveyed at the Lin-ching Kuan 臨津館 in the Nan-t'ai District (*FCTC*1 38.4a).

In 909 relations with the state of Wu in Huainan deteriorated. Yang Lung-yen 楊隆演 had just ascended the throne at Yang Prefecture vacated by the death of his brother Yang Wo 楊渥. In the fall of the year Lung-yen sent an envoy, Chang Chih-yüan 張知遠, to cultivate good relations with the new Prince of Min. Chih-yüan made the mistake of showing contempt for Shen-chih and all his works, for which he was decapitated. This meant a complete severance of relations between the two states and henceforth Shen-chih was obliged to send his regular tribute-shipments to Liang by sea rather than overland.[207] In contrast to this failure of diplomacy, good relations were cemented with Wu-yüeh on the north, and with (Southern) Han on the south. In both cases marriage alliances were contracted between the respective ruling families. Ch'ien Ch'uan-hsiang 錢傳珦, a guards officer of Wu-yüeh, and a Prince of the royal house, took a wife in Min late in 916 or early in 917, that is in the twelfth month of the second year of the reign Chen Ming.[208] In the third year of that reign (917) Shen-chih took a daughter of Liu Yen of Han for his son Yen-chün.[209]

Meanwhile, trouble developed within Min itself. Wang Yen-pin had succeeded his father Shen-kuei as Prefect of Ch'üan, and by all accounts governed very well.[210] Shen-chih had granted him the nominal title of P'ing-lu Legate 平盧節度使,[211] but this failed to satisfy the ambitious young man. Inspired by supernatural signs, he sent an envoy secretly by sea to give tribute to Liang, and request that he be made "Legate of Ch'üan Prefecture," a much more realistic designation. Shen-chih learned of this affair, and being naturally unwilling to have a relative as his peer in military authority in one of the major cities of his realm, put to death the priest

[207] TCTC 267.9a. There is a poem by Han Wo written in 910 which describes the desolation of the Min countryside between Yu-ch'i District and Ch'üan Prefecture after the passage of a marching army (ChWTS 78.1182). I am unable to discover in the histories what battle or campaign could account for Wo's statement that settlements in this area were completely deserted.

[208] TCTC 269.18b-19a.

[209] TCTC 270.5b. Liu Yen 巖 (later written 龑) designated his empire, whose capital was at Canton, Great Yüeh 大越 in 917, but later in the same year changed its name to Han.

[210] The text says, "Yen-pin governed Ch'üan Prefecture for 17 years and the populace got security through him." The statement is given as background for events of the year 920. It would therefore appear that Shen-kuei had died in approximately 903.

[211] The P'ing-lu Army had been created by Hsüan Tsung of T'ang to control Southern Jehol and Eastern Hopei. After the rebellion of An Lu-shan, it was moved south into Northern Shantung. The Liang dynasty abolished the title of P'ing-lu Legate in 915 (WTS 2.4396c, 3.4397b). Shen-chih was exceeding his authority in making an appointment to this empty post although the text may have omitted to state that he requested it of the Liang court.

who had inspired Yen-pin's pretensions and degraded Yen-pin himself to private station.[212]

Relations with Han went quickly from good to bad. In May 922, the second year of Lung Te (the last Liang reign), the Emperor Liu Yen, in preparation for an invasion, sent some Taoist adepts, posing as refugees, to spy out the western frontier of Min in the vicinity of T'ing Prefecture. The Min general, Wang Yen-mei 王延美, anticipated these plans with a raid over the frontier, but his movements were reported by the spies, and Liu Yen and his forces fled without giving battle.[213] Two years later, the Lord of Han brought his troops to the southern border of Min once more, but was attacked, defeated and put to flight.[214] With this the permanent frontier between Min and Han was established west of T'ing and Chang Prefectures.

In June 925, the third year of the Later T'ang reign of T'ung Kuang, Shen-chih took to bed with an illness that was to prove fatal, and put his son Yen-han, the Vice-Legate, in charge of the military government (權知軍府事).[215] On December 30, the Prince of Min died and was canonized "Patriotic and Estimable Prince" (忠懿王).[216]

## 3. THE KING

Yen-han, eldest son of the Prince of Min,[217] declared himself Deputy of the Wei-wu Army immediately upon the death of his father.[218] He found himself faced with a military and political crisis. A certain Ch'en Pen 陳本 raised the standard of revolt in the southwestern corner of the province and laid siege to T'ing Prefecture with a force of thirty thousand

[212] *TCTC* 271.7a.

[213] *TCTC* 271.16b.

[214] *TCTC* 273.6a. A tribute-bearing embassy from Min to T'ang is recorded for this year (March 924). See *Ts'e-fu yuan-kuei* 169.7a.

[215] *TCTC* 273.14b.

[216] *WTS; TCTC* 274.4a. The "Ancestral Temple of the Patriotic and Estimable [Prince]" (忠懿廟) was located at Shen-chih's former residence, and was the site of the "Tablet for Virtuous Government" already mentioned in Note 99 (*Min tu chi* 8.5b). This was in Hou-kuan District. The *Ch'ang-lo hsien-chih* 長樂縣志 8.38b tells of another temple bearing the same name erected east of Ch'ang-lo in the Ch'ien Lung reign (eighteenth century).

[217] *WTS.*

[218] *TCTC* 274.4a. T'ao Yüeh 陶岳, *Wu Tai shih pu* 五代史補 (*Yü-chang ts'ung-shu* 豫章叢書 edit.) 2.4b-6b states that Shen-chih was succeeded by Yen-chün—an error, and also that Yen-chün was Shen-chih's younger brother, instead of his son—another error. Yen-han himself is not mentioned.

men. A punitive expedition with Liu Yung 柳鄶 in command of twenty
thousand troops was sent against him. The rebel army was smashed in
February or March 926, the first year of the T'ang reign T'ien Ch'eng.[219]

On April 19, Yen-han received his confirmation as Legate from the
T'ang court, and on July 1 was given the court title of Titular Minister.[220]
But titles given reluctantly by a feeble and distant government were
insufficient to satisfy the vanity of the new ruler. The Emperor Chuang
Tsung 莊宗 was assassinated in this year and the time seemed ripe for a
seizure of royal power. Yen-han found justification for his ambition in
recorded history. He showed his ministers and generals a passage in the
*Historical Memoirs* of Ssu-ma Ch'ien, and pointed out that biographies of
the Kings of ancient Min-yüeh 閩越 were omitted. This he interpreted
as meaning that Fukien had never been a part of the Chinese empire. His
domain had been a kingdom (王國) from antiquity, and he was justified
in restoring the ancient dignity. Convinced by this argument, or unable
to offer effective resistance, his officialdom submitted a petition to him,
begging him to take the throne.[221]

Accordingly, on November 13, Yen-han declared himself King of
Great Min (大閩國王), ordained a regular official hierarchy (百官),
declared a general amnesty and canonized his father Shen-chih as "Radiantly
Martial Prince" (昭武王).[222] Nonetheless he left a semblance of superior
authority to Ming Tsung, the new T'ang Emperor, by continuing to employ
the reign title of the northern empire, rather than adopting a new one for
himself.[223]

But internal strife developed immediately. The King found himself
at odds with his adoptive brother Yen-ping, Prefect of Chien,[224] and
provoked the wrath of his younger brother Yen-chün, Prefect of Ch'üan,
allegedly for his rapaciousness towards the daughters of his subjects.[225] The

---

[219] *TCTC* 274.6a.

[220] *TCTC* 274.16a, 275.7a.

[221] *WTS*. In *Han shu* 95.0604d, the story of the conquest of Min-yüeh is told. The
Ch'in empire gave King Wu-chu the title of "Chieftain" (君長) and reduced the
status of his kingdom to that of Commandery of Min-chung 閩中. For aid given to
the founder of the Han dynasty, Wu-chu was restored as King of Min-yüeh in 202
B.C. It is noteworthy, however, that in the *Han shu*, Min-yüeh is not listed in the
*Monograph of Geography* (地理志), but rather in the section on foreign nations, i.e., not
as a part of the Chinese empire. Nan-yüeh, further south, was a Chinese possession
however. See also Léonard Aurousseau, "La Première Conquête chinoise des pays
Annamites (iiie siècle avant notre ère)," *B.E.F.E.O.* 23.137-264 (1923).

[222] *TCTC* 275.11a-b.

[223] *WTS*.

[224] Original surname Chou 周 (*WTS*).

[225] *TCTC* 275.12b-13a.

two Prefects laid plans for the removal of their brother, organized fleets and proceeded simultaneously against Fu Prefecture. Yen-ping reached the capital first, and defeated Yen-han's commander, Ch'en T'ao 陳陶. The victor then led a band of daredevils over the city wall, captured the wardens of the gate and seized his brother's arsenal. His soldiers penetrated the royal apartments but the terrified Yen-han found temporary safety in a side room. The following morning, January 14, 927, he was discovered, accused of the murder of Shen-chih in concert with his wife and decapitated. Yen-chün did not arrived from Ch'üan until then, and was welcomed at the city gate by his brother Yen-ping who saluted him as Deputy of the Wei-wu Army.[226] The short-lived kingdom was extinct, and Fukien remained a military garrison, nominally subject to T'ang, for six years.

## 4.  THE EMPEROR HUI TSUNG[227]

Wang Yen-chün, the new lord of Fukien, was the second son of Shen-chih. Thus his elevation to succeed Yen-han was quite correct in terms of the rule of fraternal succession, especially since Yen-ping was not the Prince's offspring. But all did not go well between the two brothers. Yen-chün gave a farewell party on February 20 as Yen-ping was on the point of returning to his post at Chien Prefecture. The Prefect addressed the Deputy in these words, "It will be well to maintain the aspirations of our parent. Do not annoy your old brother by making him return."[228] Presumably this was a warning to Yen-chün not to aim at the sovereignty. At any rate, the Deputy disclaimed any such intention but is said to have blushed.[229] Whereupon Yen-ping returned up-river.[230]

The usual appointments soon arrived from the T'ang court. Yen-chün was confirmed as Legate and given honorary rank as Secretary of State and Prince of Lang-yeh on June 5 of that year (927).[231] On August 13, 928 he was made Prince of Min.[232]

---

[226] *TCTC* 275.13a.

[227] 惠宗.  惠 " benevolent " is a substitute for 慧 " shrewd," itself a euphemism for "witless," and commonly employed in the posthumous titles of mad monarchs.

[228] I follow the language of *WTS*.  *TCTC* 275.14b is very similar.

[229] *TCTC* 275.14b.

[230] *WKKS* b.6b says he returned to Ch'üan Prefecture.  An error.

[231] *TCTC* 275.18a and *Wu Tai hui yao* 11.144.  *WTS* adds *Chien-chiao t'ai-shih* 檢校太師, without date.

[232] *TCTC* 2/6.9a and *Wu Tai hui yao* 11.144.  *Ts'e-fu yüan-kuei* 224.19b says that at this time Yen-chün created the post of Legate of Chien Prefecture for Yen-ping.

Early in 930 Yen-ping became ill and retired to his country villa.[233] He petitioned the T'ang Emperor, requesting that authority in Chien Prefecture be transferred to his son Chi-hsiung 繼雄. Accordingly the latter was appointed Prefect of Chien as of January 7.[234] It would appear that Yen-ping's strategic position above Fu Prefecture suggested grandiose plans to him, and also enabled him to communicate directly with the T'ang capital.[235] Probably the appointment of his own son as Prefect was an initial step in his scheme to make his own family dominant in Fukien. The following summer (931) Yen-ping was informed that his brother was mortally ill[236] and, quickly assembling a naval force, he descended the river towards Fu, leaving his second son Chi-sheng 繼昇 in command at Chien.[237]

Yen-ping and Chi-hsiung arrived before the prefectural city of Fu on May 5 and launched simultaneous attacks against its walls. The resistance was led by Wang Jen-ta, Commander of Galleons 樓船指揮使. Jen-ta brought about the defeat of the attackers by a stratagem. He concealed himself with a band of soldiers in an armored vessel from which he ordered the white flag of surrender to be hoisted. Chi-hsiung, assured of victory, came aboard inadequately protected. He was instantly stabbed to death, his head chopped off and exposed over the West Gate of the city where his father was leading the assault.[238] At this sight Yen-ping broke into anguished tears, his attack faltered and his host was shattered by Jen-ta's forces. Some attendants attempted to make their escape from the scene of the defeat carrying Yen-ping in a grain measure, but they were pursued and captured on May 6. The unhappy man was taken before his brother who reproached him ironically: "Indeed I have troubled my old brother by making him return." Yen-ping was imprisoned while Yen-chün sent an envoy to Chien Prefecture to round up the partisans of the former Prefect. The envoy was assassinated and Chi-sheng fled to Wu-yüeh with his younger brother Chi-lun 繼倫.[239] The following month Yen-ping was publicly decapitated and his name removed from the register of the Wang

[233] *TCTC* gives him the title of Feng-kuo 奉國 Legate at this point, but no hint is given as to whence and at what time he received such an appointment. Possibly he received it directly from the T'ang court, in view of what follows.

[234] *TCTC* 276.17b-18a.

[235] Hu San-hsing's note on *ibid*.

[236] *WKKS* b.6c states that Yen-chün actually sent a report of his own death to provoke an incident.

[237] *TCTC* 277.12a.

[238] *WTS*, *TCTC* 277.12a-b.

[239] *WTS*, *TCTC* 277.13a, *WKKS* b.6b.

clan.[240] Yen-ping's younger brother Yen-cheng became the new Prefect of Chien.[241]

The Legate, under the influence of soothsaying Taoists, now began to lay plans for the usurpation of the imperial title. He first memorialized the T'ang court: "[In view of] the death of Ch'ien Liu 錢鏐 it is requested that your servant be appointed Prince of Wu-yüeh. [In view of] the death of Ma Yin 馬殷 [ruler of Ch'u] it is requested that your servant be appointed Minister of State 尚書令."

The imperial court made no reply to this audacious request, whereupon Yen-chün discontinued his tribute missions, signalizing thereby that he no longer recognized the court.[242] This was in July 932.

All preparations were complete and all omens favorable in February 933. Yen-chün declared the foundation of the empire of Great Min with himself as first Emperor and the reign title Lung Ch'i.[242a] A general amnesty was proclaimed; Shen-chih's posthumous title was raised to "Radiantly Martial Filial Emperor" (昭武孝皇帝), with the temple name of T'ai Tsu 太祖; the five ancestral temples were erected and an official hierarchy established. The Emperor changed his personal (taboo) name from Yen-chün to Lin 璘.[243]

The great officers of the new state were designated as follows:

Li Min 李敏—Vice-Minister of State for the Left (左僕射) and Vice-Keeper of the Seal (門下侍郎).[244]

Wang Chi-p'eng—Vice-Minister of State for the Right and Vice-Secretary of State.[245]

Wu Hsü—Chancellor.

At about this time, two Commissioners for Ceremony of Patent (冊禮使)[246] arrived at the capital of Min. One of them, P'ei Chieh 裴傑, was

[240] *TCTC* 277.12b; i.e., his name was restored to Chou Yen-ch'en 周彥琛.

[241] *Ibid.*

[242] *WTS; TCTC* 277.22a.

[242a] "Dragon Disclosure," from the auspicious appearance of a dragon above his residence.

[243] This is the form in both editions of *TCTC. WTS* has 鏻. *CWTS* passes over the change in silence.

[244] The title "Minister of State" was not used in the T'ang Dynasty out of deference to T'ang Tai Ts'ung, who once held this office. Yet we have seen that Yen-chün requested it for himself. Possibly he had assumed it after the discontinuance of relations with Later T'ang, hence Li Min could hold no higher title in the Min Department of State. Similarly, Shen-chih had been Keeper of the Seal, and Li Min could only be Vice-Keeper.

[245] Yen-chün had been Secretary of State since 927, making this office unavailable as well.

[246] Delegated to bestow some patent of T'ang court rank on Yen-chün.

prevailed upon to accept appointment as Warehouse Commissioner (如京使) under the new regime, while the other, Ch'eng K'an 程侃, importuned the Emperor to be allowed to return north, but this was not permitted.[247]

In May 933 the monarch designated his son Chi-p'eng as Prince of Fu 福王, and on the 31st of that month put him in complete charge of the government[248] during a temporary retirement.[249] Yen-chün reascended the throne on August 7.[250] Late in the year he raised his mother, the Grand Lady of Lu 魯國太夫人, née Huang 黃, to the rank of Empress Dowager 皇太后.[251] In December of this year, or in January 934, he designated Fu Prefecture as the Metropolitan Prefecture of Ch'ang-lo 長樂府.[252]

Meanwhile, a certain Wu Kuang 吳光, dismayed at the depredations of the Fiscal Intendant Hsüeh Wen-chieh and concerned for his own safety, had fled with his retainers to the state of Wu where he sought to bring about a military expedition against Min. He was able to convince the Prefect of Hsin 信, Chiang Yen-hui 蔣延徽, of the merits of his plan, so that the latter, without waiting for orders from his government, initiated an attack on Chien Prefecture. Yen-chün forthwith sent ambassadors to ask armed assistance from Wu-yüeh.[253] In the first month of the first year of the T'ang reign Ch'ing T'ai (i.e., January—February, 934), Yen-hui, having achieved a victory over the Min troops at the frontier town of P'u-ch'eng, laid siege to Chien Prefecture. Ten thousand fresh troops were dispatched by Yen-chün under the command of Chang Yen-jou 張延柔, Superior Army Commissioner 上軍使, and Wang Yen-tsung 王延宗, Great General of Cavalry 驃騎大將軍, to relieve the city. This army staged a mutiny en route, refusing to advance further without the head of Hsüeh Wen-chieh, the unpopular Intendant. The anti-Wen-chieh faction at court, led by the Empress Dowager and the Prince of Fu, persuaded the Emperor to abandon his favorite. Wen-chieh was struck to the ground with a ceremonial tablet by Chi-p'eng as he left the court. He was caged in a barbarous cart of his own invention, pelted with stones by the populace and sent off to the rebellious army. His escorts got him to the camp by forced marches within two days, in order to give the lie to Wen-chieh's prophecy that he would survive if the trip took three. The Intendant was

---

[247] *TCTC* 278.5a.
[248] In charge of " all eventualities " (萬機).
[249] *TCTC* 278.6b.
[250] *TCTC* 278.7b.
[251] *TCTC* 278.13b.
[252] *TCTC* 278.15a.
[253] *TCTC* 278.14a.

dismembered by the soldiers and his flesh devoured.[254]  Meanwhile the Emperor had repented his desertion of his minister and sent a messenger with a reprieve.  It arrived too late to save the unlucky man.[255]  During this time the siege of Chien was progressing favorably for the invaders, but the matter had come to the attention of the all-powerful Wu official, Hsü Chih-hao 徐知誥.[256]  Yen-hui was the son-in-law of the founder of the Wu dynasty, Yang Hsing-mi, and an intimate of one of the Wu princes, Yang Meng 楊濛.  Chih-hao feared that if Yen-hui were successful, the prestige of the pro-Yang faction in Huai-nan might frustrate his own plans for founding a dynasty, and accordingly he sent a messenger to Yen-hui ordering his return.  The wisdom of a speedy withdrawal was made even more apparent to the general with the news that the army of Min was about to arrive, reinforced by troops from Wu-yüeh.  Therefore he raised the siege and departed.  The inspired Fukienese pursued him and inflicted a bloody defeat on his army.  Chih-hao took this occasion to degrade Yen-hui to a guard command and sent envoys to re-establish good relations with Min.[257]

On New Year's Day (February 6, 935), a new reign was inaugurated in Min—Yung Ho "Perpetual Accord," doubtless so named in honor of peace between Min and Wu, and a general amnesty was declared.[258]  Shortly thereafter the luxurious lady Ch'en, known as Golden Phoenix, was designated Empress.[259]

---

[254] *TCTC* 278.16a-b, *WTS*.  This appears to have been a kind of ritualistic cannibalism reserved especially for unpopular officials accused of being devourers of the people's substance.  Compare the case of Chang Yen-tse 張彥澤, brought to justice for the crime of plundering K'ai-feng by the Khitan Emperor in 947, and dismembered and eaten by the citizenry (*TCTC* 286.1b-2a).  A comprehensive study of cannibalism in China has been written by Kuwabara Jitsuzō 桑原隲藏.  He counts many historical instances among the following general types:  1) due to famine;  2) in besieged cities;  3) sybaritic gourmandism;  4) for hatred and revenge;  5) as medicine.  See his " Shina-ningen ni okeru shoku-jinniku no fūshū " 支那人間に於ける食人肉の風習.  *Tōyōgakuhō* 東洋學報 14.1-62 (1924).

[255] *Ibid.*  It is stated that Sheng T'ao 盛韜, the influential shaman (see below, under Religion), was put to death at this time.  The reason is not revealed.

[256] He later (937) overthrew his sovereign and founded the dynasty of Southern T'ang. *NTS* 1.3 states that he had been urged to take the throne by Min.  Chih-hao first called his state Ch'i 齊, subsequently changing it to T'ang (Later T'ang, in the north, had meanwhile given way to Later Chin).  Hsü Hsüan 徐鉉, *Chi-shen lu shih-i* 稽神錄 拾遺 (*TSCC* edit.) 5, tells that during an invasion by Wu, the Buddhist temples were occupied by the invading troops and the monks indiscriminately put to death.  It is doubtless the present campaign that is referred to.

[257] *TCTC* 278.16b.

[258] *TCTC* 279.16a.

[259] *Ibid.*

The Prince of Fu, Chi-p'eng, was now laying the groundwork for his own accession to the throne. He was an enemy of the Empress, her family and friends, and took as his instrument of vengeance a certain Li Fang, Imperial City Commissioner 皇城使. In the fall of the year the Emperor was critically ill, and the news of this is said to have provoked a pleased expression on the countenance of the Prince. Li Fang took this as a hint that Yen-chün ought not to recover. The first move was made against Li K'o-yin, the Empress' lover, who was beaten to death with cudgels on November 16. On the following day the Emperor was sufficiently improved to attend to business and Golden Phoenix complained to him about the assassination. Yen-chün assembled his court and initiated inquiries. Li Fang, in alarm, led a band of ruffians to the palace. The commotion frightened the Emperor, who took refuge in the Nine Dragon Tent, where he was found, stabbed and left writhing in agony. Also murdered were the Empress Ch'en, her relative Ch'en K'uang-sheng, the Emperor's favorite Kuei Shou-ming and Chi-p'eng's younger brother Chi-t'ao 繼韜, whom he hated and greatly feared.[260]

## 5.  THE EMPEROR K'ANG TSUNG[261]

On November 18, 935, the day following the regicide, Chi-p'eng ascended the imperial throne, changed his personal name to Ch'ang 昶, gave his father, the murdered Emperor, the appropriate posthumous titles, and declared a general amnesty. The Empress Dowager Huang was appointed "Regent" (監國), and Chi-p'eng assumed the powers of Legate in Fukien (權知福建節度事), while sending an embassy to memorialize the T'ang court of his action. His sweetheart, Spring Swallow, née Li, became Hsien Fei "Estimable Consort."[262]

The actual control of the government was now vested in the assassin,

---

[260] *TCTC* 279.20a-b, *WTS*. The Emperor had at least one man to mourn for him. This was the virtuous eunuch Lin Yen-yü 林延禹, who had been sent to Canton in connection with negotiations for the hand of the Han Princess of Ch'ing-yüan. He had remained there as a sort of consul, but also in the employ of the Han Emperor. It is reported that when he heard of the murder of Yen-chün, he asked permission to return to Min, but was refused. He then donned white garments and sat for three days facing his country, weeping (*TCTC* 279.20b).

[261] See Appendices, Table A. Chi-p'eng was the eldest son of the late monarch, whom *WTS* designates Hui Huang-ti 惠皇帝 with the temple name T'ai Tsung 太宗. These titles are not confirmed by other sources, although *Ts'e-fu yüan-kuei* 224.6a gives Hui Ti 惠帝. I follow *TCTC*.

[262] *TCTC* 279.20a-b.

Li Fang.[263] The latter, however, was uneasy at heart, in view of the common fate of king-slayers. Therefore he kept a private corps of bravos for his own protection. Chi-p'eng, for his part, took the view that his agent was a dangerous man with too much power. He therefore chose a certain officer, Li Yen-hao 李延皓,[264] to assume the role of Fang's partisan, insinuate himself into his confidence and in this way render his private bodyguard useless.[265] The plot was successful. A body of Yen-hao's guards seized Fang on December 19, beheaded him and exposed his head at one of the gates of the palace.[266] Fang's bodyguard, consisting of approximately a thousand men, attacked the palace, burned the Ch'i-sheng Gate, seized their captain's head and fled with it to Wu-yüeh. Chi-p'eng immediately published a decree blaming the deaths of the late Emperor and his party exclusively on Fang. Presumably his own role in the unsavory business was not generally known, and Fang had been the only possible informer.

The supreme military command ("Controller of the Guards of the Six Armies") was now vested in a member of the royal family, Wang Chi-yen 王繼嚴, Prince of Chien 建王, while the titles of *Hsüan-hui-shih* 宣徽使[267] and Government Councilor (參政事) were bestowed on the estimable Yeh Ch'iao.[268] This latter personage did not remain in office long. He admonished his sovereign for the special favor shown Spring Swallow to

---

[263] His official title became "Controller of the Guards of the Six Armies" (判六軍 諸衞), one of the highest titles in the administration of Min. *Min-hou hsien-chih* 50.1a preserves the names of two of the six armies: Dragon-tiger (龍虎) and Heavenly Imperium (天霸). The "Six Armies" are the armies of the Son of Heaven (see *Chou li*, "Hsia kuan, Ssu-ma" 夏官司馬).

[264] *TCTC* makes him Commander of the Kung-ch'en Division, while *WTS*, without naming the spy, states that the Army of the Great Offering (大享軍) was privy to the plot. The latter must have been one of the Six Armies, probably one whose command was given to Yen-hao, thereby making him Fang's subordinate.

[265] *TCTC* 279.21a-b, *WTS*.

[266] So *TCTC*. *WTS* says "in the marketplace." The former is more consistent with the material which follows.

[267] This title was for one of the many extra-bureaucratic offices which were established in the T'ang dynasty, but not registered in the official T'ang history. It was at first, like that of *Shu-mi-shih*, held by eunuchs. These officials were in charge of palace stores, services and accounts. In the Five Dynasties period the *Hsüan-hui-shih* was a very high-ranking state officer, not necessarily a eunuch, and the title was frequently held concurrently with that of Chancellor (*Wen-hsien t'ung-k'ao* 58.525c-526a). The term *hsüan-hui*, "manifest superbness," appears in *Pei shih* 13.2785d as the title of a minor lady-in-waiting on the Toba Emperors, analogous to "manifest enlightenment" (宣明), a similar title.

[268] This was the man elsewhere styled "National Patriarch," Chi-p'eng's mentor before his accession.

the detriment of the Lady of Liang 梁國夫人, *née* Li, his first wife,[269] daughter of the great minister Li Min and niece of Hui Tsung. When the old man become importunate in this matter, the Emperor, losing patience, sent him into retirement at Yung-t'ai, his native town. Chi-p'eng signalized this act by a pun: "A single leaf, gone with the wind, falls in the imperial drain," a reference to Ch'iao's surname Yeh, which means "leaf."[270]

In April 936—the first year of the reign T'ien Fu in the calendar of the newly established Northern Dynasty of Chin—Chi-p'eng adopted the reign title T'ung Wen.[271] At the same time he elevated Spring Swallow to the rank of Empress, and increased his grandmother's dignity with the augmented title of Grand Empress Dowager (太皇太后).[272]

That Chi-p'eng's role in the murder of his father was by now widely known or suspected is borne out by the report that the Fukienese, learning of T'ang's fate, drew an analogy between the Prince of Lu 潞王, last ruler of that dynasty, who attained the throne by murdering his predecessor, and their own ruler, and asked what would be his fate?[273] The new Emperor, seems to have been unpopular with his subjects. This may have led to his hearing rumors of revolt for we are informed that in the early summer of 937 he sent agents to all parts of the empire "to spy out hidden evil."[274]

Chi-p'eng now decided to attempt to gain recognition of his autonomy from the feeble dynasty of Chin, and in November 937, instructed his younger brother Chi-kung 恭繼, who held the old title of Legate of the Wei-wu Army, to draft a memorial to the Northern Court announcing his own succession to the imperial throne and requesting the establishment of a "residence" (邸) for him in the northern capital.[275] It will be recalled that relations with the Five Dynasties had been interrupted since 932 when Yen-chün stopped sending tribute to T'ang. This then was in the nature

---

[269] The text has 元妃, but this is not a formal title analogous to "Estimable Consort" (賢妃). It signifies simply "original mate." Cf. commentary on *Tso 'chuan* (Duke Yin 1).

[270] *TCTC* 279.21a-b.

[271] "Comprehensive culture." Actually the Chin dynasty was not established in place of T'ang until the eleventh month of this year but I follow the Chinese custom of using the reign title retrospectively to cover the whole period. It was a momentous year—the Khitans now had a grip on northern Chinese affairs, and Wang Chien 王建 of Koryŏ achieved the hegemony of the Korean peninsula with the submission to him of Silla and Paikche.

[272] *TCTC* 280.2b.

[273] *TCTC* 280.18b.

[274] *TCTC* 281.4b.

[275] *TCTC* 281.11a. *Ts'e-fu yuan-kuei* 224.19b makes Chi-kung "Legate of Fu Prefecture."

of a friendly overture, especially since token tribute was to accompany the mission.[276]  But the main issue was to achieve formal acknowledgement of the legitimacy of Chi-p'eng's own status.  This is proved by the fact that when, on November 27, 938, the Chin Emperor appointed Chi-p'eng King of Min, and sent Lu Sun 盧損 as Commissioner for Ceremonies of Patent to convey the royal grant and bestow an ochre robe on Chi-p'eng, the latter despatched an envoy to explain to the Chin government that he could not accept such a patent, since he had already assumed the purple.[277]

Lu Sun arrived in the Min capital early in 939, preceded by the news of his mission, and was not permitted an interview with Chi-p'eng who pleaded illness.  Instead he delegated Chi-kung to entertain the ambassador,[278] and presently sent Sun back to the Chin capital in company with Cheng Yüan-pi 鄭元弼, a secretary of the Board of Rites (禮部員外郎), bearing the memorial drafted by Chi-kung and carrying tribute.[279]

The spring and summer of 939 were marked chiefly by acts of violence and discrimination against members of the royal family, which led to the murder of the Emperor himself.  Chi-p'eng, envious of his uncles Yen-wu 延武 (former Prefect of Chien) and Yen-wang 延望 (President of the Board of Taxation 戶部尚書), listened to the shaman Lin Hsing 林興 when the latter revealed a spiritual oracle to the effect that these worthies planned an insurrection.  The shaman led bullies to the homes of the Emperor's uncles, and killed them both as well as their sons.[280]  Later in midsummer, envy and suspicion of the Prince of Chien, Chi-yen, a man popular with the literati, induced the Emperor to remove him from his overall military command, to be replaced by his younger brother Chi-yung 繼鏞.[281]  Meanwhile Lin Hsing's supernaturalistic impostures became known and he was banished to Ch'üan Prefecture.[282]

---

[276] WTS.

[277] TCTC 281.17a-b.  On November 29 the Chin court also announced the appointment of Chi-kung as Prince of Lin-hai Commandery 臨海郡王.  WTS says " Prince of Min " instead of " King of Min."

[278] This discourtesy provoked a certain aristocrat, Lin Hsing-tsou 林省鄒, to remark, " Our lord does not serve his sovereign [i.e., the Chin Emperor, a treasonable utterance], nor love his parents, nor pity his subjects, nor reverence his gods, nor act friendly toward his neighbors, nor act courteously toward his guest.  How can he long endure?"  TCTC 282.2a.  Chi-p'eng's neglect of Lu Sun was in part conditioned by an insult tendered the Chin ambassador to Liu I 劉乙, the dandy, who was Under-Secretary of State (中書舍人), and a member of the entertainment committee (WTS).

[279] Ibid.

[280] TCTC 282.3b.

[281] SPPY edit. has 鎔.  Chi-yen's name was changed to Chi-yü 繼裕, for reasons not apparent to the writer.  At this time also the word " Guards " (諸衛) was dropped from his title, leaving only " Controller of the Six Armies " (Ibid.).

[282] TCTC 282.4a.

These acts, and displeasure of the two guard divisions led by Lien Chung-yü and Chu Wen-chin, provoked a rebellion. Chi-p'eng suspected that Chung-yü had some knowledge of the fire which destroyed the Northern Palace, and his suspicion was reported to the commander by a certain scholar Ch'en T'an 陳郯. Fearing for his life, Chung-yü took command of the two guard divisions on the night of August 29 and led them in an attack on the Ch'ang-ch'un Palace ("Enduring Spring") to which he set fire. At the same time he sent men to look for the Emperor's uncle, Yen-hsi, "in the midst of tiles and pebbles," and hail him with the salutation "Ten Thousand Years." Chi-p'eng and his family escaped from the city with the faithful members of the Ch'en-wei Division, and spent the night in the wilderness. Yen-hsi dispatched his nephew Chi-yeh 繼業, former Prefect of T'ing, with a band of troops to capture the refugees. They were found in a little village hut. Chi-p'eng, an accomplished archer, managed to account for a number of his attackers, but finally he was overwhelmed and cast his bow on the ground, saying to his cousin, "Where is the fealty of a subject?" Chi-yeh replied, "If the sovereign lacks a sovereign's virtue, why should a subject have a subject's fealty? The new sovereign is my uncle. The former sovereign [i.e., you] is my brother. With which should I be intimate, and from which estranged?" The Emperor replied nothing to this. He was seized and taken with his family as far as T'o-chuang 阤莊 where he was stupefied with wine and garrotted. Also put to death were the Empress Li, Wang Chi-kung and the monarch's sons.[283]

## 6.　THE EMPEROR CHING TSUNG

With the assassination of Chi-p'eng, a kind of death reserved especially by heaven for the Min Emperors, one which Yen-hsi himself was not to escape, the empire once more reverted to the status of a kingdom. Yen-hsi immediately styled himself Legate of the Wei-wu Army and King of Min. He altered his given name to Hsi 曦 and adopted the reign title Yung Lung 永隆.[284] Prisoners were liberated and largess distributed. It was proclaimed that Chi-p'eng had been murdered by members of his personal guard, the

---

[283] TCTC 282.5a-b, 6a-b, WTS. Yin Chu 尹洙 (1001–1047), Wu Tai ch'un-ch'iu 五代春秋 b.8, has "a Fukienese murdered the sovereign Hu 胡." Apparently this is a misprint for Ch'ang 昶.

[284] TCTC 282.6a-b; WTS. See TCTC k'ao-i 考異 30.4a for a discussion of the date of adoption of this reign title. One authority has argued that the adoption could not have been until late in 940, when Chin bestowed the title of King on Yen-hsi. But he was already King by self-declaration.

Ch'en-wei Division. The late ruler was appropriately canonized and given the temple name of K'ang Tsung.[285] An embassy was despatched to the Chin court to declare Min a tributary state.[286]

A new minister was appointed—Li Chen 李眞, formerly T'ai-tzu t'ai-fu 太子太傅, who now became Ssu-k'ung, and concurrently Vice-Secretary of State and Titular Minister.[287]

Lien Chung-yü inaugurated the new reign with the execution of the spiritual advisers of the late monarch. The Taoist Ch'en Shou-yüan attempted to flee the court in disguise but was caught by soldiers and killed. Agents were also sent to Ch'üan Prefecture to execute the shaman Lin Hsing.[288] Chung-yü was now the most powerful individual in the state.

Meanwhile the tribute embassy sent earlier in the year by K'ang Tsung to the Chin court was continuing its journey northwards. It did not arrive at Ta-liang 大梁, the capital, until November 26, 939. The memorandum drafted by the late Chi-kung and now presented to the Chin Emperor by Cheng Yüan-pi was contemptuous of the repeated shifts of dynasty in the north, indicative of heaven's withdrawal of favor from the supposed "Emperors" of the Five Dynasties, and sought the employment of the protocol of equal sovereign states between Chin and Min. On November 28 the Emperor decreed that the tribute from Min should be rejected, and that Yüan-pi and Lin En 林恩 (the "Memorial Transmission Officer" 進奏官) should be immediately sent back to their country under escort. However, one of the Chin officials suggested to the throne that the arrogance of the note from Chi-p'eng, and his manifest usurpation, merited nothing better than the seizure of the tribute and the imprisonment of the envoys which was accordingly done.[289]

---

[285] TCTC loc. cit.

[286] Ibid.; WTS.

[287] TCTC loc. cit.

[288] TCTC 282.6b.

[289] TCTC 282.7a, WTS. T'se-fu yuan-kuei 233.12b-13b has many details of this mission. Ssu-ma Kuang (in TCTC k'ao-i 30.4b) quotes a passage from Lo-chung chi-i 洛中紀異 which states that "Ch'ang, after being rebuked by mandate of the [Northern Court], then despatched envoys across the sea to make overtures to the Khitan." The text goes on to tell how Chi-p'eng offered the Khitan the goods confiscated by the Chin court; that the Khitan chieftain forced the latter to give them up and release the Min embassy; and thereafter missions from Min to the Khitan in search of horses were frequent. Ssu-ma Kuang rejected this material from his history on the grounds that since Chi-p'eng was already dead, he could not know anything of the fate of his embassy. However, if the author of Lo-chung chi-i had an unclear notion of Min chronology he might easily have attributed these exchanges between Fukien and Manchuria to the late Emperor instead of his successor.

In February 940 Cheng Yüan-pi was brought once more into the imperial presence. He prostrated himself and apostacized completely any allegiance to the Min dynasty. "Wang Ch'ang [*i.e.,* the late Chi-p'eng]," said he, "is sovereign over barbarians and savages. He is ignorant of duty and protocol. If Your Majesty gets good words from him, there is no reason for joy, and if bad words, there is no reason for anger. Your Majesty now displays that great reliability which attracts men from distant places. Your servant is disgraced by having undertaken such a mission, and is willing to submit to the headsman's axe in expiation of the guilt of Ch'ang." Chin Kao Tsu graciously pardoned the man, had him released and sent back home.[290] This took place on February 15.

Fraternal dissension disrupted the Min state once more. Yen-cheng, Prefect of Chien, was in the habit of sending scolding letters to his brother in the capital. Yen-hsi retaliated by delegating old Yeh Ch'iao, now back in favor, to "inspect" the troops at Chien. Ch'iao and Tu Han-ch'ung 杜漢崇, another imperial spy, sent back regular reports to their king about Yen-cheng's private affairs. On one occasion Ch'iao went so far as to accuse Yen-cheng of plotting rebellion. The Prefect wished to decapitate Ch'iao but the latter managed to escape in time and, together with Han-ch'ung who was "inspecting" the Garrison of the South (南鎮軍),[291] attempted armed resistance to Yen-cheng's troops. They were defeated, however, and returned to the capital.[292] Yen-hsi forthwith despatched his "Commissioner of the Combined Armies" (統軍使), P'an Shih-k'uei 潘師逵, and a certain Wu Hsing-chen 吳行眞, at the head of forty thousand soldiers to attack Yen-cheng. Chien was besieged and Yen-cheng sent for help from Wu-yüeh. The Prince of that state (Ch'ien Yüan-kuan 錢元瓘), against the advice of his minister, sent Yang Jen-ch'üan 仰仁詮 and Hsüeh Wan-chung 薛萬忠 in command of forty thousand troops to aid Yen-cheng. This was on April 6.

[290] Actually Yüan-pi did not leave for Min until August 7, with his company of 350 persons (*TCTC* 282.12a, *T'se-fu yuan-kuei* 42.29a-b). In reporting the text of Yüan-pi's retraction, I have amalgamated the versions of *TCTC* 282.8a and *WTS*, which are virtually identical except for one line in each which is missing from the other. Yüan-pi's characterization of the Fukienese as "savages" was calculated to flatter the northerners of that day, to whom Min was still a frontier region. Despite Yüan-pi's disclaimer, he continued to serve the Min court after his return to Fu. We find him employed as Remonstrator to Yen-hsi in January 944 (*TCTC* 283.17b), which was after the latter had claimed the imperial title. His statement to the Chin Emperor was therefore insincere, or else he thought to do good as Remonstrator.

[291] This army was stationed on the border between the areas controlled by Yen-cheng and Yen-hsi, under the latter's command. See the note of Hu San-hsing on this passage.

[292] *TCTC* 282.8b-9a.

On April 12 Yen-cheng accomplished a successful sortie against one of Shih-k'uei's detachments. The following day he raided the enemy camp by night and killed Shih-k'uei. The latter's army was dispersed, and the victorious troops of Chien proceeded to the camp of Hsing-chen, which they found deserted. Yen-cheng now found himself undisputed master of upper Fukien and added two new towns to his domain, Yung-p'ing 永平 and Shun-ch'ang.[293] To all intents and purposes, the empire of Min was divided into two autonomous states.

In June of that year Yang Jen-ch'üan, the general from Wu-yüeh, finally arrived at Chien Prefecture. He was given provisions for his army and politely asked to withdraw. This did not suit Wu-yüeh policy, which was to attain as much authority in Fukien as possible, so Jen-ch'üan encamped his army northwest of the city. Yen-cheng now found himself obliged to apply to his hated brother for aid. Yen-hsi obliged him by sending Chi-yeh, Prefect of Ch'üan, to Chien with twenty thousand troops and also a letter of censure to the Prince of Wu-yüeh. At the same time he waged a guerrilla campaign against the Wu-yüeh supply lines with the result that Jen-ch'üan soon found his supplies exhausted. At this juncture, Yen-cheng carried out another successful sally, defeated the alien army and took thousands of prisoners. Jen-ch'üan and the remnants of his force fled on the night of June 26.[294] The situation looked hopeful for a reconciliation between the brothers and indeed the Emperor of Southern T'ang, successor to the Wu Emperors in Huai-nan and Chiang-nan, sent an envoy for the specific purpose of bringing about an amicable settlement between Yen-cheng and Yen-hsi. A compact between the two was sworn at Hsüan-ling 宣陵, but the brothers remained as suspicious of each other as ever.[295]

On December 24 Yen-hsi was honored by the Chin court with the empty titles of Legate of the Wei-wu Army, Secretary of State and King of Min— the latter at least he had already assumed.[296] Early in the new year (941) he created the fief of Fu-sha for Yen-cheng, and made him its Prince.[297]

But events were building up more trouble for King and Prince. Yen-hsi had reason to suspect a conspiracy between Yen-cheng and Yen-hsi 延喜, Prefect of T'ing. Accordingly he had the latter arrested.[298] He also

---

[293] *TCTC* 282.9a-b, 9b-10a. Shun-ch'ang has been noted above as the site of a temple to the deified Yen-ping. It was made a District after the conquest of upper Fukien by Southern T'ang. See *Shih-kuo ch'un-ch'iu* 112.16b.

[294] *TCTC* 282.10a-b.

[295] *TCTC* 282.10b-11a.

[296] *TCTC* 282.13b, *Wu Tai hui-yao* 11.145.

[297] *TCTC* 282.14a. The fief was located near Yen-p'ing, southwest of Chien Prefecture. See *Shih-kuo ch'un-ch'iu* 112.16a.

[298] *TCTC* 282.14b.

suspected a plot between Yen-cheng and Chi-yeh, Prefect of Ch'üan. The latter was seized, forced to commit suicide and his sons put to death. At the same time Yang I-feng 楊沂豐, a Titular Minister and intimate of Chi-yeh, was executed along with his whole family.[299] These acts of violence provoked remonstrations from Yen-hsi's ministers. One, Huang Chün, was degraded, and another, Ch'en Kuang-i 陳光逸, was hanged after a severe lashing.[300]

Yen-hsi now felt sufficiently secure and powerful and in August 941 declared himself Augustus of Great Min 大閩皇.[301] Instantly warfare broke out between him and Yen-cheng, but no conclusive engagements were fought, although on the land between Chien and Fu "the bare bones were like weeds."[302] At one time a truce was effected, but it was ineffective. Yen-cheng did not hesitate to parade his military might before the envoy of Yen-hsi, and threatened to have his own officer, P'an Ch'eng-yu, a proponent of peace, devoured.[303]

Yen-hsi remained suspicious of his nephews. Chi-yen, now Prefect of Ch'üan, was removed from office and poisoned.[304] But the monarch was unsuspicious of the young man whose party was ultimately to cast him from the throne. This was his son Ya-ch'eng, whom he had made Titular Minister and Controller of the Guards of the Six Armies in May. Later, in October, he became Prince of Ch'ang-lo 長樂王, Legate of the Wei-wu Army and Secretary of State. In April of the next year he was named Prince of Min.[305]

In November 941 Yen-hsi adopted the full title of Emperor for himself. In the same month the great minister Li Min died and Yen-cheng proclaimed himself Prime Marshal of Cavalry (兵馬元帥).[306]

War broke out between Yen-hsi and Yen-cheng once more in the late summer of 942 and its hostilities opened with Yen-cheng's siege of T'ing Prefecture. The Emperor launched a double counter-attack, sending five thousand troops from Chang and Ch'üan to relieve T'ing, and large forces under the command of Lin Shou-liang 林守亮 and Huang Ching-chung 黃敬忠 to Yu-ch'i and Yu-k'ou 尤口 respectively, as an initial move against

[299] *TCTC* 282.17a-b.

[300] *WTS*, *TCTC* 283.12a.

[301] *TCTC* 282.18a. This title is also given on the inscription on his pagoda, for which see below under Buddhism.

[302] *Ibid.*

[303] *TCTC* 282.18a-b.

[304] *Ibid.*

[305] *TCTC* 282.14b, 282.20a, 283.2a.

[306] *TCTC* 282.20b.

Chien Prefecture itself.[307]   These two armies were backed up by a third force of eight thousand infantry under the command of Huang Shao-p'o 黃紹頗.   Yen-cheng, after repeated attempts to storm the prefectural city of T'ing, withdrew.   But on August 29, his generals, Pao Hung-shih 包洪實 and Ch'en Wang 陳望, using marines from river craft, crushed Ching-chung's force at Yu-k'ou, whereupon both Shou-liang and Shao-p'o fled back to the capital.[308]   There was now no question in Yen-hsi's mind of the military supremacy of Yen-cheng, hence he despatched an envoy to his brother with a letter requesting peace, a rich gold vessel, a large sum of money and 640 letters of official appointment.   Yen-cheng, confident in his strength, refused to accept these gifts.[309]

January 943 found a new favorite in the court at Fu, Li Jen-yü 李仁遇, former Commissioner of Salt and Iron and Minister of State for the Right. He was the son of the late Minister Li Min and a sister of Yen-hsi, and was now transferred to the post of Minister of State for the Left and concurrently Vice-Secretary of State.   At the same time the Hanlin Scholar Li Kuang-chun became Vice-Secretary of State and concurrently President of the Board of Taxation.[310]

In the northwest, Yen-cheng, secure and menacing, declared himself Emperor, entitling his state "Great Yin" 大殷.   The customary general amnesty was declared and the reign title T'ien Te, "Heavenly Virtue," adopted in March.[311]   The new Emperor created two new prefectures—that of Yung 鏞 at the former District of Chiang-lo 將樂縣, and T'an 鐔 at the former garrison town of Yen-p'ing 延平鎮.   His wife, *née* Chang 張, became Empress.

Important appointments were:

P'an Ch'eng-yu—President of the Board of Personnel (吏部尚書) and Titular Minister.

Yang Ssu-kung—President of the Board of War (兵部尚書), Minister of State and Recorder of Military and State Business (錄軍國事).[312]

---

[307] *TCTC* 283.4a.   With regard to the character 尤 which occurs in these place-names, this is here simply an abbreviated form of the surname 沈 (Shen) which was very common in this area.   The pronunciation has been appropriately changed.   The modification was made to avoid conflict with 審, part of Shen-chih's taboo name.   Both were ancient *siəm* (*YTCS* 133.5a).

[308] *TCTC* 283.4a-b.

[309] *TCTC* 283.5a.

[310] *TCTC* 283.6a-b.

[311] *TCTC* 283.9a.   *NTS* 1.4 makes this event early in 939!   Possibly it has been confused with the accession of Yen-hsi in that year.

[312] *TCTC* 283.9a-b.

Shortly after this Ch'eng-yu was removed from office for his audacity in writing a memorandum to Yen-cheng, accusing him among other offenses of conscripting troops from among the people for service "in foreign lands;" of establishing new prefectures and districts in waste places, with clouds of officials to harass the people; of leaving Chien Prefecture exposed to raids from T'ang and Wu-yüeh; of not cultivating friendship with either of these nations, etc.[313]

In April, Yen-hsi took the daughter of Shang Pao-yin 尙保殷, Commissioner of the Golden Talisman (金吾使),[314] as his "Estimable Consort." In the following month his capital suffered a raid by Ch'en Wang, one of the victors of Yu-k'ou, but after initial successes the Yin troops were repulsed.[315] The ruler of Southern T'ang tried once more to effect a reconciliation between the Emperors of Yin and Min. In February 944 he sent letters to both of them decrying this fraternal conflict. Yen-hsi replied citing classical precedent for the execution of noxious brothers by the Son of Heaven[316] while Yen-cheng wrote a less pleasing note accusing the T'ang Emperor of usurping the throne of the late Emperor of Wu. Consequently T'ang broke off relations with Yin.[317]

Meanwhile, the two regicides Chu Wen-chin and Lien Chung-yü feared reprisals and to make themselves secure they contracted mutual marriage alliances. But Yen-hsi had already determined that they should die.[318] He often made loud insinuations against them at drinking parties while Wen-chin and Chung-yü tearfully protested their innocence of further designs against the throne. Now the Empress Li, daughter of the minister Li Chen, was jealous of the special favor shown the Lady Shang, and such was her resentment against her imperial husband that she made plans to take his

[313] *TCTC* 283.11a-b. For other criticisms made in this memorial, see under Court, Economy and Architecture.

[314] A kind of palace police official, whose prototype in ancient China warded off evil influences from the sacred person.

[315] *TCTC* 283.11a. See *TCTC k'ao-i* 30.4b for discussion of the form 可殷, an alternate version of Shang's name.

[316] Specifically, pointing out how the Duke of Chou had killed his younger brother Hsien 鮮 of Kuan 管 and imprisoned his younger brother Tu 度 of Ts'ai 蔡, both accused of malice against him; and how T'ang T'ai Tsung had killed his brothers Chien-ch'eng 建成 and Yüan-chi 元吉.

[317] *TCTC* 283.19b.

[318] It would appear that Wen-chin was still Commander of the Kung-ch'en Division, but Chung-yü now bore the title of Commissioner of Portals (閤門使), a kind of chamberlain. The command of the K'ung-ho Division was now held by Wei Ts'ung-liang 魏從朗. This man was put to death at this time as a partisan of Chu and Lien (*TCTC* 284.3a).

life and to place Prince Ya-ch'eng, her son, on the throne. She made the two regicides her instruments of vengeance, sending a messenger to them with this message: "The Emperor is very uneasy about you two lords. What should be done?" The two lords took immediate steps for their own safety and sent an officer of the Kung-ch'en Division, Ch'ien Ta 錢達 by name, to murder Yen-hsi as he returned from a visit to Li Chen who was ill. This assassination took place on April 8, 944.[319]

## 7. THE TYRANT (CHU WEN-CHIN)

Wang Yen-cheng was now sole Emperor in Fukien. But the regicides made no overtures to him. Instead they addressed the assembled court in this fashion: "T'ai Tsu, the Radiantly Martial Emperor, founded the State of Min. Now his sons and grandsons are licentious and cruel, and in their wildness have reached the end of their rope.[320] Heaven loathes the Wang family! It is suitable that we now choose a virtuous person and enthrone him." The officialdom preserved a becoming silence at this, whereupon Chung-yü escorted Wen-chin into the audience hall, invested him with robe and coronet and saluted him as Emperor at the head of all the lords of Min.

Wen-chin immediately ordered the arrest of every available member of the Wang family, beginning with Yen-hsi 延喜, and had them all put to death. They numbered over fifty persons, old and young. The late Emperor was canonized with a long title, eloquent of his philosophic virtues, and given the temple name of Ching Tsung. Chung-yü was rewarded with various titles, including the important one of Controller of the Six Armies.[321] The Remonstrator Cheng Yüan-pi objected to this whole proceeding and was forthwith degraded from office and sent into retirement.[322]

Great officers of the administration were now:

Pao Ssu-jun 鮑思潤—Titular Minister (former Chancellor).

Huang Shao-p'o—Prefect of Ch'üan.

Ch'eng Wen-wei 程文緯[323]—Prefect of Chang.

---

[319] *TCTC* 284.3a. *Wu Tai ch'un-ch'iu* b.8 gives the Emperor's name as 延義 (sic!), and puts his murder in the fall of the year. I follow the account of *TCTC*. *WTS* states that the emperor was assassinated as he returned drunk from a party, while *WKKS* b.8b states that he was killed as he returned from a visit to one of his favorite women. All accounts agree that he was on horseback at the time of his death.

[320] 墜厥緒.

[321] *TCTC* has "Director (總) of the Six Armies." I follow *WTS* here.

[322] *TCTC* 284.4a.

[323] *WTS* has Ch'eng Yün 程贇. I cannot tell which is correct.

Hsü Wen-chen 許文稹[324]—Prefect of T'ing.[325]

Wen-chin desired to maintain the semblance of friendly relations with
T'ang. He sent an embassy to that state which was not well received and
the envoys were jailed. That summer the T'ang Emperor made plans for
the invasion of Min but recalled them because the plague was ravaging his
population.[326] After this rebuff Wen-chin felt the need of another patron
and sent another embassy, this time to Chin, declaring himself tributary,
and so was confirmed in the titles of Legate of the Wei-wu Army and
Governor of Min 知閩國事. This was on September 3, 944,[327] the first year
of the reign K'ai Yün in the Chin empire, a title now adopted in coastal
Fukien.[328]

Meanwhile Yen-cheng undertook military operations against the
murderers of his brothers and nephews. He first sent his Commissioner of
Combined Armies, Wu Ch'eng-i 吳成義, against Fu, but this venture was
unsuccessful. Then, in the fall of the year he despatched two army groups,
one of three thousand men under Ch'en Ching-ch'üan 陳敬佺 to encamp
at Yu-ch'i and Ku-t'ien, and another of two thousand men under Lu Chin
盧進 to encamp at Ch'ang-ch'i. These detachments were presumably meant
as frontier guards until he should be able to carry out another major
operation against Wen-chin.[329]

Wen-chin's empire, however, was already crumbling. Trouble began
in Ch'üan Prefecture where Huang Shao-p'o represented Wen-chin but was
only a temporary obstacle in the rising career of a vigorous and ambitious
military officer, Liu Ts'ung-hsiao 留從效.[330] He organized a pro-Wang
faction whose more important members were Wang Chung-shun 王忠順,
Tung Ssu-an 董思安 and Chang Han-ssu 張漢思.[331] The central point of
the clique's program was support of Wang Yen-cheng, who appeared to
Ts'ung-hsiao as the man most likely to win ultimate control of Fukien.
Accordingly, the plotters gave a great banquet in Ts'ung-hsiao's home for
picked soldiers from their divisions. The troops were regaled with wine,
and told a lying tale to the effect that Yen-cheng had already taken Fu
Prefecture and had sent orders for the punishment of Shao-p'o. The men,

[324] *WTS* has Wen-shen 文縝.

[325] *TCTC* 284.4a.

[326] *TCTC* 284.5b. *NTS* 2.11 adds that the Min envoys were later released.

[327] *TCTC* 284.7a.

[328] *WTS*.

[329] *TCTC* 284.7b.

[330] Ts'ung-hsiao eventually became dictator of the Ch'üan and Chang areas. See his
biographies in *CKC* 10.100-101 and *SS* 483. *WKKS* b.11a gives his name as Lou 婁
Ts'ung-hsiao.

[331] Chung-shun and Ssu-an have biographies in *CKC* 10.101.

deceived by this story and seduced by promises of wealth and glory, rushed off to Shao-p'o's house and murdered the unfortunate Prefect. Ts'ung-hsiao then laid hands on the prefectural seal, carried it to the residence of Wang Chi-hsün 繼勳, one of the few remaining male members of the Wang clan, and asked him to take over the government of the Prefecture.[332] Ch'en Hung-chin 陳洪進, a cavalry officer, was sent to Chien Prefecture to show the head of Shao-p'o to Yen-cheng.[333] En route Hung-chin was held up at Yu-ch'i by the garrison there. He told them a false tale to the effect that Chu Wen-chin had been put to death by insurgents at Fu Prefecture, and that he was on his way to give the allegiance of Ch'üan to Yen-cheng. The story was believed and several of the notables of Yu-ch'i accompanied Hung-chin on the remainder of his journey.

On hearing the news from Ch'üan, Yen-cheng gave appointments as Division Commanders to the four officers Ts'ung-hsiao, Hung-chin, Chung-shun and Ssu-an, and appointed Wang Chi-hsün Prefect of Ch'üan and Keeper of the Seal.[334] Thereupon the military commander at Chang in the far south killed his Prefect, Ch'eng Wen-wei, and replaced him with another junior member of the Wang clan, Chi-ch'eng 繼成.[335] Finally, Hsü Wen-chen, Wen-chin's Prefect at T'ing, foreseeing the future trend of events, offered his allegiance to the empire of Yin. Of the five original prefectures only Fu remained in the hands of Wen-chin.[336] It may have been some solace to him that on January 1, 945, he received from the Chin Emperor the titles of Titular Minister and King of Min.[337]

The tyrant was now obliged to take military action. The new year found an army recruited by double stipends marching towards Ch'üan Prefecture, under the command of Lin Shou-liang and Li T'ing-o 李廷鍔, twenty thousand strong. Yen-cheng immediately sent another force of equal strength, commanded by Tu Chin 杜進, to relieve the southern city. Wen-chin's army was crushed in a sortie by Ts'ung-hsiao[338] and Yen-cheng

---

[332] *TCTC* 284.7b, *WTS*.

[333] Hung-chin's star was rising along with that of Ts'ung-hsiao. He succeeded to the control of Southern Fukien on the latter's death and later turned it over to the Sung empire. See his biographies in *CKC* 10.102 and *SS* 483.5702c.

[334] *Ts'e-fe yüan-kuei* 224.20a makes the accession of Yen-cheng (written 延正 !) and his *son* Chi-hsün's appointment as Prefect appear simultaneous. *TCTC* 284.7b states that Chi-hsün was Yen-cheng's nephew. But *NTS* 2.11 agrees with *Ts'e-fu yüan-kuei*.

[335] *TCTC* notes that Chi-hsün and Chi-ch'eng had survived the massacre of the Wang family only because of their remoteness from the capital.

[336] *TCTC* 284.7b, *WTS*.

[337] *TCTC* 284.8b. *WKKS* b.10b confirms this but states that Wen-chin adopted the T'ien Fu reign title, an anachronism.

[338] *Ch'üan-chou fu-chih* 16.31a and 17.4b tells of a spot north of the prefectural city

sent a fleet under Wu Ch'eng-i to attack Fu Prefecture. Wen-chin found it necessary to apply for aid to the kingdom of Wu-yüeh.

Meanwhile, Southern T'ang in the northwest was preparing to take steps against Yin. Operations were put in the hands of Ch'a Wen-hui 查文徽 holding the title of Pacification Commissioner of Chiang-hsi (江西安撫使) and assisted by the strategist Tsang Hsün 臧循. Preliminary reconnaissance from Hsin 信 Prefecture seemed favorable to Wen-hui and accordingly an army under the command of Pien Hao 邊鎬, Captain of Punitive Armies on the March (行營招討諸軍都虞候), was sent to support the Commissioner and to begin the invasion of Yen-cheng's territory. One force, under Wen-hui, marched out beyond Chien-yang as far as a place called Kai-chu 蓋竹[339] but when the Commissioner received the news of the capitulation of Ch'üan, Chang and T'ing to Yen-cheng, and the imminent arrival of an army of eight thousand from the new Prefecture of Yung under Chang Han-chen 張漢眞, he withdrew to Chien-yang. Tsang Hsün took another group of T'ang troops to Shao-wu but was captured in a raid by local militia, sent to Chien Prefecture and put to death.[340]

At this point the Yin general, Wu Ch'eng-i, somewhere in the vicinity of Ch'üan Prefecture, sent a deceitful message to be circulated in Fu, announcing that the T'ang armies were in Fukien only to aid Yen-cheng in punishing Chu Wen-chin. This came to the ears of Wen-chin himself who, on February 12, sent his minister Li Kuang-chun to Chien Prefecture to offer his surrender to Yen-cheng. Two days later an official of Fu Prefecture, Lin Jen-han 林仁翰, led thirty armed men against Lien Ch'ung-yü whom they found at his residence. Ch'ung-yü, also armed, put up a bold front and Jen-han's followers retreated. Jen-han, however, thrust at Ch'ung-yü with a lance, killed him and cut off his head to show to the people. He was able to incite a mob against Wen-chin and that worthy was also killed. Both heads were forwarded to Yen-cheng and Generalissimo Wu Ch'eng-i was invited to enter the city.[341] So ended the brief reign of Chu Wen-chin. But the Wang family's time also was running out.

---

called "The Grave of the Thousand Men" (千人塚), so named as a scene of carnage in the conflict between Ts'ung-hsiao and Wen-chin. Later a temple was erected there— the *Kuang-chi yuan* 廣濟院.

[339] Northwest of the prefectural city of Chien.

[340] *TCTC* 284.8b.

[341] *TCTC* 284.9b. *WTS* and *NTS* have a rather different version of these events. They tell that Ch'ung-yü, seeing things going badly with his puppet empire, killed Wen-chin himself and offered his allegiance to Yin. Later Ch'ung-yü was murdered by Jen-han.

## 8. THE TRIMMER (LI JEN-TA)

In February 945 Wang Yen-cheng, by invitation of the great ministers in Fu Prefecture, dropped the national designation of Yin and restored the name Min to his empire.[342]   He was at last ruler over the whole of Fukien. It was requested that the capital be shifted from Chien to its former site on the coast.   However, in view of the presence of T'ang troops in his domain, the Emperor found it inexpedient to make this change and instead sent his nephew Chi-ch'ang 繼昌, Titular Minister and Vice-Keeper of the Seal, to Fu Prefecture, as Overseer of All Military Affairs in the Southern Capital (都督南都內外諸軍事).   With Chi-ch'ang went Huang Jen-feng, as Police Commissioner.   The tyrannicide, Lin Jen-han, meanwhile proceeded to Chien Prefecture, where he received little reward for his merits.   Further, five thousand troops, including the Min imperial guards, were removed from Fu and marched to Chien to join in the resistance to T'ang.[343]

Ch'a Wen-hui, the T'ang commander at Chien-yang, sent a request for reinforcements to his sovereign.   Accordingly several thousand more soldiers were sent into the south with Ho Ching-chu 何敬洙, Tsu Ch'üan-en 祖全恩 and Yao Feng 姚鳳 as leading officers.   The combined T'ang armies moved through Ch'ung-an 崇安[344] and encamped at Red Range (赤嶺)[345] where they were opposed by the Min force of ten thousand headed by Yang Ssu-kung and Ch'en Wang, facing them across the river.   An argument arose between Ch'en Wang, in actual operational command of the Min soldiery, and Yang Ssu-kung, the political strategist.   Wang, praising the fitness and training of the enemy, advocated standing fast without deliberately provoking battle while Yang successfully supported the tactic

---

[342] M. Tchang in his *Synchronismes chinois* (Variétés sinologiques 24, Shanghai, 1905), p. 329, states that Wang Yen-cheng changed the dynastic name to Min and took Fu Prefecture in the sixth month of 944.   He was made prisoner by Southern T'ang in the eighth month of the same year.   Tchang seems to have confused these events somehow with the seizure of power in Min by Chu Wen-chin, which took place in that year.   If Tchang is a year too early, the synoptic chronological chart (表) in *WTS* is a year too late in giving the fall of Yen-cheng as 946 as does ch. 68 of the same source.

[343] *TCTC* 284.12a.

[344] A District (*hsien*) created in Sung times (A.D. 944).   However, it seems to have existed earlier as a village (see *YTCS* 129.4b).   It was in the mountains near the Southern T'ang border.

[345] South of Ch'ung-an.

of immediate attack. The T'ang commanders placed a large host across their vanguard and sent a detachment to the rear of the Min army. The Fukienese were crushed and routed. Ch'en Wang was killed in this action while Yang Ssu-kung barely escaped with his life.[346]

The Emperor found himself unprotected in Chien Prefecture at this juncture and summoned Tung Ssu-an and Wang Chung-shun from Ch'üan with five thousand men to defend the outposts of his capital.[347] But the threat from the north was now matched by an equal one from the south.

Li Jen-ta, a fellow-townsman of the Wang family from Kuang and Commander of the Yüan-tsung Division (元從[都]指揮使) for fifteen years, had fled to Chien Prefecture during the reign of Yen-hsi.[347a] The man was a turncoat for he returned to Fu Prefecture on the death of Yen-hsi and gave his allegiance to Chu Wen-chin, to whom he outlined a plan for the reduction of Chien. Wen-chin had no liking for the trimmer and banished him to the country. When Yen-cheng took the Prefecture of Fu and re-established the empire of Min, Jen-ta saw a new opportunity. The viceroy Wang Chi-ch'ang was a drunken weakling and extremely unpopular in the Southern Capital. Jen-ta entered the city secretly and persuaded a certain Ch'en Chi-hsün 陳繼珣, another enemy of Yen-cheng, and Huang Jen-feng, the Police Commissioner, to take advantage of Yen-cheng's preoccupation with the T'ang invaders to seize the city for themselves. The conspirators raided the perfectural palace and murdered Chi-ch'ang together with General Wu Ch'eng-i. It was Jen-ta's intention to take the imperial throne himself but he had reason to suspect that this move would not please the populace. Therefore, he brought an innocent and revered abbot, Cho Yen-ming 卓巖明, from a country temple into the city and on April 17 crowned him Son of Heaven.[348] The Chin reign title was employed however, and envoys were sent to the northern empire declaring Min tributary.[349] When the news of this usurpation reached the Min northern

[346] In two separate notes Hu San-hsing takes a dim view of Ssu-kung's abilities accusing him of urging the wrong course at Red Range and of precipitating the fall of the empire by his taxation policy. For further details of the battle, see *NTS* 2.11.

[347] *TCTC* 284.13a.

[347a] The Yüan-tsung Division, as its name implies, was constituted by the original adherents of Wang Shen-chih.

[348] Hu San-hsing observes various forms of the element *yen* in the priest's name, e.g. 儼 in *CWTS*. He concludes that 巖 was the original form, and that 偃 was his name in religion.

[349] *TCTC* states that this was the tenth year of T'ien Fu in Chin. This would be correct, since that reign began in 936, but Chin had changed the reign to K'ai Yün in 944, so that properly this was the second year of the latter reign. I am unable to explain this discrepancy. Is it possible news of the change had not been heard in Min?

capital at Chien, Yen-cheng retaliated by ordering a general slaughter of the family of the apostacized Huang Jen-feng.[350]

The Emperor also despatched a fleet carrying five thousand men down the river, under the command of Chang Han-chen, with orders to join the troops of Chang and Ch'üan Prefectures in an assault on Fu. Huang Jen-feng, mad with grief at the loss of his wife and children, led the defending forces in a sortie and inflicted a heavy defeat on the attackers. General Chang Han-chen was captured and decapitated.[351]

But Jen-feng, basically a gentleman in the old tradition, was already dissatisfied with the course of action he had undertaken. To his colleague, Ch'en Chi-hsün, he said, "What makes a man a man is his holding to loyalty, faithfulness, humanity and a sense of duty. Not long ago I had merit [in the service of the Prince] of Fu-sha. In the meantime I have rebelled against him, which was disloyal. If a man entrusts his nephew to me,[352] yet I join others in slaying him, I have been unfaithful. Recently I fought with the troops of Chien, and those I killed were my fellows, which was inhumane. I abandoned my wife and children, allowing others to oppress them, which was undutiful. This body of mine has sunk ten times and floated up nine —its death will have a superabundance of shame."[353] Chi-hsün responded with a cliché about "real men pursuing fame," but the conversation came to the ears of Li Jen-ta and both were put to death. Jen-ta, as Controller of the Six Armies, was now dictator of Fu.[354]

At last Jen-ta made up his mind to seize the supreme power in name as well as in fact. On July 4, at a grand inspection of troops by the ecclesiastical monarch, he had several soldiers break ranks, ascend the steps of the throne and stab Yen-ming to death. Jen-ta himself feigned alarm and astonishment, pretended to flee, was seized and led reluctantly to the vacant and bloodstained throne. But he took only the title of Deputy of the Wei-wu Army. He offered a double allegiance. On the one hand, he sent a petition of submission to Southern T'ang and adopted the reign title of that nation (it was the third year of Pao Ta 保大 there). On the other hand he sent a tribute-bearing mission to Chin. He also sent ambassadors to Wu-yüeh "to cultivate friendship."[355]

---

[350] *TCTC* 284.14a-b.

[351] *TCTC* 284.16b.

[352] The reference in is to Chi-ch'ang.

[353] Cf. the biography of this worthy in *CKC* 10.98–99.

[354] *TCTC* makes the interesting point, anent the general political incompetence of the priest Yen-ming, that he had invited his father to the capital and invested him as "Grand Supreme Augustus" (太上皇), a term for Emperors in retirement. Yen-ming seems to have completely engrossed in the formal privileges of the imperium.

[355] *TCTC* 284.16b-17a. The Grand Supreme Augustus, father of the late lamented

Meanwhile Yen-cheng was fighting for his life with varying fortune. His capital was besieged and the troops summoned from Ch'üan Prefecture were defeated by the T'ang army. On the other hand Hsü Wen-chen was victorious over the invaders at T'ing Prefecture. It was reported to the Emperor that the guards whom he had brought from Fu were not loyal to him, so he disarmed them, sent them back to the south, and ambushed and killed them all on the way.[356] Then the newly created Prefecture of T'an was taken by the T'ang general Pien Hao. At this pass, Yen-cheng was humiliated by having to send to Wu-yüeh for help, offering a declaration of dependency in exchange.[357]

By the end of September the long siege was making itself felt in Chien. The people were displeased and there was idle talk of abandoning the Emperor. Tung Ssu-an was approached on the matter but said, "My generation serves the clan of Wang. If I rebel against it in [times] of danger, who under Heaven would accept me?" Ssu-an seems to have been an exceptional man. His example encouraged others and the city did not surrender. It was carried by storm on October 2, the honor of being the first man to ascend the wall going to Wang Chien-feng 王建封, Engineering Commissioner of the T'ang Vanguard (先鋒橋道使). Wang Chung-shun perished in the conflict and Tung Ssu-an escaped to Ch'üan Prefecture with a band of loyal followers. The city was pillaged by the victorious troops. The Min dynasty was at an end[358] but the family line has not disappeared in modern times. The Wangs of Fukien who are descended from the Emperors of Min are distinguished as the K'ai-Min Wangs (開閩王).[359]

puppet, was murdered at this time. T'ang made the quickest response to Jen-ta's overtures. He was confirmed as Legate by that state, and named Titular Minister. At the same time the name Hung-i 弘義 was bestowed on him, and he was enrolled on the family register of the rulers of T'ang. His surname being Li no change was necessary there since the founder of T'ang was surnamed Hsü only by adoption, and had resumed the name Li after his accession. Jen-ta underwent a number of changes of name, this being the first of several which paralleled his shifting allegiances. I shall continue to refer to him as Jen-ta, however.

[356] The ambushing soldiers sliced up their victims' flesh to provide meat on the return trip to Chien. Perhaps this is another instance of semi-ceremonial eating of traitorious flesh.

[357] TCTC 284.18a-b.

[358] TCTC 285.1b. Things were made somewhat easier for the invaders by the peasantry who were dissatisfied because of the extraordinary taxes imposed by Yang Ssu-kung, and thus welcomed the T'ang soldiers to the countryside. NTS 2.12 states that the strategic defenses of Chien Prefecture were at Hsi-yen 西巖 and Yen-p'ing (i.e., T'an Prefecture), which were reduced shortly before the occupation of Chien Prefecture.

[359] Min-hsien hsiang-t'u chih 234a. The descendants of Shen-kuei are particularly localized in Ch'ang-lo (Hou-kuan-hsien hsiang-t'u chih 5.8a).

## 9.   THE WARLORD (LIU TS'UNG-HSIAO)

October 945 found most of Fukien in the hands of the conquerors from Huai-nan. Upon the fall of Chien, the Prefects of T'ing, Ch'üan and Chang surrendered to the invaders but were left in control of their Prefectures. Chien Prefecture became the Yung-an Army (永安軍).[360]

But Wang Chi-hsün, Prefect of Ch'üan, was deposed in May of 946 by the ambitious soldier Liu Ts'ung-hsiao who fought off an attack directed at him by Li Jen-ta, and was in turn made Prefect of Ch'üan by T'ang. The other two prefects, Hsü Wen-chen (at T'ing) and Wang Chi-ch'eng (at Chang), were removed from Fukien and given the same posts at Ho 和 and Ch'i 蘄 Prefectures in the Southern T'ang empire.[361] As for Yen-cheng, he was removed to the T'ang capital at Chin-ling and appointed Grand General of the Yü-lin army.[362]

In Fu Prefecture Li Jen-ta refused an order to submit peacefully to T'ang and subsquently beat off a naval attack under the T'ang general Ch'en Chüeh 陳覺 on September 17. He now gave his whole allegiance to Chin and changed his name again.[363] T'ang made another assault on his city in October and Jen-ta shifted his allegiance to Wu-yüeh, asked an army of support from that state and changed his name a third time.[364] The ruler of Wu-yüeh decided to create a buffer state at Fu Prefecture and sent an army and navy to drive out the T'ang forces. The Wu-yüeh expedition arrived at Fu on December 18 but the war with T'ang was inconclusive until April 7, 947 when a sortie of Min troops coincident with an amphibious attack by Wu-yüeh crushed the T'ang armies, and the Chekiangese entered the city.[365]

Meanwhile, a revolt in Chang Prefecture was crushed by Liu Ts'ung-

---

[360] *TCTC* 285.1b, *NTS* 2.12.

[361] *TCTC* 285.5a-b. *WTS* states that Ts'ung-hsiao became Legate of the new Ch'ing-yüan Army (清源軍) established in place of Ch'üan Prefecture. According to *NTS* this did not take place until later.

[362] *TCTC* 285.2b. Later, in 948, he was made Legate of the An-hua Army (安化軍), stationed in Jao 饒 Prefecture (*TCTC* 287.16a).

[363] This time to Hung-ta 弘達. *TCTC* 285.9b.

[364] This time to Ta 達. *TCTC* 285.9b.

[365] *TCTC* 286.11a, 12a, 13b. The war of occupation was not easy for T'ang. It is reported that after the Chin empire was erased by the Khitans those barbarians invited the T'ang Emperor to take over in the Yellow River basin. The Chinese lord replied, "We are exhausted by the Min campaign. How could we possibly contend for mastery of the Central Plain?" (*NTS* 3.15).

hsiao and T'ang made his colleague, Tung Ssu-an, Prefect of that city.[366]
Ts'ung-hsiao and Ssu-an were ordered to take part in the attack on Li Jen-ta
but as soon as Fu was occupied by Wu-yüeh, they returned to the south.[367]

Li Jen-ta, after a visit to the new ruler of Wu-yüeh, made a fourth
change of name (by royal decree).[368]   However, he owed allegiance only
to himself and thus decided to murder the commander of the Wu-yüeh
garrison in Fu and return his support to T'ang.  The plot was discovered
and he was executed with his whole family.[369]   On February 11, 948, Wu-
yüeh made a native Chekiangese Legate of the Wei-wu Army.[370]

Subsequently Liu Ts'ung-hsiao drove the T'ang garrisons out of Ch'üan
and Chang Prefectures and the partitioning of Min was complete.  This left
the regions of Chien and T'ing in the north and west to Southern T'ang,
Fu in the northeast to Wu-yüeh and Chang and Ch'üan in the southeast
independent under Ts'ung-hsiao.  Later, when the Chou dynasty had
replaced Chin in the far north, Ts'ung-hsiao offered his submission to the
victorious Emperor Shih Tsung.  His petition was refused since after the
removal of the Huai-nan area proper from the T'ang to the Chou empire,
the boundary between the two states had been solemnly fixed on the Yangtze
and Shih Tsung refused to interfere in southern politics.  Ts'ung-hsiao
continued nominally as an agent of T'ang.  On his death in 962 his territory
went to his old comrade Ch'en Hung-chin who finally ceded it to Sung
in 977.[371]

---

[366] Ssu-an at first refused because of the taboo on his father's name (Chang) but
T'ang simply changed Chang Prefecture to Nan 南 Prefecture (TCTC 285.11a).

[367] TCTC 286.14a.

[368] To Ju-yün 儒贇.  TCTC 287.7b.

[369] TCTC 287.14b.

[370] TCTC 287.15a.

[371] WTS.

# IV

# ECONOMY

## 1. PRODUCE AND TRIBUTE

THE *Sung History* lists as the most important products of Fu-chien Route (福建路) the following: silver, copper, *Pueraria* (ko 葛, presumably both the fiber-cloth and the ground medicinal root), tea, salt and products of the sea.[372] Abundant evidence in other sources confirms the accuracy of this list throughout Fukienese history.

Silver, whether in ingot form or hammered into vessels by native artisans, appears among the most frequent items of tribute sent to the courts of the Five Dynasties by the government of Min.[373] The metal was mined in the vicinity of the upland towns in the western part of the empire: specifically mentioned are Ning-hua, Chiang-lo, Chien-an and Yu-ch'i.[374] The tribute inventories usually mention rather large quantities, such as taels 6500 (in the tribute of November 929) or taels 7000 (in that of November 930).

Copper was not considered of sufficient value to submit as tribute, but

---

[372] *SS* 89.4710c.

[373] See *Ts'e-fu yüan-kuei* for the details. Tribute-bearing embassies are listed as follows (page references in parentheses): November 924 (169.8a); December 927 (169.10a); November 929 (169.11a); November 930 (169.11a-b); October 938 (169.15a-b); November 941 (169.18a); January 943 (169.19b-20a); October 908 (196.13a); August 910 (197.23a); 911 (197.23b); 912 (197.24a). Articles appearing in five or more tribute lists are silver, ivory, rhinoceros horn, aromatics, bananas (in various forms), *Pueraria* (in various forms), tea. The Min tribute system has been analyzed in detail by Hino Kaisaburō 日野開三郎 in his "Go-dai Min-koku no taichūgen chōkō to bōeki" 五代閩國の對中原朝貢と貿易 in *Shigen* 史淵 26.1-50 (1941) and 27.1 41 (1942). In this study the Chinese names for products are not specifically identified. The author also has 延鈞 in error for 延鈞, and 延義 for 延羲 as names of Min rulers.

[374] *TS* 41.3728c-d, *SS* 89.4710b-c.

the local industry flourished. It was mined in the western highlands in the same regions as silver.[375]

Cloth woven of the fibers of *Pueraria* was a major item in the industry of Min. Large quantities of it were submitted as payment of tax on commerce to the tax board of the northern government. Thus, on November 18, 941, the Chin court received 8880 pieces for this purpose.[376] The root of the same plant was powdered for pharmaceutical purposes, but I have no record that this substance was sent as tribute by Min, although it may be included in the general category "aromatics and herbs" (香藥).

In the tenth century, as in modern times, Fukien was renowned for its teas, which were in great demand in Northern China as later they were in the western world. The variety named after the Wu-i Mountains 武夷山 in the northwest, whence the English name Bohea, is now world famous, as is Oolong, the "Black Dragon" variety. These names were not yet known in the middle ages of Chinese history, but tea growing was a major industry in the Prefectures of Fu and Chien—that is, around the major cities, although it was grown far and wide in the province. The Prefecture of Chien was known for several special kinds: "Stalactite" (石乳茶) and "Dragon",[377] the latter described by Ts'ai Hsiang as "especially excellent."[378] The tribute lists of the empire of Min also refer frequently to "Great" tea (大茶). The distinction of being the best in the world is claimed for the tea produced in the roasters (*pei* 焙 "to dry over a fire") of the Northern Park (北苑) at the foot of Phoenix Mountain (鳳凰山) in the Prefecture of Chien by the *Fu-chien t'ung-chih*. In this gazetteer it is stated that during the reign Dragon Disclosure (933-934) a resident of this place, Chang T'ing-hui 張廷暉, began production of tea, and that the name Northern Park dates from this period.[379] Ts'ai Hsiang himself writes that the tea from the roasters of Northern Park has the best flavor.[380] The teas produced here became very famous in the Sung dynasty, and were sent

---

[375] *Ibid.*

[376] 度支戶部商稅 see *Ts'e-fu yüan-kuei* 169.18a.

[377] *SS loc. cit.* The notice "Dragon and Phoenix Teas" also appears (龍鳳等茶). *T'ai-p'ing huan-yü chi* 102.6b gives a "Wax" tea (蠟茶) from Chang Prefecture, and there is also a "Wax-surface (?)" tea (蠟面茶) in the tribute of 943. I have used *T'ai-ping huan-yü chi*, a valuable Sung source, to supplement *TS* and *SS*. The products given in it as typical of Fukien were doubtless found there in the tenth century. Page references are: Fu Prefecture 100.3b-4a; Nan-chien 南劍 Prefecture (a Sung creation at Yen-p'ing) 100.9b-10a; Chien Prefecture 101.3b; Ch'üan Prefecture 102.3b; Chang Prefecture 102.6b; T'ing Prefecture 102.9b-10a. It will be hereafter cited as *TPHYC*.

[378] Ts'ai Hsiang 蔡襄, *Ch'a lu* 茶錄 (edit. of *Po-ch'uan hsüeh-hai* 百川學海) la.

[379] *FCTC*1 45.1a.

[380] *Ch'a lu* 1b.

regularly as local tribute to K'ai-feng. Thus, "Chien Prefecture sent as annual tribute two catties each of 'Great,' 'Dragon,' and 'Phoenix' lump-teas (團茶), eight cakes constituting one catty."[381]

Salt factories were distributed along the seacoast, notably at Ch'ang-ch'i and Lien-chiang in the north, and in the vicinity of the Prefectures of Ch'üan and Chang in the south. Min produced large quantities but, like copper, it was not a rarity nor a unique specialty of the area, and is therefore not to be seen in the tribute records.

The coastal dwellers of Fukien have always been great sailors and fishers as well; every reference to the economy of the country mentions some aspect of this industry. If not mentioned in general terms, like "delicacies" of the sea (海味), the world generally employed is hai-ko 海蛤, presumably including clams, oysters, mussels and the like—that is to say, bivalves in general. Shellfish of this kind appear with several of the tribute shipments from Min to the north. A fish for which Chang Prefecture enjoyed some special fame was the "silver fish" (銀魚), Salanx microdon, whose flesh was regarded as a great delicacy.[382]

The foregoing constitute the typical and abundant products of the land as listed in the Sung History. Min was also the source of other products, which, if not so abundant, were valuable and much sought after by the Chinese. Most of these items should be classified as luxury goods.

Gold was sent as tribute several times, often in the form of worked vessels, as decoration on vessels of silver or in other forms. The goldworking industry produced such complexities as "gold-incrusted girdles" (in the tribute of November 924). The T'ang shu gives only one Fukienese town as a source of gold, Chiang-lo in the central uplands. T'ai-p'ing huan-yü chi, however, gives (alluvial) gold dust (麩金) as a product of Fu Prefecture.

Ivory and rhinoceros horn were frequent tribute articles. It is not clear whether these were native products in the tenth century, or were imports brought in by the traders from Southeast Asia and the Archipelago. We have seen, at any rate, that there were almost certainly herds of elephants still to be found in the remote parts of the empire, and it is possible that ivory may have occasionally been obtained directly from this source.

Herbs, aromatics and spices of all kinds were a specialty of the region, some being native products, others coming with merchant voyagers from

---

[381] Yeh Meng-te 葉夢得 (1079–1148), Shih-lin yen-yu 石林燕語 (TSCC edit.) 8.80. And cf. Ou-yang Hsiu, Kuei-t'ien lu 歸田錄 (edition of Hsüeh hsin t'ao-yüan) 2.4b: "Among the types of tea, none surpasses the 'Dragon' and 'Phoenix.' They are called lump-teas..." For more on "lump-teas" see Note 525.

[382] TPHYC.

the South Seas. Sent as tribute to the northern empire were "frankincense"
(乳香), "aloes-wood" (沈香)[383] and two less-known aromatics, "cake
aromatic" (餅香),[384] and "parched aromatic" (煎香).[385] Also in the tribute
lists, and doubtless imports, were pepper and nutmeg, but powdered ginger
(粉薑) and dried ginger (乾姜) were local products.[386] Safflower (紅花)
was grown in both Fu and Ch'üan.[387] Jasmine (茉莉, *Jasminum sambac*),
was introduced originally from Western Asia, but now cultivated in Fu and
Ch'üan.[388] Fennel (茴香) is noted in the Sung Prefecture of Nan-
chien.[389] Another aromatic, *chia-hsiang* 甲香, made from the operculum of
a local gastropod, is described in several sources as a special product of
Chang.[390] Deer horns appear from Fu, and were doubtless used medicinally
in powdered form.[391] "Dragon brain" (龍腦), an aromatic crystalline
substance called borneol, resembling camphor and produced by the tree
*Dryobalanops camphora,* appears in the tribute lists, but was probably
imported from Indonesia.[392] *Chiang-chen-hsiang* 降眞香, an aromatic
derived from a forest tree which I cannot identify, and by most texts said
to be native to Kueichou, is given as a product of T'ing.[393]

Here follow various fruits and vegetable products of some importance:

[383] Tribute of 941.

[384] Hung Ch'u 洪芻, *Hsiang p'u* 香譜 (*TSCC* edit.) a.4 lists a *p'ing-hsiang* 瓶香 (lit.
" vase aromatic ") as a kind of " frankincense." I do not know if this is the same
substance.

[385] Tribute of 943. 煎香 is possibly the 甲煎香 made by mixing 甲香 (see below)
with various other aromatics and herbs, and was used as lip rouge (口脂). See *Pen-ts'ao
kang-mu* 本草綱目 (Commercial Press edit.) 46.42.

[386] Tributes of 941 and 943, and in *TPHYC* as from Fu.

[387] *SS* 89, and *TPHYC* as from Ch'üan.

[388] *TPHYC.*

[389] *TPHYC.*

[390] *TS, SS, TPHYC.* *TS* 43.3431b describes it as a product of Canton, but it is also
especially abundant on the Fukien coast. The mollusc is *Eburna japonica* 海蠃, its
operculum being definitely identified with *chia-hsiang* by Li Shih-chen. This writer
cites the *Nan-chou i-wu chih* 南州異物志 of Wan Chen 萬震 (pre-T'ang, see *Sui shu*
33.2448a) to the effect that the operculum is mixed with other aromatics and burned
for increased fragrance, but has an unpleasant odor if burned alone (*Pen-ts'ao kang-mu*
46.41). He also cites the *Pen-ts'ao yen-i* 本草衍義 of K'ou Tsung-shih 寇宗奭 to the
effect that it is used in combination with aloes (沈), sandal (檀), borneol (龍) and
civet (麝) (*ibid.* 46.42). Mixed with aloes, civet and various herbs and flowers, writes
Shih-chen, it makes a lip rouge and incense (焚爇) called 甲煎 (*loc. cit.*).

[391] *SS* 89.

[392] Stuart, *Materia Medica* 157 says that it " is also said to be found in Kuangtung
and Fukien, although there seems to be no Chinese name for it recorded in the books."

[393] *TPHYC.* The name implies that the substance, burned as incense, will cause the
immortals to descend. See Stuart, *op. cit.* 428–9, for further information.

quinces (木瓜);[394] "Chinese olive" (橄欖, *Canarium*), a source of water-proofing oil for ships' bottoms;[395] bananas, for fruit, fiber-cloth and beauty;[396] the "dragon's-eye," longan, (龍眼, *Nephelium longana*), related to the lichee and almost equally famous;[397] various leafy vegetables,[398] among which *Asparagus lucidus* is mentioned by name: *t'ien-men-tung* 天門冬;[399] pine-nuts (松子) from Ch'üan;[400] sugar cane (甘蔗);[401] the citron called "Buddha's Hand" (佛手柑, *Citrus medica,* var. *chirocarpus*);[402] the kumquat (金橘, *Citrus nobilis,* var. *microcarpa*);[403] the loquat (枇杷, *Eriobotrya japonica*);[404] and the Chinese "gooseberry" (羊桃, *Averrhoa carambola*).[405]

Outstanding among the admired flora of Min was the lichee.[406] This plant had been known to North China since the reign of Chao T'o in the south, and is mentioned in the *Shang-lin fu* 上林賦 of Ssu-ma Hsiang-ju with the graphs 離支. Ts'ai Hsiang regarded the lichee of Fukien as superior to that of Kuangtung, but perhaps was biased in favor of his native province. His opinion, however, is confirmed by T'ao Ku, who writes that the lichee of Lingnan does not equal that of Min.[407] Two varieties of the fruit are said to date from the Five Dynasties period, or at least to have been named in that period: one, called "eighteenth maiden lichee" (十八娘荔枝), is said by tradition to have been named for the eighteenth daughter of one of the Kings of Min who was fond of this particular variety. Ts'ai Hsiang, a century later, writes that trees which bear it stand by the Princess' grave at the Pao-kuo Close 報國院 east of Fu Prefecture. Another variety,

---

[394] Tribute of 938.

[395] *TS* 41 and *TPHYC*. *Canarium* is also a source of timber, and the fruits are eaten.

[396] All sources. *TPHYC* mentions the *Musa coccinea* (美人蕉) of Fu Prefecture in particular. This was much admired for its handsome red flowers.

[397] *TPHYC*.

[398] *SS* 89. Among these was *tzu-ts'ai* 紫菜, identified in modern dictionaries as *Porphyra tenera*. *FCTC* records a tradition that a particularly fine variety of this plant grew near Ch'ang-lo District. Wang Shen-chih sent this north as tribute each year, and forbade private persons to gather it. (*FCTC*1 40.1b). The site where it was gathered was sometimes known as Taboo Rock (禁石) (*Min tu chi* 26.16b).

[399] *TPHYC* as from Ch'üan. The *root* is the part employed. See Stuart, *op. cit.* 55.

[400] *SS* 89.

[401] *TPHYC* as from Fu and Ch'üan.

[402] *TPHYC* as from Fu.

[403] *TPHYC* as from Nan-chien.

[404] *TPHYC* as from Ch'üan.

[405] *TPHYC* as from Fu. *Yang-t'ao* is the Fukienese term for this plant, elsewhere called *Wu-lien-tzu* 五斂子.

[406] *SS* 89 and *TPHYC*, mentioned in particular for Fu and Ch'üan.

[407] *CIL* a.40b. An anecdote about the lichee of Fukien is given in *ibid.* a.43b.

the "General Lichee" (將軍荔枝), found at Fu Prefecture, is supposed to have been planted by an anonymous general of the Five Dynasties period.[408]

The following are various luxury items produced in the empire: bamboo of many varieties;[409] shark-skins from Chang on the southern coast;[410] tortoise shell, quite frequent on the tribute lists;[411] tortoise carapaces;[412] the native banyan (榕, *Ficus Wightiana* var. *Japonica*), so typical of Fu that the prefectural city came to be known as "Banyan Town" (榕城).[413] Pearls and glass (琉璃) both were sent by Min as tribute to the north, but I do not know that these were products of the region.[414] The mole (鼴鼠 *Mogera wogura*) is listed as from T'ing—presumably its skin was regarded as valuable.[415] The coastal cities of Fu and Ch'üan were sources of "python bile" (蚺蛇胆), doubtless for medicinal use.[416]

Manufactured goods, other than textiles follow: *T'ai-p'ing huan-yü chi* makes the two south coastal Prefectures of Ch'üan and Chang the sites of shipbuilding industries, specifically of "ocean-going vessels" (海舶).[417] Various kinds of decorated fans were made at Fu.[418] Arrows of various kinds, including "fire-arrows," presumably smeared with pitch;[419] wax

---

[408] Ts'ai Hsiang, *Li-chih p'u* 荔枝譜 (edit. of *Po-ch'uan hsueh-hai*) 1a, 1b, 6b.

[409] Noted by *TS* 41 as a specialty of Chien.

[410] *TS* 41 has 鮫革; *SS* 89 has 鮫魚皮; *TPHYC* has 沙魚皮.

[411] This was called 玳瑁; contrast the next item.

[412] *TPHYC*, 龜甲.

[413] At least from Sung times. See *FCTC*2 62.2b. It is listed as a " product of the soil " (土產) in *TPHYC* 100.3b, but its use is not clear.

[414] There were important pearl fisheries at Ho-p'u in Southern Han at any rate.

[415] *TPHYC*. But Li Shih-chen gives medicinal uses for the cooked flesh (*Pen-ts'ao kang-mu* 51.67–68).

[416] *TPHYC*. *Ling-piao lu-i* 嶺表錄異 c.9b (edit. of *Wu-ying-tien chü-chen-pan ch'uan-shu*) tells that certain people of P'u-an 普安 (in Kueichou, but possibly an error for Chin-an 晉安, that is Fu Prefecture?) raised pythons for the purpose of extracting bile, which was dried and submitted as tribute. Li Shih-chen (*op. cit.* 43.68) states that pythons are native to Lingnan, but cites T'ao Hung-ching 陶弘景 of Liang to the effect that the serpent is found around Chin-an 晉安 (晉安, cf. *Ling-piao lu-i*), and Chang Tsu 張鷟 (eighth century) in his *Ch'ao-yeh chien-tsai* 朝野僉載 (*TSCC* ed.) 1.2 tells that the local magistrates of Ch'üan Prefecture collected python bile for tribute. A certain traveler there was cured of a serious disease by eating the snake's flesh.

[417] It is clear from this, and from the many records of naval warfare in Min, that the Fukienese still retained the nautical skill that had characterized them from the earliest times. Writing of these people when they were still near-savages (in the Han dynasty), the Prince of Huai-nan emphasized that " they are practised in aquatic warfare and accustomed to the use of boats " (*Han shu* 64.0516c-d).

[418] *TS* 41, *TPHYC*, and the tribute lists. Among the kinds found in the latter was " five-colored *t'ung*-bark fans " (五色桐皮扇子).

[419] 火箭, from the Prefecture of Chien (*SS* 89). Arrow types whose names I have been unable to translate satisfactorily are 通槽箭 of the tribute of 929, and 通節箭 of the tribute of 938.

candles from T'ing;[420] leather boots;[421] baskets made of rattan (白藤, *Calamus sp.*), manufactured in Fu and Ch'üan;[422] refined sugar, manufactured at Fu;[423] paper, including a glossy transparent variety from Ch'üan;[424] finally, "flower-drums" (花鼓).[425]

The empire produced a great variety of textile goods, among which that woven from *Pueraria,* already mentioned, was the most notable. Next to it in importance were the goods woven from banana fiber, called *chiao-ko* 蕉葛 or *chiao-pu* 蕉布.[426] Fukien also produced ramie cloth (made from *Boehmeria nivea,* called *po-chu-pu* 白苧布).[427] In addition there were hempen sackcloth (紵布),[428] coarse silk cloth (絲布),[429] fine pongee (輕絹),[430] fine brocaded silk (錦綺羅),[431] white and red cotton stuffs (白氎紅氎),[432] "cicada-gauze" (蟬紗), so called because it was as sheer as the cicada's wing,[433] and silk cloth dyed red with madder (茜緋, from *Rubia cordifolia*).[434]

Not mentioned as one of the chief products of Fukien, nor figuring in tribute to the imperial court, but worthy of note as important in the local economy, was iron. Deposits are observed by the *T'ang History* in the vicinity of each of the prefectures with the exception of Chang.

Nothing has been said so far about the chief crop in the local economy, namely rice. This important cereal was grown in flooded fields wherever

420 *TS* 41, *SS* 89. See Stuart, *op. cit.* 237–239 for an account of the wax insect and its properties.

421 The tribute of 938 includes 麖靴. The *ching* was a mythological one-horned deer, but has more recently been identified with the *Cervus unicolor* of South Asia and Indonesia. There is a possibility that we have here an error for 麋 or 麞, yet *Ch'uan-chou-fu chih* 19.22b lists 麖 as a native of this area, separate from 麢 and 麞.

422 *TPHYC.*

423 *TPHYC*, 乾白沙糖.

424 *TPHYC*, 蠲符紙.

425 In the tribute of 943.

426 Mentioned in all sources.

427 *TPHYC*, as from Nan-chien. Stuart, *op. cit.* 70 states of this cloth, "Prior to the eleventh century there is no record of where it was produced, although it was known from ancient times as a textile plant. Su-sung, who wrote in the eleventh century, said that it was at that time grown in Fukien, Szechuan, Chekiang, and Kiangnan."

428 *SS* 89 and *TPHYC*, from Fu.

429 *TPHYC*, from Fu.

430 *Ibid.*

431 Tribute of 929.

432 Tribute of 929.

433 Tribute of 943.

434 *TPHYC.*

the water was available, except in salty areas near the coast. Evidently the rice crop was more reliable than elsewhere in China, for the *Sung History* tells us that the fields of Fukien were fertile and did not suffer bad years.[435] Two crops a year were customary in this semitropical land. The rulers of Min, in their religious fervor, took care that the priesthood should be well provided for, and gave the best rice fields to the Buddhist and Taoist temples, leaving the inferior fields for lay farmers.[436] Especially interesting is the variety of rice known as "Champa paddy" (占城稻), a drought-tolerant kind, which imported from Fukien to the Yangtze basin in A.D. 1011 by imperial decree after a long drought in Central China. It may be presumed that this variety was known in Fukien in the previous century, and the name suggests that it was brought thither from Champa.[437]

## 2.   COURT EXPENDITURES AND TAXATION

All sources agree that Wang Shen-chih was personally frugal, even parsimonious, and that his administration was prudent and economical in contrast to that of his successors who are all accused of extravagance, the imposition of unusually heavy taxes and hence of unworthiness and unpopularity. This pattern, repeated in the official histories of other states of this age, seems to represent, in part at least, an orthodox Confucian attitude, to wit: Shen-chih was nominally an agent of the T'ang dynasty, and although he was in fact sole administrator of his province, he was careful never to assume any outward prerogatives which might be construed as belonging only to the Son of Heaven. His sons and grandson, however, aspired openly to imperial dignities in greater or less degree, and since later historiography has given legitimacy to the rulers of the "Five Dynasties," convention demanded that these "usurpers" should be regarded as bad administrators, cursed with the vice of overliberality with the people's money. While I feel sure that this attitude was at work in phrasing the accounts of Min left us by the Sung historians, nonetheless it is also natural that Shen-chih, an old campaigner unused to luxury, should have spent less in his government than the Princes who followed him—they were born to the purple, maintaining staffs of courtiers and domestics analogous to those at K'ai-feng in the north, and addicted to the construction of secular and religious buildings of the most elaborate sort.

[435] *SS* 89.4710c.
[436] *SS* 173.4907b.
[437] *SS* 173.4904a; *FCTC1* 59.1b. For a study of Champa rice see Katō Shigeru, 加藤 繁, *Shina-keizaishi-kōshō* 支那經濟史考證, (Toyobunko Publications Series A, No. 34, Tokyo, 1953) Vol. 2, pp. 659–675.

At any rate, the state is said to have enjoyed both "public and private prosperity" under Shen-chih. He lightened the tax burden, and was careful to send annual tribute to Liang by sea when that dynasty came to power, even though a great portion of this was lost through shipwrecks.[438] His immediate successor Yen-han ruled for only a few months, and there is no material available on the national fiscal situation during this period. After him, however, all the sovereigns of Min were plagued with income troubles.

Yen-chün found it impossible to balance his budget by readily available means. He therefore appointed a ruthless military officer, Hsüeh Wen-chieh, as his Fiscal Intendant (國計使), who supplemented the national income by means of blackmail. He carried out secret investigations of the wealthy, and wherever he found anything in their lives that might be interpreted as a misdemeanor, he confiscated their property for the state. He also forced the reluctant to part with their riches by the application of torture. Flogging and branding with bronze flat irons are specifically mentioned in the text. One member of the gentry, Wu Kuang, of the Prefecture of Chien, when almost in Wen-chieh's toils, fled with ten thousand rebellious men north into the state of Wu. Lather he returned with the Huainanese to attack Chien, and brought about the execution of Wen-chieh.[439] Perhaps a portion of the financial difficulties of Yen-chün was the result of the loss of income attendant on the policy of permitting the state to support three million Buddhist priests.[440] The text uses the word "support," which I take to mean that the priesthood was tax free, and possibly also that the temples actually received income for food, clothing and building from the pro-Buddhist monarch.

Chi-p'eng's money troubles were also due in part to his extravagant religious fervor, in his case directed towards the Taoists rather than the Buddhists. It is recorded that he used "several thousand catties of yellow gold" to cast images of the Precious August and of Lao-tzu (as the deity *Yüan-shih t'ien-tsun t'ai-shang lao-chün* 元始天尊太上老君). In addition he burned large amounts of expensive aromatic woods before these divinities in his search for the divine elixir.[441] Another drain on the imperial treasury was the expenditure of great sums on his special band of praetorian guards, the Ch'en-wei Division, which Chi-p'eng created out of mistrust of the older divisions. He is said to have dressed these men in fine silk and silver girdles,

---

[438] *TCTC* 267.9a. See below for the sea route to Shantung.

[439] *WTS*, *TCTC* 278.8a. The appointment of Wen-chieh took place in August 933, that is, when Yen-chün ascended the imperial throne.

[440] *WKKS* b.6a. There are some extravagances in this source, and the number may be exaggerated. See below under Religion.

[441] *WTS*.

fed them from golden dishes and paid them salaries much greater than those allotted to the other palace guards.[442] He sought to supplement his resources by the accepted means of increasing the taxes on fruit, vegetables, chicken and pork. He also strengthened his tax collectors' hands by decreeing the punishment of flogging for persons who concealed their age to avoid listing on the tax rolls and death for persons who misrepresented the size of their families (隱口者). But finding the revenues from taxes insufficient he resorted, in the summer of 937, to less usual means. In short, he systematized the sale of public offices. His Director of Finances (判三司) and Vice-President of the Board of Personnel, Ts'ai Shou-meng 蔡守蒙, essentially an honest man, was outraged when his Emperor asked him about methods of bribe-taking. But finally under pressure of threats, he was forced to carry out Chi-p'eng's scheme, to rule out incompetence as a bar to public office, and to make all appointments proportional to the bribe received, the money going into the treasury instead of into ministerial pockets. In addition, the Emperor made a former apothecary (醫工), Ch'en Kuei 陳究, his "Agent for Blank Commissions" (空名堂牒使).[443] The title refers to the practice of selling offices by vending blank appointment forms, in which the name of the new officeholder and his title were inserted at the time of sale. Ts'ai Shou-meng, for his part, like the majority of the fiscal agents of the Min rulers, came to a unfortunate end. He was executed for "taking bribes" after the accession of Yen-hsi.[444]

Yen-hsi too is described in the histories as "extravagant," and the tale of his predecessors is repeated for him, with the difference that he does not seem to have condoned the practice of selling offices at first, but relied rather on the ingenuity of his collectors. His Fiscal Intendant was Ch'en K'uang-fan 陳匡範, who contracted to show a daily income of ten thousand in gold on his books, for which promise he was rewarded with the title of Vice-President of the Board of Rites, and Yen-hsi boasted publicly at a palace entertainment that K'uang-fan was "a jewel among men." The means by which the Intendant proposed to raise the guaranteed gold was an exceptionally heavy poll tax on merchants. Unfortunately the amount received from this source did not come up to expectations, and in order to retain the imperial favor, K'uang-fan supplemented this income by making levies on the working funds of various government agencies. He is said to have died of anxiety lest the truth be disclosed. After his death the departments which were short of funds by reason of K'uang-fan's depredations complained to the Emperor, who ordered the late Intendant's grave

[442] *WTS, WKKS* b.7b.
[443] *TCTC* 281.6b.
[444] *TCTC* 282.6b.

opened and his corpse dismembered.[445]   His successor was a man named
Huang Shao-p'o, who, with imperial sanction, reinstituted the practice of
selling offices, at a price range of from one hundred to one thousand strings
of cash, in accordance with a careful estimate of the candidate's birth,
reputation and so forth.[446]   Yen-hsi had the talent to seize on a providential
situation to make additional money.   The anecdote is told of Yü T'ing-ying,
Prefect of Ch'üan, who forged an edict authorizing himself to obtain girls,
ostensibly for the imperial harem but actually for his own enjoyment, from
local families.   When the Emperor learned of this, he summoned the culprit
to the capital, but instead of putting him to death, accepted one hundred
thousand in cash by way of commutation, with the euphemism "payment
for a feast," and then exacted an equal sum as "local tribute" from the
Prefecture to the Empress.   This precedent started the custom of annual
tribute from all of the Prefectures of Min "for the Empress."[447]

Yen-cheng, the last of the Emperors of Min, seems to have emulated
Shen-chih in some respects, since he wore coarse robes instead of fine silks,
and avoided elaborate ceremony.[448]   Nonetheless, the tax collector he
appointed on his accession, Yang Ssu-kung, earned the imperial favor and
popular resentment through his skill.   He also earned the title "Yang the
Flayer."   He increased "field and fallow taxes" (田畝山澤之稅) and
doubled the taxes on fish, salt, green vegetables and fruit.[449]   Three months
after Yen-cheng's assumption of the purple, in June 943, the President of
his Board of Personnel, P'an Ch'eng-yu, presented a memorial to the throne,
comprising ten separate items of criticism.   Among other things he attacked
the superabundance and weight of both taxes and forced labor, in particular
pointing out the hatred of the people toward Yang the Flayer.   He also
criticized the custom of awarding offices to members of wealthy families (did
Yen-cheng sell offices after all?) and the unwise practice of inflicting heavy
penalties on tax defaulters.   He objected also to the levies made at "the
fords of Yen-p'ing," that is at the crossings of the river Chien, on fruit,
vegetables, fish and rice, which raised little income, but created much anger
among the people.   This doubtless refers to a tax on products brought for
sale in Chien from outside the prefecture—fish and salt (mentioned above)
were coastal products.[450]   It is interesting and perhaps pertinent that Hu

---

[445] *TCTC* 282.17a-b.   *TCTC* gives the appointment of K'uang-fan as taking place in
July 941, two years after Yen-hsi's accession.

[446] *Ibid.*

[447] *TCTC* 283.5b.

[448] *WKKS* b.9a.

[449] *TCTC* 283.9b.

[450] *TCTC* 283.11a-b.

San-hsing, the commentator on Ssu-ma Kuang, attributes the downfall of the empire to the exactions of Yang the Flayer rather than to the loss of the war against Southern T'ang.[451]

Meanwhile in the Prefecture of Fu, before that city offered its allegiance to Yen-cheng, the new and temporary Emperor, Chu Wen-chin, on his accession in April 944, attempted to gain popular approval by instituting economy measures intended to afford a marked contrast to the fiscal administration of Yen-hsi: he dismissed the hordes of palace girls and put a stop to architectural construction. These attempts to cut down the court expenditures did not suffice to save his life, since he was the puppet of an ambitious man.

From the early Sung we have a report of a regular poll tax (丁錢) exacted in the various prefectures of Min, but the source, which is reliable, does not tell at what period the tax was instituted, describing it only as operating under the "spurious" Min (僞閩).[452]


## 3.  CURRENCY[452a]

We are informed that Shen-chih circulated both copper and lead currency in his princedom: this independent policy, which corresponds with the downfall of the T'ang dynasty, since the coins were issued at about the turn of the year 916-917, seems to have been dictated by the need for a reliable kind of money in the area under his jurisdiction. We do not know whether this currency continued in use after his acceptance of Liang.[453]   Later texts also speak of iron coins cast by Shen-chih. These latter bore the popular legend *K'ai-yüan t'ung-pao* 開元通寶, already used for many T'ang issues, and some at least bore the character 閩 on the reverse.[454]

Yen-chün apparently cast two coinages, named for his reigns Lung Ch'i

---

[451] *TCTC* 284.13a.  Ssu-ma Kuang tells that the Legate appointed by T'ang to rule Northern Fukien from the Prefecture of Chien, Wang Ch'ung-wen 王崇文, " governed with liberality and simplicity, and the people of Chien were consequently secure." *TCTC* 285.5b.

[452] Ts'ai Hsiang, *Tsou chuan Chang Ch'uan Hsing-hua ting-ch'ien su* 奏鐲漳泉興化丁錢疏, cited in *T'u-shu chi-ch'eng* Chih-fang tien 職方典 1032.

[452a] For this note see bottom of p. 79.

[453] *TCTC* 269.19a.

[454] Liang Shih-cheng 梁詩正 (1697–1763), *Ch'ien lu* 錢錄 (*TSCC* ed.) 9.164–5 has a woodcut of the coin with plain reverse, but Arthur B. Coole, *Coins in China's History* (Tientsin, 2nd edit. 1937) 37 reproduces a photograph of this coin with 閩 on reverse. *Ch'ien lu* states that the Fukienese referred to this issue as 銛刄 ; a gloss adds that the pronunciation of the first character is unknown, while that of the second is like 貨. *Ch'ien lu*'s source is T'ao Yüeh (Sung) 陶岳, *Chu'an-huo lu* 泉貨錄, not available to me.

(龍啓) and Yung Ho (永和), but I have no information as to their composition.[455] If Chi-p'eng made a new coinage, it has not come to my attention.

Yen-hsi, in September-October 942, had cast the issue of *Yung-lung t'ung-pao* 永隆通寶, made of iron, and valued at one per hundred lead cash.[456] Shortly thereafter, in February 944, Yen-cheng issued another iron currency, named after his own reign *T'ien-te t'ung-pao* 天德通寶, also at the rate of one to a hundred.[457] The immediate effect of these measures on the fiscal administration of the nation is not clear, but in any case Min was close to its end.

From another part of China, however, we have some thoughtful analyses of the effects of debasing the currency. When the King of Wu-yüeh decided to create a buffer state in Min in the fall of 946, he proposed to cast iron money to pay his troops. His relative, Ch'ien Hung-i 錢弘億, admonished him, and among the arguments which he adduced against the new currency was the economic principle known in the West as "Gresham's Law." Some of his points follow: "When the new currency has been circulated, the old currency will all flow into neighboring countries"; "It may be used in our country, but not used in other countries, so that the merchants will not travel, and produce will not circulate"; further he argued that if copper was prohibited, the people would become counterfeiters since iron implements were abundant everywhere. Finally he pointed to the disturbances in Min where an iron coinage had been established. The clinching argument pointed out that Ch'ien (錢, "cash") was the imperial surname, and that to change the currency would augur ill for the dynasty. The King abandoned his plan.[458]

## 4. FOREIGN TRADE

It is clear that the trade both with the other nations of China and with overseas lands to the south was considerable, but it is difficult to estimate its extent with any precision.

Despite the troubled times and the multiplicity of national boundaries

---

[455] *Min-hou hsien chih* 49.1a-b.

[456] *TCTC* 283.5a. *WTS* says that Yen-hsi cast "great iron coins," valued at one to ten. Perhaps the comparison is with copper coins. See also *Ch'ien lu* 9.165–166. *Min-hou hsien chih loc. cit.* mentions both copper and iron cash of the Yung-lung period.

[457] *TCTC* 283.19b. See *Ch'ien lu* 9.166–167 for illustration. Actually there were two T'ien Te issues, the second bearing the legend 天德重寶, with 殷 on the reverse.

[458] *TCTC* 285.11a.

in China during this era, there is abundant evidence that merchants traveled with freedom from state to state.[459] Indeed it is apparent that they had an easier time making their ways across frontiers than had any other class, certainly more so than the official class. Hence it was customary to employ merchants in various capacities extraneous to their legitimate business. Thus Yen-hsi, after his accession, sent traveling tradesmen to the capital of Chin to declare himself tributary to that empire.[460] In the following year he again sent merchants with his petition for autonomy (自理), which brought him the title of King of Min.[461] Such was the comparative ease with which merchants could travel into neighboring countries that frequently an official would be sent on a mission disguised as a man of commerce. Thus Liu Ts'ung-hsiao, the successor to the dynasty of Wang in Ch'üan Prefecture, sent a certain officer named Ts'ai Chung-hsing 蔡仲興 to offer his submission to Chou Shih Tsung, garbed as a trader on the way.[462] Because of their familiarity with the topography of the lands in which they sought business and through which they traveled, merchants were a source of valuable strategic information, and useful as spies to the rulers of the various nations. An instance is the case of Tsang Hsün of Southern T'ang, who, having become familiar with the landscape of Fukien after frequent business trips there, gave abundant data to his native state for drawing plans of the assault on the Prefecture of Chien early in 945.[463]

We know something of the sea routes from Fu to the north from the records of the tribute missions sent to the courts of the Five Dynasties. Doubtless these routes were used by ordinary traders as well as by official missions. The ships from Fukien made port at Teng 登 or Lai 萊 in modern North Shantung, and the embassies proceeded overland thence to K'ai-feng. The trip was considered perilous however, for it is recorded that Shen-chih lost four-fifths of the tribute cargoes sent to Liang.[464] Hu San-hsing gives the stages of the overland journey that had been in use prior to the occupation

---

[459] An anecdote: a merchant from Ching 荆 and a merchant from Min were quarrelling at an inn. The former said to his rival, "Your belly contains worms," and the latter retorted, "You people have weapons in your belly!" (*CIL* a.19b). This is a graphic joke, based on the characters 閩 and 荆.

[460] This was in the early fall of 939. *TCTC* 282.6b.

[461] *TCTC* 282.13b.

[462] *WTS*.

[463] *TCTC* 284.8b, also *NTS* 2.11. Nonetheless it should be noted that it was not impossible for nonmercantile individuals to travel from kingdom to kingdom: we sometimes read of literary persons doing so. As an example, the poet Hsü Yin, a native of Fukien, frequently travelled to the Liang capital to compose rhapsodies for Chu Ch'üan-chung. See his reconstructed biography in *Shih-kuo ch'un-ch'iu* 95.3b-4a.

[464] *TCTC* 267.9a.

of Huai-nan by the Yang family of Wu: the successive Prefectures passed through by the northbound traveler were Ch'ü 衢, Hsin 信, Jao 饒, Ch'ih 池, thence across the Long River, via Shu 舒, Lu 廬 and Shou 壽 through the Huai area, and so to the capital. Now the Chu family of Liang and the Yang family of Wu on its southern frontier were not on good terms, so that it became necessary for the travelers to and from the south, especially those bearing tribute to Liang, which the monarchs of Wu might well prefer to see in their own treasury, to take the sea route and thus avoid Huai-nan altogether. According to Hu San-hsing, the vessels departed from Fu Prefecture, passed via Wen 溫, T'ai 台 and Ming 明 Prefectures, the Harbor of Lieh 冽港,[465] and thence, abandoning the coast, across the open sea to Teng and Lai.[466] Min had, in fact, already made use of the sea route before the occupation of Huai-nan, but the kingdom of Wu-yüeh had depended entirely on the overland route until 918, when it became necessary for them to take to the sea also.[467]

The coastal cities of Min—Fu, Ch'üan and Chang—still engaged in overseas trade with the countries of the South China Sea and the Indian archipelago, as they had during T'ang. We have already seen that the latter two Prefectures were centers of the shipbuilding industry. Ch'üan seems to have been especially prosperous as a result of this commerce, although that port could not yet compare with Canton in the empire of Han in the

---

[465] I am unable to locate this harbor with certainty. Recent geographical works give a Lieh Harbor 烈 (sic) 港 at Chin-t'ang Island 金塘山 in the Chou-shan Archipelago, off Ningpo (ancient Ming Prefecture). This would be consistent. See for instance Hu Tsung-hsien 胡宗憲, Ch'ou-hai t'u-pien 籌海圖編 5.48b (a Ming work, sixteenth century).

[466] TCTC 267.9a.

[467] In 918, the Wu nation began to extend its power south from Huai-nan proper, and the three powers to the south of that state found it expedient to band together for mutual aid. The struggle became critical at the Prefecture of Ch'ien 虔 (in the south of modern Kiangsi). This prefecture was controlled by T'an Ch'üan-po 譚全播, who, in the capacity of Commissioner of Defense (防禦使) appointed by the Liang court, governed in relative security until attacked by Wu. The prefectural city resisted stoutly until a new Huainanese commander, Liu Hsin 劉信, arrived to press the siege in the seventh month of 918. The Commissioner then requested aid of Wu-yüeh, Ch'u and Min, that is of the rulers of Chekiang, Hunan and Fukien. Each state sent an army to T'an's relief since all feared the rising power of Wu, and preferred Ch'ien Prefecture to remain a buffer city which owed nominal allegiance to distant Liang, on their frontiers. However, a detachment of the Wu army smashed the Hunanese in a night raid, and the allies from Wu-yüeh and Min, demoralized by news of this defeat, withdrew. Ch'ien was taken in the eleventh month, and Commissioner T'an was captured and given a military title in the host of Wu. Thus Wu-yüeh and Min found territory belonging to the Yang clan along their western borders. See WTS 29.4434c, TCTC 270.11b, 13a-b and 14a.

bulk of imports from overseas.[468]   Nonetheless, it is reported that Wang Yen-pin, the nephew of Shen-chih and Prefect of Ch'üan until his degradation early in 921 for displaying imperial pretensions, brought great prosperity to his Prefecture through his administration, whose economy was chiefly supported by foreign trade represented by the ships of the "Southern Outlanders" (蠻舶).  For his success in encouraging this business, he received the popular title of "Treasure-beckoning Secretary" (招寶侍郎).[469]

Shen-chih himself gave great attention to waterborne commerce, and "summoned the barbarian merchants from overseas."[470]   He was personally, however, not given to extravagance and seems to have been rather contemptuous of foreign luxuries:  "Boy, I hate their empty shows, Persian garlands I detest. . ."[471]   It is related that he once received a vase of glass as a gift from the "South."  He broke it disdainfully as a symbol of all the useless gewgaws from the outlands.[472]   His interest in international commerce, which chiefly brought much sought after luxury goods into China, must have been merely to keep his budget balanced and the treasury full.[473]   In this he differs from his successor Yen-chün, who sent a special mission to Champa[474] to obtain a crystal screen for his new palace.[475]

## 5.   POPULATION CHANGES

Information available regarding population changes can be best presented in tabular form.  Note that all figures are for taxable families:

[468] In early Sung, despite attempts to force increased foreign trade in the northern ports of Ch'üan, Ming and Hang 杭, Canton was still by far the most flourishing. See Chu Yü 朱彧, P'ing-chou k'o-t'an 萍洲可談 (TSCC ed.) 2.17.

[469] WKKS b.9b, and cf. TCTC 271.7a.

[470] WTS. Min-hsien hsiang-t'u chih 23a states that overseas trade was managed by a certain Chang Mu 張睦, a fellowtownsman of Shen-chih.

[471] Q. Horatius Flaccus, Odes I.38, trans. by William Cowper.

[472] WKKS b.5b.

[473] For a list of exotic products brought into China by sea in early Sung, certainly much the same as under the Min rulers, see SS 186.4946d.

[474] 日南, the T'ang name of a "province" only nominally Chinese.  It was now the northernmost part of the Cham empire on the boundary of the Annamese lands, which were to become independent in a few years as the empire of Đại Cồ-Việt 太瞿越 (G. Maspero, "La Géographie politique de l'Indochine aux environs de 960 A.D.," Etudes Asiatiques 2.83–84, Paris, 1925).  Between Min and Champa, then, were Southern Han and embryonic Annam.

[475] CFWC.  The screen doubtless gave its name to the "Crystal Palace."

### TABLE OF POPULATION CHANGES

| Prefecture | Early 8th Century[476] | Early 9th Century[477] | Late 10th Century[478] | Early 12th Century[479] |
|---|---|---|---|---|
| Fu | 34,084 (31,067) | 19,455 | 94,470 | 211,552 |
| Chien | 22,770 (20,800) | 15,480 | 195,043 | 403,721 |
| T'ing | 4,680 ( — ) | 2,618 | 24,007[480] | 81,454 |
| Ch'üan | 23,806 (50,754) | 35,571 | 130,288 | 264,563 |
| Chang | 5,346[481] (1,690) | 1,343 | 24,007[480] | 100,469 |
| Totals | 90,686 (104,311) | 74,467 | 467,815 | 1,061,759[482] |

[476] Figures for early eighth century are for the K'ai-yüan reign as reported in *Chiu T'ang shu* 40.3223 and *TS* 41.3728. Data in parentheses are for the same period, but according to *Yuan-ho chun-hsien chih* 30.

[477] Figures for early ninth century are for the Yüan-ho reign as reported in *Yuan-ho chün-hsien chih*.

[478] Figures for late tenth century are for the T'ai-p'ing hsing-kuo reign as reported in *TPHYC* 100–102. These are broken down in the text into resident families (主) and guest families (客), i.e. new settlers. I report the totals. Sung dynasty figures, are not exactly comparable to those for T'ang, because of changes in the administrative divisions of the province. Thus the new Prefecture of Nan-chien was created from Yu-ch'i District (formerly in Fu Prefecture) and Yen-p'ing, Sha and Chiang-lo Districts (formerly in Chien Prefecture). Also the Shao-wu Army 邵武軍 was created from Shao-wu, Kuei-hua and Chien-ning Districts (taken from Chien Prefecture). I include the figures for Nan-chien and Shao-wu with Chien Prefecture. The Hsing-hua Army 興化軍 was created from P'u-t'ien, Hsing-hua and Yu-hsien Districts (taken from Ch'üan Prefecture), therefore I include the figures for Hsing-hua with Ch'üan Prefecture. Other minor changes, for which I can make no compensatory changes on my chart since I lack statistics for individual Districts, are Te-hua District 德化 carved out of Fu Prefecture and added to Ch'üan, and Ch'ang-t'ai District 長泰 taken from Ch'üan and added to Chang.

[479] Figures for early twelfth century are for the thirty-second year of Shao-hsing (1162) as reported in *SS* 89.4710.

[480] Figures given as identical for T'ing and Chang, evidently in error.

[481] Here I follow *Chiu T'ang shu*. *TS* has 5,846.

[482] *SS* gives total number of families in Fu-chien Route, as of the same reckoning, as 1,390,565. I do not know where the other 33,000 are. Total population (taxable *persons*) for 1162 is given as 2,828,852. I do not have population figures (persons) for other periods except the eighth century—*Chiu T'ang shu* gives 411,587. The decrease shown between the eighth and ninth centuries was probably attendant on the rebellions of An Lu-shan and Shih Ssu-ming. A guess for the population of the Min empire would be approximately a million persons of taxable age.

[452a] After this volume had already gone to press, I discovered a valuable book on the currencies of the Five Dynasties and Sung periods: Miyasaki Ichisada 宮崎市定, *Go-dai Sō-hatsu no tsūka-mondai* 五代宋初の通貨問題 (Kyōto, 1943). Information on the Min coinages may be found on pages 52–55. I lack some of Prof. Miyasaki's information on the lead coinage of Shen-chih, but he lacks my data on the two coinages of Yen-chün.

# V

# ARTS

## 1.  ARCHITECTURE

THE two most famous palaces of the imperial court of Min are the Ch'ang-ch'un Palace (長春宮) and the Shui-ching Palace (水晶宮), both in the District of Hou-kuan.[483]  The former is also referred to as the Southern Palace (南宮).[484]  It was located on the grounds of the former Headquarters of the Wei-wu Army in the north central part of the city.[485]  Tradition has it that the palace was constructed by Yen-chün especially for his Empress, Golden Phoenix.[486]  It (or some of its buildings) was destroyed by fire on the night of August 29, 939, at the hands of Lien Chung-yü and his men during their rebellious attack on Chi-p'eng.[487]  The details of its construction and form are not preserved.  Rather more is known of the Shui-ching Palace, built over the West Lake, three *li* west of the prefectural office of Fu, outside the wall of the city.[488]  It is said that in Yen-chün's time it consisted of more than a hundred separate apartments (室).[489]  A "double way" (複道), that is, a passage constructed with both upper and lower ways, led out to it from the city proper through the *lo-ch'eng* 羅城, and the palace girls were accustomed to stroll out this way, while the

[483] *FCTC*1 39.1b-2a.

[484] This would appear from the fact that on July 14, 939, Chi-p'eng moved to the Ch'ang-ch'un Palace.  *TCTC* 282.4a.  *WTS*, with reference to the same event, tells that he moved to the Southern Palace.

[485] *FCTC*1 39.2a.

[486] *CFWC*.

[487] *TCTC* 282.5a-b, 6a-b.

[488] *FCTC*1 39.1b-a, *YTCS* 128.11a.  King Ho-lü 闔閭 of the ancient kingdom of Wu (Ch'un-ch'iu period) is said to have constructed a "crystal palace."  See Jen Fang 任昉, *Shu-i chi* 述異記 (in *Han Wei ts'ung-shu* 漢魏叢書) a.20a.

[489] *FCTC*1 39.1b-2a.

populace stared.[490]

The names of five other palaces in the capital are preserved in *Yü-ti chi-sheng*: Pao-huang 寶皇, Ta-ming 大明, Tzu-wei 紫微,[491] Tung-hua 東華 and Lung-yüeh 龍躍 Palaces. These were built at different times, and according to the gazetteers, were all located on the grounds of the Ch'ang-ch'un Palace, which, then, must have been the name for the "imperial city" itself.[492]

The Palace of the Precious August (Pao-huang), built by Yen-chün in 931, will be discussed below under Religion. Of the Ta-ming Palace I know nothing beyond its name. The Tzu-wei Palace, built in 937 by Chi-p'eng, will also be treated under Religion. The Tung-hua Palace was built by Yen-chün for the Lady Spring Swallow, who later became Chi-p'eng's favorite.[493] We are told that the kingposts supporting the rafters (梲栭) of this palace were of coral, the lintels and the tiles (櫺瓦) of glass (琉璃), the beams (梁棟) of sandalwood and nanmu (檀楠), the screens (簾幙) of pearls (眞珠) and the pillars and plinths (柱礎) of gold leaf (汇金). The Tung-hua Palace survived in some form for a considerable period for it was renamed Yüan-miao Kuan 元妙觀 in the Yüan dynasty;[494] a temple once attached to it, the T'ai-shan Miao 泰山廟, was later known as the "Traveling Palace of the Eastern Sacred Mountain" (東嶽行宮).[495] The Lung-yüeh Palace was the pre-imperial home of Yen-chün, and will be treated under Religion.

Pavilions (殿) erected by the monarchs of Min on the grounds of the Ch'ang-ch'un Palace were as follows:[496]  Wen-te 文德, Wen-ming 文明, Ta-p'u 大酺, Ming-wei 明威 and Chiu-lung 九龍 Pavilions.  I can find

[490] *Ibid.*  In modern times the Fukienese have believed the islet in the middle of the West Lake to be the ruins of this palace but this is incorrect.  See *Min tu chi* 9.7a-b.

[491] *YTCS* has the characters 紫薇, but in view of the Taoist associations with the structure, I prefer the reading of *TCTC* 281.4b.  If the former were correct, the palace would have been named after the plant *Lagerstroemia indica*.  But the term "Purple Subtlety" is an ancient name for the imperial throne.  The Wei-yang Palace 未央宮 of the Han Emperors in Ch'ang-an is said to have been also called "Palace of Purple Subtlety" (Hsin——辛氏, *San Ch'in chi* 三秦記 [*Shuo fu* edit.] 2b).

[492] *YTCS* 128.14a lists the Ch'ang-ch'un Palace co-ordinately with these palaces. *FCTC*1, however, treats them as parts of the Ch'ang-ch'un Palace and lists the Shui-ching Palace separately.  The map in *Min tu chi* shows the location of these palaces within the imperial enclosure.  The text of *FCTC*1 goes: 長春宮在舊威武軍內有寶皇宮 etc.

[493] The splendid substances of which the palace was made are given in *CFWC* and may therefore be suspect.

[494] *Min tu chi* 11.5a.  *yüan* 元 is probably a substitute for *hsüan* 玄 in this text.

[495] *FCTC*2 15.2b.

[496] *YTCS* 128.14a.

details of human activity in connection with only two, the Ta-p'u and Chiu-lung Pavilions.  The former was the scene of great drinking parties in the palace, named for the ancient custom[497] of ordering drinking festivals throughout the empire in honor of important events in the court, such as the appointment of an Heir Apparent or the adoption of a new reign title.[498] Yen-chün held a party at this pavilion on New Year's Night (元夕),[499] and feasted his army there in the autumn of 935 on the evening of his assassination.[500]  The "Nine Dragon" Pavilion was the scene of dalliance between Yen-hsi and his concubine Shang-kuan, but was constructed at the order of Yen-chün by Li K'o-yin.  More precisely, K'o-yin was the manufacturer of the Nine Dragon Tent from which the pavilion took its name.  The tent was appliqued with gold (縷金) and decorated in various bright colors, with eight dragons woven on the outside, the ninth being the Emperor within.[501]

These palaces and pavilions, together with the gates of the imperial enclosure, enumerated above under Landscape, marked the residence of the Emperor, his male and female relatives, the officers of the court and the hordes of servants and underlings who supported them.  This was the so-called "Southern Palace."  The identity of the "Northern Palace," vacated by Chi-p'eng because of unfavorable omens and destroyed by fire shortly before the incineration of the Ch'ang-ch'un Palace, is more difficult to determine.  In view of the special status and isolated position of the Shui-ching Palace, it is at least possible that this was the Northern Palace.

Little can be told of the secular building of pre-imperial Min.  Shen-chih's frugality seems to have prevented him from indulging in extensive architectural construction.  The only record of a nonreligious structure dating from the period of his rule is a notice of a watchtower on the seacoast in Fu-ch'ing District.[502]  This had as its purpose the sounding of alarms with horns and drums, and came to be known as the Drum Tower (皷樓).  Such

---

[497] e.g. *Shih chi* 28.0116a:  " A universal great bacchanal was ordered." (令天下大
酺).  This was on the occasion of the change of reign title by Han Wen Ti in 163
B.C.

[498] Professor Shou-yi Ch'en of Pomona College has collected considerable information
on these national festivals, the occasions for holding them and the methods of financing
them.  He says that they were extremely popular in the early T'ang dynasty, but that
none were held after 755 because of the poverty of the court.  It is not clear
whether the parties of Yen-chün held at the pavilion were parts of nationwide celebrations, or merely court festivals in imitation of those held by the T'ang rulers.

[499] *CFWC*.

[500] *WTS*.

[501] *CFWC*.

[502] *FCTC*1 40.8.  This was located at the village of Lung-jen (隆仁里).

a relic is consonant with the practical temperament of the old war lord. His brother, Shen-kuei, for his part built a *Chao-hsien yüan* 招賢院 at the District of Nan-an, to attract eminent scholars, presumably refugees from the T'ang court.[503] Yen-han, despite his short reign, was able to erect fine buildings in Fu Prefecture, although none of their names have been handed down. It is simply recorded that when he declared himself King, "he erected palaces and pavilions."[504]

The major construction works of Yen-chün and Chi-p'eng, especially of the former, have already been alluded to. A little additional data is available. The location of the Eastern Palace (i.e. the residence of the Heir Apparent) built by Yen-chün after his assumption of the purple, was still known in Sung times.[505] Also surviving then was the Ancestral Temple of Shen-chih, bearing the designation Chung-i Wang Miao 忠懿王廟.[506] It is not known whether this was constructed by Yen-han or Yen-chün, although it was probably the latter. Chi-p'eng is said to have erected buildings even more elaborate and elegant than the Tung-hua Palace,[507] that magnificent achievement of his father. Yen-hsi had perforce to construct a palace to replace the Ch'ang-ch'un, destroyed by fire. What name he gave the new imperial residence is not told. History tells us only that in January 940 he built a "new palace" (新宮).[508] Of architectural work carried out by Yen-cheng in Chien Prefecture we know only that he commanded buildings consonant with his imperial pretensions. They are referred to in the famous memorial of P'an Ch'eng-yu, which gives, as its tenth accusation against the government's fiscal policy, the charge of extravagance in these words, "Palaces, apartments, terraces and villas (榭, i.e. a terrace with a building on it) are elevated and decorated without limit."[509]

Constructions of members of the royal family other than the Emperor are seldom mentioned. There is, however, the Kao-t'ing Palace 高亭宮 built in 934 at Kao-t'ing Mountain in Lung-ch'i District 龍溪 (Chang Prefecture) by the Prefect Wang Chi-ch'iung 王繼瓊.[510] A contemporary source also speaks of a *Kan-lu t'ang* (甘露堂) as a favorite haunt of palace ladies—this was then doubtless located in the capital.[511]

---

[503] *FCTC1* 42.16a and *Ch'üan-chou-fu chih* 17.6b.

[504] *TCTC* 275.11a-b.

[505] *YTCS* 128.14a. This was in the Sung District of Huai-an 懷安, originally the northern part of Min District.

[506] *YTCS* 128.14b, *Min tu chi* 8.5b. Cf. footnote 216 above.

[507] *CFWC.*

[508] *TCTC* 282.8a.

[509] *TCTC* 283.11a-b.

[510] *FCTC1* 43.1b.

[511] *CIL* b.4a-b.

Hardly deserving a place under Architecture are the tombs of various worthies of Min, many of which are listed in *Yü-ti chi-sheng*.[512] Nonetheless several are included here because of special interest. In view of the relationship by marriage between the courts of Min and of Southern Han (one or two of Yen-chün's consorts were Princesses of the house of Liu from Canton), it is interesting that the Liu clan resided in Fukien before shifting to Kuantung where it ultimately gained imperial power. The ancestor of the Han Emperors was a certain Liu An-jen 劉安仁 who made his home in Min for commercial purposes. His grave was located at Nan-an.[513] A memorial tablet from the grave of one of the Min Princesses, the wife of that eccentric character, Han Hsi-tsai 韓熙載 of Southern T'ang, is the subject of a fine tale, worth repeating in its entirety:[514] "A certain native of Shao-wu, surnamed Wei 危, buried a relative in the second year of Ta Kuan 大觀, at the side of the road beneath the pagoda enclosure west of the Commandery. When a month's rain had passed, he looked at the side of the mound, where there were traces as if of something hidden. He dug there and obtained two silver wine goblets, a bronze water pot and a mirror with an inscription. He also found an inscribed burial tablet, whose text read, 'The daughter of the Prince of Lang-yeh, surnamed Wang, wife of Hsi-tsai of Chiang-nan: in the intercalary seventh month of the *ping-shen* year was buried west of the stone city-wall.' All of the utensils were made in the old style, with fine skill unattainable by the artisans of our time." The biography of Han Hsi-tsai will be found in chapter 13 of the *Nan T'ang shu* of Ma Ling. He is most remembered for his large collection of singing girls and concubines, whom he treated most indulgently.[515]

From the western part of the empire we have the record of a wall (城) built by Yen-cheng, fifty *li* west of T'ing Prefecture, for defense against the invading troops of Southern T'ang.[516] This was known in Sung times as "the old wall" (古城).

The monarchs of Min raised many structures in the interests of religion,

---

[512] For instance, the tomb of Han Wo near Ch'üan Prefecture (*YTCS* 132.7a), and that of Huang T'ao near Hsing-hua (*YTCS* 135.8a).

[513] *YTCS* 130.11a.

[514] *YTCS* 134.9b citing *I-chien chih* 夷堅志.

[515] The only possible *ping-shen* year was 936, but at this time Shen-chih (who was Prince of Lang-yeh under T'ang) was already dead (since 925). This daughter then must have been born late in Shen-chih's life and died early. Hsi-tsai himself was still a young man at this time. He died in 970 A.D. at the age of sixty-three, and therefore his wife died in his twenty-ninth year. 936 was the last year of the Kingdom of Wu, and it may be that the lady was killed in the troubles attendant on the end of the dynasty.

[516] *YTCS* 132.7a.

and the more important of those devoted to the practise of Buddhism will be mentioned under Religion. The names of many others may be found in the poems of such Min writers as Han Wo. Here I list a few which have some recorded human associations. Han Wo himself, a refugee from the disorders of the central plain, resided at Nan-an in the Lung-hsing Temple (龍興寺).[517]  Another poet, Hui-leng 慧稜, also a Buddhist priest, was invited to reside in the *Ch'ang-ch'ing Yüan* (長慶院) at Ch'ang-lo.[518]  In Hou-kuan District there was a Lo-han Temple (羅漢寺), at the foot of Wu-shih Mountain (烏石山). The story relates that Wang Shen-chih once dreamed of a pair of juniper trees and a priest at this spot, and visiting it the following morning, found it just as in his dream.[519]  There is a record of a stele at the An-kuo Temple (安國寺), erected in 930, during the reign of Yen-chün.[520]  In the southeast part of the city was a Ti-tsang t'ung-wen Temple (地藏通文寺), obviously erected by Chi-p'eng, since it bears the name of his reign.[521]

## 2.  MISCELLANEOUS ARTS

Records of sculpture and image casting in Min are fairly abundant. Some of these will be discussed later under Religion, as the images in the Pagoda of Yen-hsi. Indeed the art of reproducing the human figure seems to have been restricted largely to iconography, particularly Buddhist, though we have seen that images of Taoist divinities were also cast under imperial patronage. A mountain range even took its name from the abundance of bronze statues of the Buddha erected there during the tenth century. This was the Buddha Range (佛嶺) at Yung-ch'un District in Ch'üan Prefecture.[522]  Not all images were cast in metal, however. For instance,

---

[517] *ChWTS* 75.1137.

[518] *ChWTS* 87.1326.  For more on Hui-leng, see Tokiwa Daijō, *Shina Bukkyō no kenkyū* p. 459.  His biography appears in *Sung Kao Seng chuan* 13.787a (Taishō Tripitika).

[519] *YTCS* 128.13b-14a.  *Min-hou hsien-chih* 20.4a styles this "The Temple of the Five Hundred Arhats" and elaborates the story somewhat:  In year 919, Shen-chih dreamed of several hundred bonzes clad in glory and a pair of junipers by a pond.  One of the priests asked the prince for support.  Next day Shen-chih located the spot, and built a hall there, naming the pond "The Bath of the Holy Ones" (浴聖) and the junipers "The Rest of the Holy Ones" (息聖).

[520] *YTCS* 128.19a.

[521] *Min tu chi* 5.3b.  This text gives the date of erection as "Ch'ing T'ai fifth year," which would give 938 A.D., but Ch'ing T'ai was a one-year reign.  However, that date must be approximately correct.

[522] *YTCS* 130.7a.

there was a representation of the [Buddha of the] Golden Millet (金粟像) "modelled" (塑) at the Wan-sui Temple (萬歲寺) in Fu Prefecture during the overlordship of the Wang clan.[523]

Some notices of minor arts (other than those already listed with articles of tribute above) practiced in tenth century Fukien have been preserved. There is, for example, a record of a bronze bell (銅鐘) cast by the Min dynasty at Chiang-lo District for the *Pao-hua Yüan* 寶華院.[524] Presumably masterpieces of the art of pottery making were cups (盞) with "francolin spots" (鷓鴣斑點), much valued by the tea tasters (試茶家) of Min.[525] Court celebrations during the reign of Yen-chün featured illumination by hundreds of "Gold Dragon Candles" (金龍燭), the name doubtless describing the form.[526] At these same festivities, the maids-in-waiting carried goblets and dishes of jasper (?瓊瑤), agate (瑪瑙), amber (琥珀) and glass.[527] North of the capital city was a pottery kiln (陶竈) built by Shen-chih, apparently used chiefly for brickmaking. The anecdote is told that the bricks produced there all bore the character 錢, which was later taken to be an omen of the invasion of Min by the Ch'ien family of Wu-yüeh.[528]

I have no record of any painter who practised his art under the Min Emperors.

Some notices verify the popularity of music at the Min court but none tell of its form. We know only that it was the conventional "strings and wind instruments" (絲竹弦管).[529] Singing was also popular, and if we may rely on her *Biography*, Golden Phoenix was wont to sing while the

---

[523] *YTCS* 128.11a. Further data on religious architecture and sculpture may be found in Tokiwa Daijō, *op. cit.* 460–1.

[524] *YTCS* 133.11a.

[525] *CIL* a.62a. The same source (b.44a) tells of objects bearing the named "Weight-carriers" (耐重兒) made of "tea-grease" (茶膏) bound in gold wire. Eight of these strange artifacts were presented to Yen-hsi, to be stolen by a courtier after the assassination of the Emperor. *Shih-kuo ch'un-ch'iu* 91.9b cites this passage, and adds that these "were made with strange flavors" (製以異味). It may be presumed that they were tea bricks of the type already mentioned under Economy as "lump-teas," especially manufactured for the Emperor. Compare Chang Shun-min 張舜民 (eleventh century), *Hua-man lu* 畫墁錄 (in *T'ang Sung ts'ung-shu* 唐宋叢書) 19a-b: "Ch'ang Kun 常袞 was Prefect of Chien during the Chen Yüan reign (貞元, end of eighth century), and he was the first to refine it [tea] by steam roasting (蒸焙而研之), calling this 'refined grease-tea' (研膏茶) ... during T'ien Sheng (天聖, eleventh century), small lumps [in contrast with the earlier 'large' lump tea] were made ... and each cake of 'small-lump' was wired (縷) with gold."

[526] *CFWC.*

[527] *Ibid.*

[528] *Min tu chi* 25.3b.

[529] *CFWC.*

imperial party drifted in pleasure boats on the artificial lakes of the capital, accompanied by the unison chanting of the palace girls.[530]   A curious anecdote relates to the Prefect Wang Yen-pin, who was a connoisseur of singing-girls.  He would engage only northerners in this role, and it is told that when he obtained a new geisha, he required that she paint her own portrait, and write a song with the picture as its theme.  Hence he was able to judge her for talent as well as for beauty.[531]

## 3.   LITERATURE

The Fukienese were considered a rather uncultured people until recent times.  Certainly few pre-Sung natives of Min enjoyed sufficient reputation as literati to deserve biographical mention in the histories or in the provincial gazetteers.  The *Book of T'ang* goes so far as to state that the people of Fukien were quite lacking in literary learning until Ch'ang Kun was appointed Observator of that province in about A.D. 780.  This official instituted local schools (鄉校) and gave personal lectures on literary composition.[532]  The province was in fact a frontier area, culturally related to the basins of the Yangtze and the Yellow River in approximately the same way that twentieth-century Texas is to New England.  Wang Shen-chih, at the end of the ninth century, must be regarded largely responsible for the rise in Min of a group of talented persons sufficiently skilled in the use of the traditional literary forms to attract the attention and admiration of the arbiters of taste in the north.  Indeed, it would appear that he was the only Min ruler in the tenth century under whom literature really flourished, a condition directly due to his patronage of poets and scholars, both natives and refugees from the disorders of the north.[533]  Shen-chih did more than encourage these men; he founded four academies for their edification and use.[534]

Although others among the Ten Kingdoms enjoyed some glory in later centuries for their contributions to the liberal arts (Southern T'ang and Shu are the instances cited most frequently), Min is usually grouped with the

---

[530] *Ibid.*

[531] *WKKS* b.9b.

[532] *TS* 150.4004d.   See note 525 above for Ch'ang's relation to the tea industry in Fukien.

[533] See Yang Yin-shen 楊蔭深, *Wu Tai wen-hsüeh* 五代文學 (Commercial Press, Shanghai, 1935).   Chapter 14 is devoted to Min.  *WTS* 68 gives Wang T'an 王淡, Yang I 楊沂 and Hsü Yin as scholars holding T'ang doctoral degrees (進士) who found refuge with Shen-chih.  Only the last of these has a literary reputation.

[534] *WTS*.

motley surplus of states not regarded as worthy of special mention.
Nonetheless, orthodox criticism singles out for praise four literati of Min,
namely Han Wo, Huang T'ao, Weng Ch'eng-tsan 翁承贊 and Hsü Yin.[535]

Of these Han Wo is the most honored. The sceptical historian will
find the reason for this in the fact that Wo was a native of Ch'ang-an and,
after a distinguished career at the T'ang court, fled to the patronage of Wang
Shen-chih when he had incurred the enmity of the famous scoundrel Chu
Ch'üan-chung. He was a Fukienese by adoption in the last years of his
life, and this doubtless explains why he is the only one of the four "Greats"
distinguished by a biography in the *Book of T'ang*.[536] One critic
characterizes his verse as having the rich and luxuriantly beautiful quality
typical of the best work of late T'ang.[537] Two hundred ninety-five of his
poems are reproduced in the *Complete Poetry of the Five Dynasties*.[538] His
compositions are also readily accessible in the collection *Yü-shan Chiao-jen
chi* 玉山樵人集.[539] He plays no important role in Min history, being
remembered chiefly for his impromptu composition at a "Great Bacchanal"
(大酺) Festival.[540] It has also been observed that one of his poems contains
one of the earliest literary references to the custom of footbinding.[541]

The most eminent among the natives of Min whose literary arts graced
the modest court of Shen-chih was Huang T'ao, a native of P'u-t'ien. One
hundred and ninety of his poems are included in the *Complete Poetry of
the Five Dynasties,* and may also be consulted in the collection *Huang Hsien-
sheng wen-chi* 黃先生文集 and *P'u-yang Huang Yü-shih chi* 莆陽黃御史
集.[542] His style has been described as sensuous yet clear.[543] T'ao was host
and sponsor for all of the famous gentlemen who sought protection in Shen-
chih's capital, and must be considered as the most distinguished and
influential of the Fukienese literati of this age.

[535] See for instance Cheng Fang-k'un 鄭方坤, *Wu Tai shih-hua* 五代詩話 (*Yüeh-ya-tang
ts'ung-shu* 奧雅堂叢書 ed.) 2a of Introduction. This is a Ch'ing work.

[536] *TS* 183.4064c-d.

[537] Yang Yin-shen, *op. cit.* 109.

[538] *ChWTS* 75–79. Here also will be found a comprehensive catalogue of sources
which refer to him and to his writings.

[539] Edition of *SPTK*.

[540] *CFWC.* See note 147 above.

[541] The poem is " An Air about Pattens '' (咏屧子). See Cheng Fang-k'un, *op. cit.*
6.11b.

[542] *ChWTS* 84–85 also lists biographical and critical sources. The two other collections may be found in the *SPTK* and *TSCC* collectanea respectively. Special studies of
his work are Lin Yüan-han 林元漢, *P'u-yang T'ang Sung wen-hsien i-p'ieh* 莆陽唐宋文獻一瞥
(*Fu-chien wen-hua* 1.8.10–14) and Kuo Yü-lin 郭毓麟, *Fu-chien T'ang-tai-ti chi-ko shih-jen*
福建唐代的幾個詩人 (*ibid.* 1.7.11–15). The latter also includes material on Hsü Yin.

[543] Yang Yin-shen, *op. cit.* 111.

Hsü Yin,[544] with 243 poems in the *Complete Poetry of the Five Dynasties*[545] was, like Huang T'ao, a native of P'u-t'ien, but his career was less closely identified with the Min court. He found official life uncongenial to his unconventional temperament, and the latter part of his life was spent in retirement. Romantic melancholy has been detected in some of his work[546] as may be seen by consulting his collected poems in *Hsü Kung tiao-chi wen-chi* 徐公釣磯文集.[547]

Slightly less famous than the men just described was Ts'ui Tao-jung 崔道融, a good friend of Huang T'ao, considered by one authority as especially adept at the *chüeh-chü* form.[548]

The *Complete Poetry of the Five Dynasties* contains compositions by thirty-nine Min poets. A few are anonymous folk singers, and one is a ghostly "palace girl of Min" who recited her verses in a dream to a man of later times. Single compositions of members of the Wang family, while displaying no unusual literary merits, are of interest as biographical data. I have quoted elsewhere Chi-p'eng's epigram on Yeh Ch'iao,[549] and the song of Golden Phoenix composed for a water festival.[550] Yen-hsi, although no original efforts of his pen have come down to us, had a classical education, since he recited a couplet from Po Chü-i to reproach and terrorize the conspirators Chu Wen-chin and Lien Chung-yü.[551] Wang Yen-pin and Chi-hsün each have one poem preserved.[552]

The modern critic Yang Yin-shen gives the names of two prose writers of Min with whose work I am not personally familiar. These are Ch'en Ch'iao 陳嶠, a drafter of memorials and other official documents, and Liu Shan-fu 劉山甫, author of *Chin-ch'i hsien-t'an* 金谿閒談 and of the grave inscription for Hsü Yin.[553]

---

[544] Sometimes written 寅 instead of 貧.

[545] *ChWTS* 80–83.

[546] Yang Yin-shen, *op. cit.* 111–112.

[547] Edit. of *SPTK hsu-pien.*

[548] Yang Yin-shen, *op. cit.* 110. See also *ChWTS* 86 and Cheng Fang-k'un, *op. cit.* 6.24a.

[549] See under History, The Emperor K'ang Tsung, and the original in *TCTC* 279.21b and in *ChWTS* 75.

[550] See note 147 above.

[551] *TCTC* 284.3a.

[552] *ChWTS* 75.

[553] Yang Yin-shen, *op. cit.* 114.

# RELIGION

## 1. GENERAL

THE Fukienese of the Sung dynasty have been characterized as ardent believers in the gods, fond of religious sacrifices and devoted to the teachings of the Buddha (浮屠).[554] That this was equally true of the tenth century has been amply proved by the contemporary scholar Wei Ying-ch'i who described Min of the Five Dynasties period as a "society of religion and mythology." He quotes a poem by Hsieh Pi 謝泌, written at the beginning of the eleventh century, as evidence of the abundance of religious activity in Fukien at that time—a condition of earlier origin which has persisted down to recent times:

> In lakes and fields they plant the paddy,
>     Double they harvest the grain.
> On ways and roads you meet the people,
>     Half of them are monks.
> On the three hills within the city,
>     Are a thousand clustered temples.
> In the seven pagodas in the night,
>     Are a myriad separate candles.

Professor Wei, on the basis of an exhaustive analysis of medieval texts, states that many of the Buddhist temples of Fukien were of great antiquity, and that the Wang family of Min added 267 to those already existing. He cites epigraphic data preserved in *Ch'üan T'ang wen* (chs. 893 and 841) as

---

[554] *SS* 89.4710c. Chang Ch'an 張闡, the twelfth century naval strategist, characterized the region of Ch'üan Prefecture as a "Buddhist Country" (佛國). See *Chuan-chou-fu chih* 20.2a and *SS* 381.5478d.

evidence of the great numbers of images cast and holy texts written during the rule of Shen-chih.[555]  His estimates of the number of Buddhist temples at various periods follows: from the late Chin to 885 A.D., about 320 erected; between 885 and 945, about 337 in existence.  Great destruction must have taken place immediately before and after the Sung unification of the empire since from 945 to 977 he gives a total of only 141.[556]  Mr. Wei has also made a special study of commonly held metaphysical beliefs in tenth-century Fukien, especially those referring to the destined rule of Wang Shen-chih.  These include such ideas as the following: that the Wang family was destined to reign over Min; that it was incumbent upon the populace to obey the will of heaven; that there was a master principle guiding actual events; that exorcism, prayer and the like can determine fortune, longevity and other human values; that it is possible for men to understand the supernatural world; that the human soul survives after death and can affect the fortunes of the living; and the *samsara* and *karma* exist.  Some of these beliefs were surely the common possession of the Chinese.  Especially emphasized in Min were the Buddhist interpretations.  Unique there, of course, was the link with the Wang clan.[557]

I shall not attempt to paraphrase or repeat further the results of the original researches of Mr. Wei but shall add such additional material (with which he was doubtless familiar) as I have encountered.  If I may find a small fault in his unfinished study, it is that he has omitted Taoism from his consideration.  Although enthusiasm for the doctrines of Buddhism persisted throughout the period of the Min empire, the courts of Yen-chün and Chi-p'eng, at least, were dominated by the adepts and attitudes of the Way.

## 2.  BUDDHISM

The rulers of Min were from the first devoted to the doctrines of Buddhism and gave bountiful support to the priests and temples of that religion.  There can be no doubt that popular enthusiasm for Buddhism matched that of the court—indeed, a Buddhist priest became Son of Heaven for a time, a dignity given him as a demagogic maneuver to win support

[555] Wei Ying-ch'i, *op. cit.* 7.75 (April 3, 1929) 5 (see footnote 5 in Introduction).

[556] *Ibid.,* p. 9.

[557] The remaining chapters of Mr. Wei's study are chiefly a catalogue of religious structures in Fukien, with dates of erection and other pertinent facts. See *ibid.*, 76.9–28, 76.11–31, 78.23–31.

from the populace for a faction opposing the rule of the Wang family.[558]

The religious inclinations of Wang Ch'ao are not known, although we have a record of at least one Buddhist structure raised during his prefectship —the "Close of Manjusri" (文殊院) built by him in 893 A.D.[559]

Shen-chih, first Prince of Min, was a patron of the religion. Most of the available information about his activities in its behalf are to be found in the writings of the poet Huang T'ao who had a great influence on his lord and also wrote inscriptions for many monuments and religious buildings in Min, particularly for Buddhist temples. Among these is an inscription for a memorial tablet at the Pao-en ting-kuang to-pao Pagoda (報恩定光 多寶塔) which tells that Shen-chih, then Legate of the Wei-wu Army and Prince of Lang-yeh, had taken an oath in 901, swearing by all the spirits to erect this pagoda at the K'ai Yüan Temple (開元寺) in the Prefecture of Fu.[560] This temple is worth mentioning as the only Buddhist temple to have escaped the persecution of Wu Tsung of T'ang. It was beautifully rebuilt by Shen-chih.[561] Huang T'ao also relates that in 906 his lord cast a gold and bronze image sixteen feet high (probably of Shakyamuni but not named in the text) and one of a Bodhisattva twenty-three feet high. The statues had bronze "flesh" and gold "skin."[562] These instances by no means exhaust the data to be found in the pages of Huang T'ao's writing which allude to the strenuous pro-Buddhist activities of Shen-chih, but they are typical. The biography of Wang Yen-ssu, Shen-chih's nephew, preserved in the *Fu-chien t'ung-chih*,[563] doubtless because of his pious Confucian moralizing tendencies, but not included in the standard contemporary sources, supports this evidence. The biography states that the people of Min were devoted to Buddhism and that "Shen-chih too was infatuated with that doctrine, and quite exhausted building materials in raising Indian edifices."

Another nephew of Shen-chih, Yen-pin, who enjoyed a long and fairly

---

[558] See Tokiwa Daijō, *op. cit.* 454–465 for an excellent study of Buddhism in Min. A small error—Tokiwa refers to the empire as "Min-yüeh" (閩越) throughout.

[559] *Min tu chi* 5.11a.

[560] *P'u-yang Huang Yü-shih chi* 325–6. *T'ang hui yao* 48.11a (Wu-ying-tien edit.) states: "On the twenty-ninth day of the tenth month of the first year of T'ien Shou (天授) a Ta-yün Temple (大雲寺) was established in the two capitals and each of the prefectures of the empire. On the first day of the sixth month of the twenty-sixth year of K'ai Yüan, all were changed to K'ai Yüan Temples." These dates correspond to 690 and 738 respectively. *FCTC2* 62.12b says that the K'ai Yüan Temple of Fu Prefecture dates back to the year 549 under various names.

[561] *Min-hou-hsien chih* 19.1b. This text gives the names of a great many other temples built during this period. See chapters 19–20.

[562] *P'u-yang Huang Yü-shih chi* 289.

[563] *FCTC1* 171.3a.

honorable dictatorship in Ch'üan, was as attracted to the foreign religion as his uncle. It is said that he "liked to discuss Buddhist doctrine" and "was much frequented by ... Zen priests."[564] The name of one of his friends, the Buddhist poet Hui-leng, who later went to the Min capital,[565] is known.

Wang Yen-chün, the first Emperor of Min, although a partisan of the Taoists (something never alleged of Shen-chih) did not neglect the Buddhists. Early in 929, that is, four years before ascending the imperial throne, he "fixed twenty thousand as the limit for Buddhist monks among the populace, and after this there were many monks in Min-chung."[566] If we may rely on a text which tends to preserve sensational tradition more than conservative history, Yen-chün, after his "usurpation" in 933, became troubled due to his concern about his legitimacy and ultimate end. He achieved peace of mind by allowing the support of three million Buddhist priests and the compilation of three hundred collections (藏) of sutras.[567] The first figure is hardly credible but may be taken as representing a utopian objective rather than a realized situation.

The Taoist party continued its control of the court during the reign of Chi-p'eng. We do not read of overt support given by him to Buddhism, yet it continued in the land as a whole. Buddhist images were certainly dedicated to the monarch, for one in clay, painted in polychrome, was preserved in the Sung dynasty in the T'ai-p'ing hsing-kuo Temple 太平興 國寺, donated by Chi-p'eng.[568] One finds traces of popular Buddhist activities in the pious dedication, said to have been written in 938, at the I Well (義井) in Min District.[569] There is also the interesting case of a certain Lin Hsing-tsou 林省鄒 who, dissatisfied with the administration of Chi-p'eng, proposed to flee northwards in monk's clothing.[570] This was in the late summer of 939. The incident may be taken as an indication of the relative freedom of a monk to move about in this land without suspicion, and also of the abundance of Buddhist priests, since the best disguise is one which is a commonplace.

There are no indications that Yen-hsi was under Taoist influences. It appears likely that he drove the sectarians of that religion from the court in reaction to the indignities he had suffered at the hands of Chi-p'eng and

---

[564] *WKKS* b.9b.

[565] *ChWTS* 87.1326. Cf. above under Architecture, and below.

[566] *TCTC* 276.11b. The meaning of the quotation is that permission was granted for the expansion of the priesthood to the officially stated limit.

[567] *WKKS* b.6a. For further data on compilation of Buddhist scriptures in Min, see Tokiwa Daijō, *op. cit.* 461.

[568] *YTCS* 133.7b-8a. This was at Sha District.

[569] *FCTC*1 38.17b.

[570] *TCTC* 282.2a.

his minions. He was doubtless a pious Buddhist for we read that he "permitted the people to become Buddhist monks. Many of the people became monks in order to avoid the heavy taxation; in all the limit was fixed at eleven thousand persons."[571] This decree was issued in the summer of 940. The figures do not seem compatible with those given above for Yen-chün's reign but the latter, as noted, were doubtless grossly exaggerated. The details of a pagoda dedicated by Yen-hsi in 941 have been preserved in the *Fu-chien t'ung-chih.*[572] This was the Ch'ung-miao pao-sheng chien-lao Pagoda 崇妙保聖堅牢塔, a restoration of the T'ang pagoda Wu-hou ching-kuang t'a 無垢淨光塔 built in 799.[573] A tablet on the fourth of its seven stories tells that it was erected by Yen-hsi on behalf of himself, his family and all of the people. Each story is dedicated to a different form of the Buddha and each has prayers inscribed asking various blessings for important people such as members of the imperial family. These data may be summarized as follows:

1st story—dedicated by Hsi, the Augustus of Great Min, to the Kanaka-cakra-rāja Buddha (金輪王佛).[574]

2nd story—dedicated by Lady Li, a nineteenth daughter, Empress of Great Min, to Anāgata Maitreya Bhagavan Buddha (當來下生彌勒尊佛).

3rd story—dedicated by Wang Ya-ch'eng, Prince of Min, and by his wife the Lady Yü 余氏, a thirteenth daughter, Lady of the State of Yüeh (越國夫人), to Amitāyus Buddha (無量壽佛).

4th story—dedicated by Lady Wang, a twenty-sixth daughter, Princess of Fu-ch'ing (福清公主), and by the Titular Minister Ch'en Wen-chih 陳文質 (her husband?), to the Prabhūta-ratna Buddha (多寶佛).

5th story—dedicated by the Vice-Legate Wang Chi-ch'ien 王繼潛, the Commissioner of the Palace Parks (宮苑使) Wang Chi-yüan 王繼源 and the following three ladies, all of the Wang family: the Princess of Shun-ch'ang 順昌, a twenty-seventh daughter, the Princess of Chien-an 建安,

---

[571] *TCTC* 282.12a.

[572] *FCTC1* 39.27a-28a. The dedicatory inscription is by Lin T'ung-ying 林同穎 and the calligraphy by the monk Wu-i 无逸. See *Min-hou-hsien chih* 49.3a.

[573] *San-shan chih* 三山志, cited in *FCTC1*, states that this was the case. See also *FCTC1* 68.23a-b for a record of an inscription, the "Incised Record of the Stele in the Stone Pagoda" (石塔碑刻記) in one *chuan*, which must refer to the same pagoda, and compare *Min tu chi* 10.27b. Tokiwa Daijō (in *op. cit.* 463–4) doubts that this is indeed a restoration of the T'ang pagoda. He cites evidence to show that the latter was a wooden construction on the site of whose remains Yen-hsi erected the new stone pagoda. A photograph of this structure and of the relief image of the Kanaka-cakra-rāja Buddha from its first story will be found among the plates in Tokiwa's book.

[574] I am greatly indebted to Professor F. D. Lessing for Sanskrit versions of the Chinese names of the Buddha. He tells me that the rendering "kanaka" for 金 is purely hypothetical.

a twenty-eighth daughter, and the Princess of T'ung-an 同安, a twenty-ninth daughter, to Bhaiṣajaya-guru Vaidūrya-prabhā Buddha (藥師琉璃光佛). The dedicatory inscription here is very interesting for its Taoist allusions in a Buddhist environment. The Princesses invoke the Goddess of the Moon (月娥) and the Constellation Wu (星婺).[575]

6th story—dedicated by Lady Shang 尚氏, a fifteenth daughter, the Estimable Consort, to the Nāgeśvara Buddha (龍自在佛). Here too there is a strong Taoist note in the inscription, which asks that "the Immortals of the Islands of P'eng 蓬島 may each send down talismans for extending life (延齡之籙)."

7th story—dedicated by the Titular Minister Li Chen and by his wife Lady Ch'en 陳氏, Lady of the State of Chao (趙國夫人), and by other notables and their wives many of the latter being royal Princesses, to Śākyamuni Buddha (釋迦牟尼佛).

Cho Yen-ming is the only instance of an ordained priest being raised to the status of Emperor in China, to my knowledge. Li Jen-ta, that wily turncoat, uncertain of the affection of the mob, made this man, whom he took from a temple on Snowy Peak, Son of Heaven, giving as evidence of his right to rule the "double pupil" of his eyes and the length of his arms for his hands hung below his knees.[576] Yen-ming, before his remarkable accession, had been Abbot of the Shen-kuang Temple (神光寺) on the aforesaid mountain.[577] His reign was short and his executive abilities were not spectacular—perhaps a good thing in a puppet. It is recorded that when Yen-cheng's army attacked the Prefecture of Fu in May-June 945 Yen-ming "had no better strategy than to spit water and scatter beans on top of a pavilion, and to perform various rituals—nothing more."[578]

Of Yen-cheng's preferred religion I know nothing.

An abundance of data pertaining to Buddhist temples in Min and to their priests, especially eminent Zen masters, is to be found in the writings of contemporary poets, in particular those of Han Wo and Hsü Yin. One

[575] The destinies of South China were bound to this constellation which was known as 婺女 or 女宿. Thus, " Wu-nü is Yang-chou " (婺女揚州, in *Han shu* 26.0401b) and " Wu-nü is Yüeh " (粤也, in *Han shu* 26.0402d). Presumably this constellation was thought of as guarding the fate of Min and was especially appropriate, with its feminine name, to the prayers of a princess.

[576] *TCTC* 284.14a-b, *WTS*.

[577] *WKKS* b.11a. Tokiwa Daijō, *op. cit.* 457–460 gives the lives of some eminent priests of Min, the most important being I-ts'un 義存, an intimate of Shen-chih. These biographies are based on sources which for the most part I do not have. The center of I-ts'un's activities was this same Snowy Peak whence came a number of the master's disciples, including Hui-leng, already mentioned earlier.

[578] *TCTC* 284.16b-17a.

of the most noted of the priests of that time was the Zen master Ho-lung Miao-k'ung 和龍妙空 in honor of whom Wang Chi-hsün wrote some verses.[579]  Another poem addressed to the same priest by a certain (surname missing) Hung 鴻 is preserved.[580]  Other priestly figures placed in the landscape of Fukien by contemporary poetry are Ch'ang-ya 常雅;[581]  Wen-chü 文炬 who bore the style "Nirvana" (涅搬)[582] and is the same priest who predicted the fall of Liu Ts'ung-hsiao, namely Miao-ying Ta-shih Huang Nieh-p'an 妙應大師黃涅槃;[583] and finally the Zen master Ch'ao-chüeh 超覺禪師.[584]  The latter is none other than the priest Hui-leng already mentioned in connection with Buddhist architecture and with literature.  Hui-leng's biography in the *Sung Kao-seng chuan* tells that he was a native of Hang Prefecture who came to Min when "he heard that there was a school of Zen in the South."  The imperial family gave him the unofficial posthumous title of Ch'ao-chüeh (閩國王氏私誄之大師號超覺).  It is clear that Fukien was an important center of the Zen sect in this period.


## 3.  TAOISM

While there are no indications of the extent of the popularity of Taoist beliefs and practices among the people of Min, the sectarians of Huang Ti and Lao-tzu had great influence at the courts of some of the Emperors, in particular at that of Yen-chün, the first of the Wang family to assume the imperial title.  There is a certain inner⋅logic in this for the humilific tendencies of Buddhism might be suitable for a Prince like Shen-chih who did not aim above his allotted station whereas Taoism could provide supernatural sanctions rooted in the Chinese imperial tradition to support the ambition of one who sought the Mandate of Heaven.

The first indications that Yen-chün desired the title of Emperor are linked with his raising of the adept Ch'en Shou-yüan 陳守元 and the three shamans Hsü Yen 徐彥, Lin Hsing 林興 and Sheng T'ao 盛韜 to power at court.[585]  These worthies prevailed upon their ruler to erect a temple to

---

[579] *ChWTS* 75.1136.

[580] *ChWTS* 87.1322.

[581] *ChWTS* 87.1326.

[582] *ChWTS* 87.1327.  For the biography of this priest whose surname was Huang, and the lives of other eminent divines of Min, see *Shih-kuo ch'un-ch'iu* 99 and *FCTC2* 60.6a.

[583] *ChWTS* 87.1330.

[584] *YTCS* 128.14a.

[585] I follow the *SPTK* edition of *TCTC* 277.14a in identifying three shamans here. *SPPY* has only two.  The following parallel passages will make the situation clear:

the Precious August (寶皇宮) with Shou-yüan as its Chief Priest (宮主). This took place in the summer of 931.[586]   In this connection it should be noted that many presages of the coming dignity of Min were circulated among the people, largely Taoist in origin.   These are discussed under the heading Folklore and Popular Religion.   In January of 932 Yen-chün's spiritual advisers recommended that he resign his position temporarily in order to receive the Tao, after which spiritual purification he would reign as Son of Heaven for sixty years.   On February 2, the future Emperor gave up his princely rank, leaving his son Chi-p'eng as acting dictator in all affairs of state.   Yen-chün received the talisman (籙) purporting to convey the supernatural orders of heaven and adopted the Taoist name of Hsüan-hsi 玄錫.[587]   On April 30 he returned once more to his secular duties.[588]   In July of the same year he had Shou-yüan ask the Precious August about his future *after* the reign of sixty years.   Shou-yüan reported that Yen-chün was fated to become Chief of the Immortals of Ta-lo (大羅 仙主), the most exalted of the Taoist heavens, and this destiny was confirmed by a report from the Ch'ung-shun Wang 崇順王[589] of the Northern Temple (北廟) who had interviewed the Precious August and transmitted his words through the mouth of the shaman Hsü Yen.[590]   With these matters clearly set forth by divine oracles and the appropriate dragon omen having appeared, Yen-chün allowed himself to be invested as Son of Heaven in February 933.   In May of that year he appointed the Heir Apparent, Chi-p'eng,

1.   *SPTK* (227.14a) 徐彥林興盛韜.   *SPPY* 徐彥林與盛韜.
2.   *SPTK* (277.22a) 徐彥等.   *SPPY* 徐彥林等.
3.   *SPTK* (282.3b) and *SPPY* 林興.

In short, *SPPY* reads 與 for 興 in the first instance, demanding the translation " Hsü Yen-lin and Sheng T'ao," whereas *SPTK* requires the translation " Hsü Yen, Lin Hsing [and] Sheng T'ao."   *SPPY* contradicts itself by recognizing the independent existence of Lin Hsing in the third instance.   It must be concluded that *SPTK* is correct and that three men are involved.   Moreover, *WTS* gives Hsü Yen rather than Hsü Yen-lin.

[586] Hu San-hsing dates the beginning of the decline of Min from the rise of these personages—an orthodox Confucian view.

[587] *TCTC* 277.15b-16a, *WTS*.   The term *hsüan-hsi* "sombre tin" occurs in Huai-nan-tzu (修務訓, p. 57a of the *Erh-shih-erh tzu ch'üan-shu* 二十二子全書 edition).   The sense may be " lead," to judge from a comment of Li Shih-chen, who writes, " the ancients gave lead (鉛) the name of 'black tin'" (黑錫).—*Pen-ts'ao kang-mu* 8.15.   This identification may be dubious; at any rate Huai-nan-tzu speaks of a newly cast mirror as lacking the power to reflect until " it is powdered (covered) with 'sombre tin.'"   He refers to " learning" (學) as the tin on the surface of the natural man.

[588] *TCTC* 277.17a.

[589] Another Taoist divinity exalted by Yen-chün.   See below under Official Cult for more details on this god.   *Shun* has the sense of " to obey or follow [the Right Way]" hence " orthodox" in the Taoist context.

[590] *TCTC* 277.22a.

Commissioner to the Palace of the Precious August (寶皇宮使).[591] This association was to bear fruit for the Taoists whose prestige at court continued after Chi-p'eng's succession to the throne. Meanwhile Yen-chün fell increasingly under the spell of these wizards who imposed shamelessly on his credulity. Their power over the mind of the Emperor was made use of by the Fiscal Intendant Hsüeh Wen-chieh to get rid of his enemy the Chancellor Wu Hsü 吳勗.[592] An elaborate plot was evolved by the Intendant in collaboration with Sheng T'ao whereby Hsü was advised to tell the emissaries of the Emperor inquiring after his health that he was suffering only from a headache. Meanwhile they had informed Yen-chün that Hsü had been plotting rebellion, and hence the Ch'ung-shun Wang was pounding a bronze nail into the Chancellor's skull with a golden mallet. The report of the emissaries seemed to confirm the truth of this revelation and Hsü was tortured into making a false confession and put to death with his whole family to the great indignation of the populace, probably because of its dislike for the ingenious tax collector.[593] These events took place late in 933.

Ch'en Shou-yüan and Lin Hsing remained in power under Chi-p'eng, a true devotee of shamans and Taoist adepts. We also hear of another adept, T'an Tzu-hsiao 譚紫霄, honored by the Emperor with the title "First-born of Upright Unity" (正一先生).[594] Ch'en Shou-yüan, for his part, was given the title "Heavenly Master" (天師) in addition to the one he held already ("First-born of the True-ones of the Grotto" 洞真先生).[595] He now had virtually dictatorial powers in the government, with full authority to appoint and to dismiss. He took bribes and it is reported that

---

[591] *TCTC* 278.6b.

[592] *WTS* has Ying 英 instead of Hsü. Hu San-hsing calls this an error.

[593] *TCTC* 278.13b-14a, *WTS*.

[594] *WTS*. Cf. *CIL* b.60a which tells how each month Chi-p'eng presented Tzu-hsiao with a marvellous "Landscape Aromatic" (山水香). The expression *tzu-hsiao* "purple cirrus" is a fairly common poetic phrase but it is sometimes used as a fanciful term for the exalted position of the Son of Heaven, e.g., "He rose to the cinnabar land of the purple cirrus" (*Nan shih* 62.2690a). But it also has Taoist connotations, to judge from analogy with such terms as "Purple Subtlety," etc. My translation of *hsiao* is based primarily on the *Kuang yün* 廣韻 definition, "vapor close to heaven" (近天氣也). The title "Upright Unity" is closely associated with the names of eminent Taoists. *Tz'u hai* 辭海 states that Chang Cheng-ch'ang 張正常, a remote descendant of the famous Chang Tao-ling 張道陵 of Eastern Han, was given the title "正一 . . . 貞人" at the beginning of the Ming Dynasty. There is no doubt that it was a Taoist term of great antiquity, however, judging from the usage in our text. And cf. *TS* 196.4086d where a Taoist mentions a "Technique of Upright Unity" (正一法).

[595] *TCTC* 279.22a, *WTS*. Date: January 936. The title "Heavenly Master" is familiar as having been held by Chang Tao-ling and his descendants since Han times.

the number of his clients was so great that "his gateway was like the market-place."[596]  The shaman Lin Hsing was powerful enough to bring about the execution of Yen-wu and Yen-wang, the uncles of the Emperor, against whom he had a grudge, by quoting the spirits to the effect that they had planned an insurrection.[597]  This was in April-May 939.  At this time it would appear that this wizard (妖人) had replaced Shou-yüan as highest spokesman for the gods for we are told under the same date that the administration was entirely in his hands, and that he now conveyed the words of the Precious August.[598]  Meanwhile Chi-p'eng was even more active than his father in the magnificence of his architectural constructions on behalf of the Taoists.  In May-June 937 he built the Tzu-wei Palace, decorating it with crystal, "twice" as splendid as the Palace of the Precious August.[599]  In the spring of 939 Chi-p'eng also constructed the "Terrace of the Three Clear Ones" (三清臺),[600] a structure of three stories on the grounds of the imperial palace.  For its sanctuary he had cast gold images (the text says "several thousand catties") of the Precious August Great Deity (寶皇大帝) and of the Heavenly Venerable Ancient Sovereign (天尊老君), that is, Lao-tzu.[601]  Here he burned great quantities of rare aromatics, such as borneol and pistachio, and had musical performances conducted, searching for the Elixir of the Great Returning (大還丹).[602]  Another religious building erected by Chi-p'eng was the Po-lung Temple (白龍寺), a Buddhist one to judge by its name.  The occasion for its erection, however, was the report of a Taoist adept that a white dragon had appeared at Lo Feng 螺峯,[603] where the temple was later raised.[604]

[596] *TCTC* 279.22a.

[597] *TCTC* 282.3b.

[598] *Ibid.*

[599] *TCTC* 281.4b.

[600] I.e., the Supernal Clear One (上清), the Jade Clear One (玉清) and the Grand Clear One (太清).  See commentary of Hu San-hsing.

[601] *TCTC* 282.3b, *WTS.*

[602] *WTS.*  *TCTC* says simply " the divine elixir " (神丹).  " Great Returning " and " Small Returning " are phrases used in Huai-nan-tzu (天文) with reference to the course of the sun.  They were employed in later Taoism as alchemical terms, referring to kinds of elixir (converted cinnabar).  Thus a poem of Hsiang Ssu 項斯 (cited in *Tz'u hai*, article *hsiao-huan*):  " After having swallowed the ' Small Returning ' one thinks oneself able to fly."  The terrace is referred to as a Pavilion (殿) of the Three Clear Ones in *CFWC*.  This doubtless refers to the chief building on the terrace.  The same source tells how Tzu-hsiao led Spring Swallow and the other palace ladies to prayers there.

[603] *FCTC2* 3.8b gives a Lo Feng " Gastropod Peak " in Hou-kuan District north of the city, in the vicinity of modern Lung-yao Mountain (龍腰山).

[604] *TCTC* 281.6b.  This was in July 937.  Chi-p'eng was not unfamiliar with Bud-

That the religious infatuation of the sovereign was imitated by some of his courtiers, sincerely or otherwise, is certain. An illustration of this point, which does not tell us the extent of the practice, is the case of the Government Councilor (參政事) Yeh Ch'iao. This learned and upright man, Chi-p'eng's preceptor before the latter's accession, was ignored when his pupil came to the throne and tried to leave the court "wearing the garment of a Taoist adept."[605] This was in December 935. A case of external Taoism not matched by belief is that of Chi-p'eng's uncle, Yen-hsi, who became the third Emperor of Min after the death of his nephew. This man pretended witlessness in order to avoid the suspicion of the monarch and the latter dressed him in Taoist robes and set him up as a priest in the Wu-i Mountains.[606] However, there is no evidence that he (Yen-hsi) favored Taoism in any way, and the only traces of Taoist influence I find from his reign are the allusions in the dedicatory inscriptions in his pagoda to the Buddhist divinities.

## 4.   OFFICIAL CULT

Notices of attention given to the official "Confucian" cult by rulers of Min are not common. Yet such a conscientious vassal as Shen-chih—not to mention his successors who must inevitably have performed the orthodox rites to support their imperial pretensions—surely did not allow his patronage of Buddhism to interfere with the prescribed rituals of the ancient cult. However, the instances I have are largely trivial. Some may best be regarded as classifiable under Popular Religion although they possess characteristics which make them identifiable with official Confucianism as well, in that they are concerned with the duties of the magistrate as representative of the Son of Heaven. The first case is that of a temple (廟) at the village of Tien-ch'i (玷琦里) in the District of Min which, in accordance with the request of Shen-chih, was "enfeoffed" as the Chao-fu Temple (昭福祠) by the Liang court late in 907.[607] The circumstances of the request are not stated. Shen-chih also did his duty by the rice crop since there is a tradition

dhism, if we may rely on the testimony of *CIL* a.35a, which has him quoting the " Amitabha Sutra " (彌陀經) at a palace garden festival. Other sutras current in Min were the Lotus Sutra (法華經) and the Diamond Sutra (金剛般若經). The latter is referred to in a poem by Hsü Yin addressed to his wife, the Lady Yüeh-chün 月君 (see *ChWTS* 80.1204 and 1228 ; the poem is quoted from the *Yung-ch'uang hsiao-p'in* 湧憧小品.

605 *TCTC* 289.21b.
606 *TCTC* 282.5a-b.
607 *Wu Tai hui-yao* (*TSCC* ed.) 11.147.

that a mound (墩) beneath the Drum Tower in the District of Fu-ch'ing represents the spot where the Prince prayed for the new sprouts of paddy.[608]

Yen-chün obtained from the Later T'ang court the title of Fu-i Wang 富義王 for the ancient ruler of Min-yüeh, King Wu-chu, to be used in sacrifices at his temples in Fukien. This was in the seventh month of 931.[609] At Wu-shih Mountain in the southwest corner of the prefectural city of Fu was the altar to the fertility spirits (社稷壇), erected earlier but reconstructed by Min.[610] The only notice I have found indicative of the Imperial Sacrifice to Heaven, which must have been performed by all of the monarchs of Min after Yen-chün, gives the location of a "suburb altar" (郊壇) constructed by Yen-cheng on his accession to the throne of Yin. This altar was located three *li* south of Chien Prefecture at Mount Sheng 昇山.[611] This was, of course, the place where the Emperor performed the greatest of the imperial rites, the *nan-chiao* 南郊.

Meritorious followers of the Wang family, in particular military heroes, were sometimes deified. A case in point is the temple (廟) to the *Kuang-wei chen-yüan chiang-chün* 光威振遠將軍—his original name is not known —erected in 940.[612] Similar is the case of the Ch'ung-shun Wang, already mentioned under Taoism. This god had appeared to mankind as a general named Liu Hsing-ch'üan 劉行全 serving in the army of Wang Hsü, the rebel leader under whom the Wang brothers began to achieve fame. He was given the posthumous title of Wu-ning Hou (武寧侯) in 897 during the prefectship of Wang Ch'ao and was raised to supernatural kingship in 919.[613] Another associate of Shen-chih was a certain Ch'en 陳 to whom a temple was raised near Min-ch'ing District west of the capital city. In later times this was called the *Chao-hsien Miao* 昭顯廟.[614] A popular deity, formerly a native of Ch'ang-lo District—his name has not been preserved —was worshipped by the people there in remembrance of his meritorious acts of giving away his fields for the construction of Peach-branch Lake (桃枝湖), and his home for the erection of the Buddhist Ta-tse Temple (大澤寺).[615]

[608] *FCTC1* 39.8a.
[609] *Wu Tai hui-yao* 11.147, *Ts'e-fu yüan-kuei* 33.11b.  *Min tu chi* 14.7b tells of a temple erected to Wu-chu south of the city wall in 930.
[610] *FCTC2* 15.1b.
[611] *YTCS* 129.10b.
[612] *Min tu chi* 5.11a.
[613] *Ibid.*, 24.15a-b.
[614] *Ibid.*, 29.2b.
[615] *Ch'ang-lo-hsien chih* 16.28b.

## 5.  MANICHAEISM

The persistence of the followers of Mani in Fukien Province long after they had disappeared from the rest of China is a familiar fact or belief. But a chronological link is missing between the Manichaeism of T'ang, that age of tolerance and exoticism, and the Manichaeism of Sung, a barely discernible remnant. The link may perhaps be found in a paragraph of the *Fu-chien t'ung-chih*. The gazetteer tells of a Mani Temple (摩尼宮) in the modern District of Fu-ting 福鼎 in northeast Fukien. Its ruins are located in the vicinity of a shrine on the Mo-hsiao Peak (摩霄峯) of T'ai-mu Mountain (太姥山). Here among fragments of stone and brick was an image to which prayers were offered for the realization of dreams. In the gazetteer this temple is listed for the Five Dynasties period, but it is not certainly attributable to the period of the rule of the Wang family. In any event, the tradition which ascribes this Manichaean place of worship to the tenth century may be reliable in the absence of evidence to the contrary.[616]

## 6.  FOLKLORE AND POPULAR RELIGION

As elsewhere in China, belief in the existence of supernatural beings of all kinds not directly connected with one of the major organized cults was prevalent in Fukien. Contemporary literature has preserved a few samples from the tenth century. One instance concerns the opening of the new harbor at Yellow Point by Shen-chih.[617] The story, doubtless largely apocryphal, tells that the Prince dreamed of the approach of a deity in golden armor, calling itself the Prince of Wu-an 吳安王, who promised to aid

---

[616] *FCTC*1 47.4b, 14.9a. See P. Pelliot, "Les traditions manichéennes au Fou-kien," *T'oung Pao* ser. 2, 22.193–208 (1923) and Ch'en Yüan 陳垣, Mo-ni-chiao ju Chung-kuo k'ao 摩尼教入中國考, *Kuo-hsüeh chi-ka'n* 國學季刊 1.203–240 (1923). The imagination is dazzled by the reference to a "stone image." Could it still be there? In regard to the use of the word *kung* for a Manichaean temple, see the same word in the text translated by Pelliot (*op. cit.*, 199, 206) and his note that this is normally Taoist terminology. In the T'ang period Manichaean temples were usually called *ssu* 寺 in conformity with Buddhist practice (see for instance Ch'en Yüan, *op. cit.*, 215, 219), and one from the tenth century (not in Fukien) was named a *yüan* 院 (*ibid.*, 223). The possibility that *mo-ni* may here mean "pearl" (Skt.) is not excluded but the use of *kung* for a Buddhist edifice is very unlikely.

[617] See chapter on Landscape.

Shen-chih in his cherished project of abolishing the hazards to navigation at Yellow Point.  Shen-chih instructed his subordinate, Liu Shan-fu,[618] to go to the coast and offer sacrifices.  When this was done all the spirits of the sea appeared.  In the end came a weird thing, "neither fish nor dragon," with yellow scales and red fins, and after a violent storm of three days duration the new harbor suddenly appeared.[619]  The opinion of the Fukienese generally was that this prodigious event was the direct outcome of the virtuous life of their lord.[620]  There is another tale, a ghost story, involving the ruling family: when Yen-ping first came to Chien Prefecture he pillaged a Buddhist temple in the mountains and killed a priest in anger when the latter did not rise in respect but continued to intone the Lotus Sutra.  Later Yen-ping saw apparitions of this unfortunate priest, which sometimes took the form of his brother Yen-chün.  This made him justifiably apprehensive, and the story is given by our source as an omen of the future fratricide.[621]  At least one text relates that the Lady Ts'ui, villainous wife of Yen-han, was killed by an evil spirit.[622]

From this time too come tales of "inanimate" objects controlled by supernatural beings, or at least symbolic of divine power.  The first is true of the magic sword of Wang Ch'ao.  When the time came to elect a new leader for the band of the unlamented Wang Hsü, the members took an oath of brotherhood, smearing their lips with the blood of the sacrificial victim. Then each saluted in turn a sword placed in the ground.  When Ch'ao did so, the weapon leaped from the earth and he was accordingly given the command.  This mystic event marks the beginning of the power of the Wang family in Fukien.[623]  Not clearly "magical" but certainly wonderful and probably regarded as a talisman was the precious sword sent to Chi-p'eng by the King of Silla.  The Emperor displayed the sword to his minister, Wang T'an 王倓, at a banquet and asked its use, to which T'an replied, "To decapitate anyone who is your servant and not loyal!"  Yen-hsi was present at this episode and since he had already envisaged seizing the throne "he shivered and changed complexion."[624]  A second sword was

[618] See chapter on Literature.

[619] *T'ai-p'ing kuang-chi* 太平廣記 313.2a-b, citing *Pei-meng so-yen*.

[620] *WTS*.

[621] *WKKS* b.6b.-7a.

[622] *WTS*.

[623] *CWTS* 134.4371a-b.  *TS* 190.4075b states that the sword jumped for Shen-chih who ceded his rights to his elder brother.

[624] *TCTC* 283.12a.  Cf. Helen B. Chapin, *Toward the study of the sword as dynastic talisman: the Feng-ch'eng pair and the sword of Han Kao Tsu* (Ph.D. Thesis, University of California, Berkeley, 1940), *passim*, for magic swords, often in pairs, which function as protectors of a dynasty.

brought by the ambassadors of Silla during Yen-hsi's reign and that monarch, as evidence of the aversion of the omen from himself, used the weapon to dismember the corpse of T'an, long since dead. It is said that the cadaver was still lifelike in appearance and flowed blood at the cut of the sword.[625] All of these swords, like certain Malayan kris, must be regarded as pregnant with the essence of kingly power. To the same genus belongs an iron staff, once the property of Wang Shen-chih. This had been a family heirloom of Liu Chen-ling 柳眞齡 of Min who gave it to the Prince. The latter bequeathed it to Ch'ien Liu, ruler of Wu-yüeh, who in turn gave it to a priest. Ultimately it came into the hands of the great poet Su Shih who wrote some verses in gratitude. He remarks that the staff was possessed by a spirit.[626] It would appear to have always been owned only by men of abundant virtue.

Various forms of divination and prognostication were widely practised in Min and we have a number of anecdotes in connection with these arts which involve eminent personages of the age. The rise to power of the Wang family was alleged to have been prophesied by a "Monk of the Shattered Stone" (碎石僧) in a couplet which, translated, reads:

The cliff is high but falls before the tidal waters.
The tide recedes and an arrow and mouth come forth.[627]

This involves two puns and a graphic puzzle. The cliff is [Ch'en] Yen [陳]巖 who fell before the might of the tide, [Wang] Ch'ao [王]潮. Ch'ao in turn receded and in his place appeared [Shen-]chih. The graph for *chih* 知 is composed of 矢 "arrow" and 口 "mouth".[628] Another story about Ch'ao and his brother tells that they visited a diviner (日者) who scrutinized them both and finally made the pronouncement, "One will overcome one," that is, one of you brothers will be more glorious than the other. It is said that Shen-chih left in a sweat.[629] We have, moreover, the story of a man who prophesied his own death, something usually withheld from clairvoyants. This was the unhappy Hsüeh Wen-chieh, an expert at prognostication, who, when Chi-p'eng sent him under guard to the army for slaughter early in 934, announced that he would suffer no harm if he managed to eke out another three days of existence. His guards traveled by forced marches, bringing him to the military encampment in less than that time and Wen-chieh met a dreadful death.[630] I do not know that diviners were attached

---

[625] *TCTC* 283.12a and *WTS*.

[626] *Tung-p'o ch'i-chi* 東坡七集 (*SPPY*) 12.4a.

[627] 巖高潮水沒，潮退矢口出.

[628] *WKKS* b.5a.

[629] 一个勝一个 *Ibid.*

[630] *TCTC* 278.16a-b, *WTS*.

to the armies of Min as a regular practice although this seems probable. At
any rate, when Yen-hsi's general, Huang Ching-chung, was about to engage
the troops from Chien Prefecture at Yu-k'ou in August 942, he desisted on
the advice of diviners, thus losing the advantage of the offensive, and was
defeated and killed.[631] A final episode illustrates the use of a (pretended)
skill at physiognomizing for the purpose of seducing men to murderous
deeds. Late in 944, when Liu Ts'ung-hsiao wished to seize control of
Ch'üan Prefecture, he chose some bravos to murder the minion of Chu
Wen-chin acting in Ch'üan, and promised them wealth for a successful
assassination in these unequivocal words: "When I regard your countenances
[I see that] they are not long [destined] for poverty."[632]

An anecdote, perhaps hardly worthy of inclusion here, but interesting
for its supernatural overtones, follows: a certain villager of Yen-p'ing
dreamed of a person who told him to go into the forest and get "something."
The rustic, at first unsuccessful in obtaining anything worthy of his efforts,
finally found some red soil like cinnabar. This stuff was luminous and he
took it home. Wang Yen-cheng heard of its remarkable properties and
took it to decorate his palace.[633]

The most frequent supernatural manifestations to be recorded in
historical and semi-historical books are premonitory happenings. Omens
have always played an important role in Chinese politics, and agents of
men who aspired to ascend the imperial throne must have been very active
in collecting and spreading rumors of supernatural sanction for their masters'
ambitions or of divine discontent with the reigns of incumbents. A large
number pertaining to Min have been preserved.

Omens of the glory of Shen-chih are particularly prominent in
contemporary sources. The case of Sweet Pear Harbor has already been
mentioned. It is also related that a certain monk of I Shan (懿山) told
Shen-chih about the length of his future dynasty in these words, "A great
king will come on horseback, and depart on horseback." The source for
this tale states that the veracity of the priest is proved by the fact that Shen-
chih obtained Min in a horse year (丙午) and that the dynasty fell in a
horse year (also 丙午).[634] Unfortunately this is true only in the loosest
way. The only applicable *ping-wu* years are 886 and 946. In the former,
Wang Ch'ao seized Ch'üan Prefecture,[635] and while this may be taken as
a mark of the founding of the dynasty, it was definitely not the year of

---

[631] *TCTC* 283.4a-b.
[632] *TCTC* 284.7b.
[633] *Chi-shen lu* 5.40, and also in *T'ai-p'ing kuang-chi* 374.9a.
[634] *WKKS* b.9a.
[635] *TCTC* 256.16b.

Shen-chih's ascendancy. Similarly, the collapse of the Wang clan was complete in 945, not in 946.

Another miraculous tale is connected with Wang Ch'ao. When he became Prefect of Ch'üan, there was an earthquake with a noise as of hundreds of drums in Peach Forest Village, north of the prefectural seat. The following day it was discovered that the grain crops had quite disappeared. The ground was dug up and the stalks found buried. The text tells us that in this year Shen-chih took possession of all of Min—an overstatement as in the previous case. Sixty years later (this is not quite accurate) the same disaster overtook the growing fields and Wang Yen-hsi was murdered.[636]

Two omens are connected with Shen-chih's nephew and contemporary, Yen-pin, Prefect of Ch'üan. In his case they were somewhat misleading. Yen-pin is said to have been born in a Buddhist temple in Ch'üan. A white sparrow nested there at the time of his birth and disappeared at his death.[637] It is also reported that a white deer and some of the auspicious purple fungus, Fomes japonicus (紫芝), were seen, and a monk, Hao-yüan 浩源, interpreted these properly as tokens of a rising monarch (王者). After this Yen-pin became "arrogant" and was reduced to the status of a commoner by his uncle. The monk was put to death.[638]

Especially wonderful were the portents associated with the name and destiny of the first Emperor of the Min dynasty, Yen-chün. A certain man reported the appearance of a dragon over Yen-chün's residence (眞封宅). Yen-chün accordingly changed the name of the mansion to "Palace of the Dragon's Prance" (龍躍宮). Immediately thereafter he went to the Palace of the Precious August to receive the tablet of investiture and, ascending the throne, adopted as title of his reign "Dragon Disclosure."[639]

Soon after his accession Yen-chün felt obliged to resign the throne temporarily in view of a cosmic hint in the form of an earthquake, his avowed purpose being "to cultivate the Way." This was on May 31, 933.[640] More strange portents are reported for the period immediately preceding his

[636] *Chi-shen lu* 5.39–40.

[637] *WKKS* b.9b.

[638] *TCTC* 271.7a. Reported for January or early February 921. Omens are ambiguous. The white deer, for instance, has been interpreted as a fell sign. Thus, "King Mu [of Chou] having obtained a white wolf and a white deer, the heritage of [Kings] Wen and Wu declined therefrom." (*SS* 61.4629d). White is usually interpreted as an unlucky color as in *TS* 35.3716c where the comment on the appearance of white deer is that "there will be a great mourning." Also *TS* 35.3716d, "White is a symbol of war." In our text, however, the white deer is obviously an auspicious sign.

[639] *TCTC* 278.5a. *WTS* notes that this was a yellow dragon.

[640] *TCTC* 278.6b. Cf. his earlier retirement discussed under Taoism.

death. The Emperor saw a red rainbow-dragon (赤虹) in his room and this prodigy vanished only after drinking up the water in a golden basin. Also, just before his assassination the *Fomes* fungus sprang up by the palace gate.[641]

It was popularly believed that the rise of the Min empire was predetermined by fate. When the embassy sent by Chi-p'eng to the Chin court in the north arrived at Ta-liang, it presented a "notification of auto-cracy" which began with the words, "Since the ascendancy of the State of Min was destined . . ."[642] This belief was supported by a legend concerning the name of Chi-p'eng, which has been preserved from oblivion by the commentator Hu San-hsing.[643] He cites the story as from the *Chiu Wu Tai shih* of Hsüeh Chü-cheng but the passage does not appear in the extant versions of that work which is admittedly a patchwork job. Here is the story: "In the Prefectural City of Fu there was an 'Altar of Wang Pa' 王霸,[644] and a 'Smelted Cinnabar Well' (鍊丹井). At the side of the altar was a blackpod tree (皂莢木)[645] which had long been withered. One day it suddenly put forth branches and leaves. In the well, a white tortoise floated to the surface. When the ground was excavated a stone was found with the engraved text 'Posterity of Wang Pa' (王霸裔孫). Ch'ang [i.e. Chi-p'eng] regarded this as [referring to] himself. In response to this he erected the Precious August Palace at the altar's side." The *Wu Tai shih pu* 五代史補 of T'ao Yüeh 陶岳 tells a rather different story about this Wang Pa who was alleged to have been a remote ancestor of the Wang clan and to have lived in seclusion at I Shan (怡山) in Fu Prefecture as a Taoist recluse. He built an altar, says the tale, under two blackpod trees and under it buried a prophecy of the future rule of one of his descendants in the territory. The inscription was found in the ninth century by another Taoist who interpreted it as indicating that Wang Ch'ao would found a dynasty.[646]

[641] *WKKS* b.6a. See *TS* 34.3714b : "A red vapor is a symbol of blood."
[642] *TCTC* 282.7a. This was on November 26, 939, when Chi-p'eng was already dead.
[643] *TCTC* 277.15b-16a.

[644] As will become clear this is intended to be read as a personal name; but *wang-pa* also means "King and Warlord" or, better, "Rex-Imperator."

[645] Genus *Gleditschia*, a leguminous plant related to the acacia.

[646] The event is supposed to have taken place about ten years before Ch'ao was appointed Legate—perhaps he started the legend. *Wu Tai shih pu* which has a preface dated 1012 A.D. and is therefore a primary source, is a valuable supplement to Hsüeh Chü-cheng's history. It was used as a source by both Ou-yang Hsiu and Ssu-ma Kuang (see *Ssu-k'u ch'üan-shu tsung-mu* 51.4b-5a'). The passage about Wang Pa will be found at 2.4b-6b. *Min-hou-hsien chih* 104.3a has a biography of Wang Pa, an accomplished alchemist of the Liang dynasty.

The rainbow spirit appeared in the palace once more in the summer of 938 during the reign of Chi-p'eng. The shaman Lin Hsing interpreted the omen as pointing to insurrection within the royal family and brought about the execution of the Emperor's uncles, Yen-wu, Yen-wang and five of their sons.[647] In the summer of 939 the Seers of Auras (望氣者) reported an evil portent in the Northern Palace. As a result Chi-p'eng shifted his residence to the Southern Palace and soon after a disastrous fire broke out in the palace just vacated. This too did not precede an imperial death by long.[648]

Meanwhile the rising star of Yen-hsi was heralded by the emission of white smoke from a stone in that worthy's courtyard. The Taoist High Priest Ch'en Shou-yüan was summoned to exorcise the spirit, but instead he interpreted the augury as favorable. Yen-hsi shortly succeeded his hated nephew on the throne of Min.[649] However, Yen-hsi's own bloody end was presaged by unmistakable signs. On the very day of his murder the Emperor visited the apartment of the Lady Shang-kuan 上官, his consort. As he left the Nine Dragon Pavilion the flowers were brushed from his head by a curtain, and he found that he could mount his shying horse only with the greatest difficulty. Soon after he was cut down by the golden lances of his own guards.[650] The miscreants who plotted the regicide, Chu Wen-chin and Lien Chung-yü, had also used supernatural arguments to rally popular support to their cause, announcing to the folk on April 8, 944, that "Heaven loathes the Wang family. . ."[651]

The priestly usurper who held the throne of Min briefly was himself the center of marvellous tales indicating his future eminence. Li Jen-ta, his chameleon-hided backer, announced to the people that a red serpent had once emerged from the nose of Cho Yen-ming when the prelate was asleep in the temple—a sign of a person greatly favored by heaven.[652]

Finally, the collapse of the Min empire before the victorious troops of Southern T'ang was predicted by a nameless priest called "The Mad Monk of Chien Prefecture." This man was regarded as an able prognosticator and his most fantastic deeds were thought to have profound significance. In 943 the monk cut down all of the trees on the north side of a certain

---

[647] *WTS*. Cf. *TS* 36.3718c, where a rainbow signifies " the imperial consorts secretly oppress the sovereign" (后妃陰脅王者).

[648] *TCTC* 282.4a, *WTS*.

[649] *WKKS* b.7b.

[650] *WKKS* b.8b. Perhaps the allusion made by *WKKS* earlier to the " Great King " of Min " departing on a horse " refers to this particular incident.

[651] *TCTC* 284.3a.

[652] *WKKS* b.11a.

road (the text says, "the south-facing trees"—symbolic of the Emperor?).
He was asked to explain this strange maneuver and said, "So as not to hinder
the banners." When the conquering army from Chiang-nan invaded Fukien
it actually passed along this route. Again when someone asked him "How
long must we wait for peace?" he replied, "You will have peace when I
am gone." And indeed Min was finally "pacified" after his death.[653]

An important source of prophecies was the monk Shang-lan 上藍 of
Hung 洪 Prefecture. To him are credited the verses:

Fear not the sheep entering your room,
Fear only the cash entering your belly.

Here "sheep" (羊) stands for the Yang 楊 clan of Wu, hereditary enemies
of Min, and "cash" (錢) to the ruling family of Wu-yüeh which ultimately
occupied Fu Prefecture.[654]

All of these marvels I relate as fact although some may be entirely
fanciful. Certainly most are a combination of both. It is important to note
that these omens are reported with monotonous regularity in connection
with the most important political schemes designed to sway the opinions of
commoner and Emperor alike.[655]

[653] Chi-shen lu shih-i 拾遺 p. 5 (TSCC).

[654] Min-hou-hsien chih 106.1b, citing Ch'uan T'ang shih-hua 全唐詩話. The whole text
of the poem is 不怕羊入屋只怕錢入腹. Ibid., for another similar prophetic warning.
Wu Tai shih pu also contains anecdotes about Shang-lan, who is said to have saved
Wang Ch'ao's life by diverting the jealousy of a rival warlord by means of a judicious
prophecy which linked the fortunes of the two men. The same monk is said to have
cryptically predicted the fall of Chekiang into the hands of the Ch'ien clan.

[655] For traces of traditional popular religion in Fukien, especially of snake and dragon
worship and of various mountain spirits, see W. Eberhard, "Lokalkulturen in alten
China" (II), Monumenta Serica Monograph Series 3(1942), pp. 14, 32, 37, 228, 251,
348, 409.

# APPENDICES

# MAP OF MIN

*Prefectures* 州
Chang 漳
Chien 建
Ch'üan 泉
Fu 福
T'an 鐔
T'ing 汀
Yung 鋪

*Districts* 縣
Chang-p'u 漳浦

Ch'ang-ch'i 長溪
Ch'ang-lo 長樂
Ch'ang-t'ing 長汀
Chiang-lo 將樂
Chien-an 建安
Chien-yang 建陽
Chin-chiang 晉江
Fu-ch'ing 福清
Hou-kuan 候官
Hsien-yu 仙遊
Ku-t'ien 古田

Lien-chiang 連江
Lung-yen 龍巖
Lung-ch'i 龍溪
Min 閩
Min-ch'ing 閩清
Nan-an 南安
Ning-hua 寧化
Ning-te 寧德
P'u-ch'eng 浦城
P'u-t'ien 莆田
Sha 沙

Shao-wu 邵武
Te-hua 德化
T'ung-an 同安
Yu-ch'i 尤溪
Yung-chen 永貞
Yung-ch'un 永春
Yung-t'ai 永泰

*Garrisons* 鎮
Yen-p'ing 延平

# TABLE A. THE WANG DYNASTY OF MIN

| RULER | TITLES | POSTHUMOUS TITLES | REIGNS |
|---|---|---|---|
| 王　潮 | 泉州刺史<br>威武軍節度使 | 司空 | |
| 王審知 | 威武軍節度使<br>閩王 | 忠懿王<br>昭武王<br>昭武孝皇帝<br>太祖 | |
| 王延翰 | 威武軍節度使<br>大閩國王 | | |
| 王延鈞ª<br>(王璘，鏻)ᵇ | 威武軍節度使<br>閩王<br>大閩皇帝 | 齊肅明孝皇帝<br>惠宗 | 龍啓<br>永和 |
| 繼鵬王<br>(王　昶) | 大閩皇帝 | 聖神英睿文明<br>廣武應道大弘<br>孝皇帝<br>康宗 | 通文 |
| 王延羲<br>(王　曦) | 閩國王<br>大閩皇 | 睿文廣武明聖<br>元德隆道大孝<br>皇帝ᶜ<br>景宗 | 永隆 |
| 王延政ᵈ | 富沙王<br>大殷皇帝<br>大閩皇帝 | | 天德 |

a. Harvard-Yenching Institute Sinological Index Series, Supplement I *Chinese Chronological Charts with Index* (February 1931) gives 均, a form which appears only rarely in the texts.

b. Yen-chün's later name (Lin) is omitted in the *Chronological Charts*.

c. The inscription on the tablet of Yen-hsi's pagoda (see above, chapter on Religion) gives what appears to be a garbled version of this title, namely 睿明文廣武聖光德隆道大孝皇帝. The errors must, however, be attributed to the editors of the *Fu-chien t'ung-chih*, not to the original stone cutter.

d. *Chronological Charts* gives 正, an error, apparently based on *Ts'e-fu yüan-kuei*.

# TABLE B.  ORTHODOX AND MIN REIGN TITLES

| A.D. | T'ANG | | MIN | |
|---|---|---|---|---|
| 894 | Ch'ien Ning | 乾寧 | | |
| 898 | Kuang Hua | 光化 | | |
| 901 | T'ien Fu | 天復 | | |
| 904 | T'ien Yu | 天祐 | | |
| | **LIANG** | | | |
| 907 | K'ai P'ing | 開平 | | |
| 911 | Ch'ien Hua | 乾化 | | |
| 915 | Chen Ming | 貞明 | | |
| 921 | Lung Te | 龍德 | | |
| | **T'ANG** | | | |
| 923 | T'ung Kuang | 同光 | | |
| 926 | T'ien Ch'eng | 天成 | | |
| 930 | Ch'ang Hsing | 長興 | **MIN** | |
| 933 | | | Lung Ch'i | 龍啓 |
| 934 | Ying Shun | 應順 | | |
| | Ch'ing T'ai | 清泰 | | |
| 935 | | | Yung Ho | 永和 |
| | **CHIN** | | | |
| 936 | T'ien Fu | 天福 | T'ung Wen | 通文 |
| 939 | | | Yung Lung | 永隆 |
| 943 | | | T'ien Te | 天德 |
| 944 | K'ai Yün | 開運 | | |

# BASIC SOURCES

# BASIC SOURCES

1. *CFWC*: Anon., [*Ch'en*] *Chin-feng wai-chuan* 陳金鳳外傳. I have not seen an original copy of this book. Chin Yün-ming 金雲銘 in his *Fu-chien wen-hua yen-chiu shu-mu* 福建文化研究書目 (*Fu-chien wen-hua* 1.2.14, Fukien Christian University, February 1932) states that it is in one *chüan*, and that a preface by Wang Yü 王于 says that it was supposed to have been dug up, enclosed in a stone box, by a farmer of Fukien in the Wan-li period (sixteenth century). Chin Yün-ming also offers his opinion that the book is a forgery. More detailed circumstances of the find appear in *chüan* 23 (25b-26a) of the *I-wen chih* 藝文志 of the *Fu-chien t'ung-chih* 福建通志 of Ch'en Yen 陳衍 (published 1922-42). The peasant is supposed to have discovered a number of other artifacts together with the book, including a bronze stove, and a bronze knife bearing the date 乾德五年 (A.D. 967) in seal characters. The paper and ink of the book were in poor shape but the text could be read. Yü got the book from the farmer, and checking it with standard historical sources, found nothing inconsistent in it. He and his friend Hsü Po 徐𤊾 made a restoration of the text. Its subsequent history is obscure, but it seems to have passed through the hands of Hsü T'ung 徐熥, Po's brother, who is sometimes credited with its authorship. I am uncertain as to its reliability, but many distinguished Chinese scholars have not hesitated to refer to it as an original source. I have reconstructed my own version of the text (doubtless an incomplete one) from quotations in such works as *Ch'üan Wu Tai shih* 全五代詩, *Shih-kuo ch'un-ch'iu* and *Shih-kuo kung-tz'u* 十國宮詞. As Wang Yü observed, there are no apparent anachronisms in the text, or variations from contemporary sources where the same events are referred to. The new material it contains is very colorful, and I have not hesitated to use it, especially in the chapter on the court life under the first Emperor of Min.

2. *CIL*: T'ao Ku 陶穀, *Ch'ing-i lu* 清異錄, edition of Hsi-yin-hsüan ts'ung-shu 惜陰軒叢書. A collection of curious customs and strange terms, explained by anecdotes, many on Min court life. Tenth century.

3. *CKC*: Lu Chen 路振, *Chiu-kuo chih* 九國志, edition of Ts'ung-shu chi-ch'eng 叢書集成 (elsewhere abbreviated as *TSCC*). Originally contained lives of Emperors of Southern Dynasties, but now only biographies of eminent men. An important source. Tenth-eleventh centuries.

4. *CWTS*: Hsüeh Chü-cheng 薛居正, *Chiu Wu Tai shih* 舊五代史. *Chüan* 134 has a little on Min, but hardly worth mentioning. Tenth century.

5. *ChWTS*: Li T'iao-yüan 李調元, *Ch'üan Wu Tai shih*, edition of *TSCC*. The complete poetry of the Five Dynasties and the Ten Kingdoms. Eighteenth century.

6. *FCTC1*: Ch'en Shou-ch'i 陳壽祺, *Fu-chien t'ung-chih*, edition of 1867. Important for epigraphic, archaeological and traditional material.

7. *FCTC2*: Hsieh Tao-ch'eng 謝道承, *Fu-chien t'ung-chih*, edition of 1737.

8. *NTS*: Ma Ling 馬令, *Nan T'ang shu* 南唐書, edition of *TSCC*. Includes various data on relations between T'ang and Min, especially pertaining to the invasion of the latter by the former. Twelfth century(?).

9. *SS*: T'o-t'o 脫脫, *Sung shih* 宋史. Very little on Min, since that empire had perished before the Sung conquest. Contains biographies of great Fukienese of the late tenth century, such as Liu Ts'ung-hsiao and Ch'en Hung-chin in *chüan* 483. Thirteenth century.

10. *TCTC*: Ssu-ma Kuang 司馬光, *Tzu-chih t'ung-chien* 資治通鑑, edition of *Ssu-pu ts'ung-k'an* 四部叢刊 (elsewhere cited as *SPTK*), the photolithographic version of the Sung edition in the Han-fen-lou 涵芬樓 library. I have compared this with the text in the *Ssu-pu pei-yao* 四部備要 edition (elsewhere cited as *SPPY*), a lead-type version, which contains the useful

commentary of Hu San-hsing 胡三省 (1230-87). Extremely important. Eleventh century.


11. *TS*: Ou-yang Hsiu 歐陽修, *T'ang shu* 唐書. Especially useful for biographical material on Wang Ch'ao, Wang Shen-kuei and Wang Shen-chih, the founders of the empire of Min (*chüan* 190). Eleventh century.


12. *WKKS*: Anon., *Wu-kuo ku-shih* 五國故事, edition of Chih-pu-tsu-chai ts'ung-shu 知不足齋叢書. Anecdotal, largely supernatural tales; material for the states of Wu, Southern T'ang, Shu, Southern Han and Min. Early Sung.


13. *WTS*: Ou-yang Hsiu, *Wu Tai shih* 五代史. *Chüan* 68 devoted to Min. Less trivial and partial than Chü-cheng's account, but lacking the details of Ssu-ma Kuang. Eleventh century.


14. *YTCS*: Wang Hsiang-chih 王象之, *Yü-ti chi-sheng* 輿地紀勝, edition of 1849. Important for archaeological, topographical and traditional material about Min still current in Sung. Thirteenth century.

# INDEX

# INDEX

Abdication, temporary, of Wang Yen-chün 王延鈞, 97, 106

Academies, founded by Wang Shen-chih 王審知, 87 ; *see also* Schools

Accounts, of palace, 43 n. 267 ; *see also* Expenditures, Taxation

*Acorus,* 4

Agate, dishes of, 86

Agent for Blank Commissions 空名堂牒使, 72

Alchemist, 107 (n. 646) ; *see also* Cinnabar, Elixir, Taoism

Aloes-wood, 66, 66 (n. 390)

Altar, to fertility spirits, 101 ; to Heaven in suburb, 101 ; of Wang Pa, 王霸 107

Ambassador, 45 ; *see also* Diplomacy, Embassies, Envoys, Tribute

Amber, dishes of, 86

Amitabha Sutra 彌陀經, 100 (n. 604)

Amphibious operations, *see* Marines

An Lu-shan 安祿山, 34 (n. 211), 79 n. 482

An-hua Army 安化軍, 61 (n. 362)

An-kuo Temple 安國寺, 85

An-t'ai Gate 安泰門, 9

Anāgata Maitreya Bhagavan Buddha 當來下生彌勒尊佛, 94

Ancestral temple, 17, 18 (n. 119), 39, 101 ; of Wang Shen-chih 35 (n. 216), 83

Annam, 36 (n. 211), 78 (n. 474)

Apotropaic, emblem, 52 (n. 314) ; rituals, 95

Apricot, 3

Archer, Wang Chi-p'eng 王繼鵬 as, 22, 46

Archers, military, 8

Architecture, ix, 27, 70, 74, 80–85, 99 ; *see also* Buddhism, Taoism, Temples

Aromatics, 63 (n. 373), 64, 65, 66, 98 (n. 594), 99

Arrows, 68, 68 (n. 419)

Artisans Institute, Commissioner of 百工院使, 21

*Asparagus lucidus,* 67

Assassinations, 36, 38, 42, 44, 45, 46, 53, 53 (n. 319), 55, 56, 59, 82, 86 (n. 525), 105, 106, 107

Astrology, *see* Constellation Wu

Augustus of Min 閩國皇, 18, 50, 94 ; *see also* Wang Yen-hsi

Auras, seers of 望氣者, 108

Aurousseau, Léonard, 36 n. 211

Auspicious, *see* Destiny, Fungus, Omen, Prophecy

Autonomy, of Northern Fukien, 49

*Averrhoa carambola,* 67

Bamboo, 68

Bananas, 3, 63 (n. 373), 67 ; cloth, 69

Banyan, 68

" Banyan Town " 榕城, 68

Barbarians, foreign merchants as, 78 ; Fukienese as, 48, 48 (n. 290) ; *see also* Fukienese

Baskets, 68

Battleships, 11 ; *see also* Commander of Galleons, Fleets, Naval Warfare, Warships

Bear, 4

Bell, cast for *Pao-hua Yüan* 寶華院, 86

Bhaiṣajaya-guru Vaidūrya-prabhā Buddha 藥師琉璃光佛, 95

Black Dragon Tea, 64

Blackpod tree, 107

Blood, from a corpse, 104 ; to seal oath, 103

Board of Personnel, President of 吏部尚書, 51, 73 ; Vice-President of 吏部郎中, 72

Board of Rites, Secretary of 禮部員外郎, 45 ; Vice-President of 禮部郎中, 72

Board of Taxation, President of 戶部尚書, 45, 51

Board of War, President of 兵部尚書, 51

Boat races, 22 (n. 147)

Bodhisattva, 92 ; *see also* Buddhism

Bodyguards, private, 43, 46 ; *see also* Guards

*Boehmeria nivea,* 69

Bohea tea, 64

*Book of T'ang,* see *T'ang shu*

Boots, leather, 69

Borneol, 16, 66, 66 (n. 390), 99 ; see also *Lung-nao*

Bowra, E.H., ix

Bribes, officially condoned, 72 ; taken by Taoists, 98

Bricks, made near Fu Prefecture 福州, 86

" Bridled Crane " 控鶴, name of army, repository, and guard division, 24 (n. 158)

Brocade Village 錦里, 18

Brocaded silk, 69

Bronze, branding irons, 71 ; statues of the Buddha, 85, 92 ; supernatural nail of, 98 ; temple bell, 86 ; water pot, 84

Buddha, forms of in pagoda of Wang Yen-hsi 王延義, 94–95 ; in Fukien, 90 ; of the Golden Millet 金粟像, 86 ; Buddha Range 佛嶺, 85

" Buddha's Hand " 佛手柑, 67

Buddhism, Buddhist, 16, 91–96 ; Priests and Monks, 41 (n. 256), 85, 85 (n. 519), 90, 93, 94, 95, 103, 105, 106, 108, 109 ; Temples, 11 (n. 72), 12, 41 (n. 256), 70, 71, 85–86, 90, 91, 92, 93, 100 (n. 604), 102 (n. 616), 106 ; *see also* Cho Yen-ming

" Buddhist Country ", Ch'üan Prefecture 泉州 as, 90 (n. 554)

Buffer, Ch'ien Prefecture 虔州 as, 77 (n. 467) ; Fu Prefecture 福州 as, 61, 75

Building, *see* Architecture

" Cake aromatic " 餅香, 66

*Calamus,* 68

Calligraphy, 94 (n. 572)

Camphor, 4, 66

*Canarium,* 67, 67 (n. 395)

Candles, 69, 90 ; " Gold Dragon " type, 86

Cannibalism, 41, 41 (n. 254), 60 (n. 356)

*Canon of the Hundred Repentances* 百悔經, 24

Canton 廣州, 20 (n. 139), 34 (n. 209), 42 (n. 260), 66 (n. 390), 78 (n. 468), 78, 84 ; *see also* Kwangtung, Southern Han

Captain of Punitive Armies on the March 行營招討諸軍都虞候, 56

Cassia, 3

Catalpa, 3

Catamite, 21 (n. 141)

*Celosia cristata,* 4

Ceramics, *see* Pottery

*Cervus unicolor,* 69 (n. 421)

Ch'a Wen-hui 查文徽, 56, 57

*Chamaerops excelsa,* 4

Champa, crystal screen from, 22 (n. 147) ; mission to, 78 ; rice from, 70

Chan Tun-jen 詹敦仁, 5

Chancellor 樞密使, vii, 39, 43 (n. 267), 53 ; see also *Men-hsia shih-chung*

Chang 張, Lady *née,* 51

Chang Ch'an 張闡, 90 (n. 554)

Chang Cheng-ch'ang 張正常, 98 (n. 594)

Chang Chih-yüan 張知遠, 34

Chang Han-chen 張漢眞, 56, 59

Chang Han-ssu 張漢思, 54

Chang Mu 張睦, 78 (n. 470)

Chang Prefecture 漳州, 4, 5, 26, 35, 50, 53, 54 (n. 330), 55, 56, 59, 61, 62, 62 (n. 366), 64 (n. 377), 65, 66, 68, 69, 77, 79 (n. 478, 480), 83

Chang Tao-ling 張道陵, 98 (n. 594, 595)

Chang T'ing-hui 張延暉, 64

Chang Tsu 張鷟, 68 (n. 416)

Chang Yen-jou 張延柔, 40

Chang Yen-tse 張彥澤, 41 (n. 254)

Chang-p'u 漳浦 (District), 31

Ch'ang K'un 常衮, 86 (n. 525), 87

Ch'ang-an 長安, 8, 81 (n. 491), 88

Ch'ang-ch'i 長溪 (District), 54, 65

*Ch'ang-ch'ing Yüan* 長慶院, 85

Ch'ang-ch'un Palace 長春宮, 46, 80, 80 (n. 484), 81, 81 (n. 492), 82, 83 ; *see also* Palace of Enduring Spring, Southern Palace

Ch'ang-lo 長樂, Metropolitan Prefecture of, 40 ; Prince of, 50 ; *see also* Fu Prefecture

Ch'ang-lo 長樂 (District), 13 (n. 83), 35 (n. 216), 60, (n. 359), 67 (n. 398), 85, 101

*Ch'ang-lo hsien-chih* 長樂縣志, 13 (n. 83), 35 (n. 216)

Ch'ang-t'ai 長泰 (District), 79 (n. 478)

Ch'ang-t'ing 長汀 (District), 12

Ch'ang-ya 常雅 (priest), 96

Chao, Lady of State of 趙國夫人, 95

Chao Kao 趙高, 19, 20 (n. 133)

Chao T'o 趙陀, 67

Chao Tsung 昭宗 (of T'ang 唐), 24 (n. 158), 32

Chao-fu Temple 昭福祠, 100

*Chao-hsien Miao* 昭顯廟, 101

*Chao-hsien yuan* 招賢院, 83

Ch'ao Prefecture 潮州, 5

Ch'ao-chüeh 超覺禪師 (priest), 96 ; *see also* Hui-leng

*Ch'ao-yeh chien-tsai* 朝野僉載, 68 (n. 416)

Chapin, Helen B., 103 (n. 624)

Chavannes, Edouard, ix

Chekiang 浙江, 109 (n. 654) ; *see also* Wu-yüeh

Chen-an Army 鎭安軍, 29

Chen-Min Terrace 鎭閩臺, 9

Chen-wu Army 鎭武軍, 29

Ch'en 陳, Lady *née* (consort of Wang Yen-chün 王延鈞), *see* Golden Phoenix

Ch'en 陳, Lady *née* (wife of Li Chen 李眞), 95

Ch'en 陳, name of deified mortal, 101

Ch'en Chi-hsün 陳繼珣, 58, 59

Ch'en Ch'iao 陳嶠, 89

*Ch'en Chin-feng, Unofficial Biography of* 陳金鳳外傳, 21–22 (n. 147), 119

Ch'en Ching-ch'üan 陳敬佺, 54

Ch'en Chüeh 陳覺, 61

Ch'en Hung-chin 陳洪進, 55, 55 (n. 333), 62

Ch'en Kuang-i 陳光逸, 50

Ch'en K'uang-tan 陳匡範, 72, 73 (n. 445)

Ch'en K'uang-sheng 陳匡勝, 20, 42

Ch'en Kuei 陳宄, 72

Ch'en Pen 陳本, 35

Ch'en Shou-en 陳守恩, 20

Ch'en Shou-yi 陳受頤, 82 (n. 498)

Ch'en Shou'yüan 陳守元, 47, 96, 97, 98, 99, 108

Ch'en T'an 陳鄲, 46

Ch'en T'ao 陳陶, 37

Ch'en Wang 陳望, 51, 52, 57, 58

Ch'en Wen-chih 陳文質, 94

Ch'en Yen 陳巖, 32, 104

Ch'en-wei Division 宸衞都, 24, 25, 46, 47, 71

Cheng Yüan-pi 鄭元弼, 45, 47, 48, 48, (n. 290), 53

Ch'eng K'an 程侃, 40

Ch'eng Wen-wei 程文緯, 53, 55

Ch'eng Yün 程贇, 53 (n. 323)

*Chi-shen lu shih-i* 稽神錄拾遺, 41 (n. 256)

Ch'i 齊 (Tenth century state), 41 (n. 256)

Ch'i Prefecture 蘄州, 61

Ch'i-sheng 啓聖門, 8, 9, 43

*Chia-ch'eng* 夾城, 6

*Chia-hsiang* 甲香, 66, 66 (n. 390)

Chiang Yen 江淹, 4

Chiang Yen-hui 蔣延徽, 40, 41

*Chiang-chen-hsiang* 降眞香, 66

Chiang-hsi 江西, 77 (n. 467) ; Pacification Commissioner of 江西安撫使, 56

*Chiao-ko* 蕉葛, 69

Chiang-lo 將樂 (District), 51, 63, 65, 79 (n. 478), 86

Chiang-nan 江南, 22, 49, 109 ; *see also* Southern T'ang

*Chiao-pu* 蕉布, 69

Chicken, tax on, 72

Chien 建, Prince of, 43

Chien Prefecture 建州, 6, 7, 10, 11, (n. 66), 12, 14, 16, 18, 18 (n. 122), 26, 28, 29, 29 (n. 189), 36, 37, 37 (n. 232), 38, 39, 40, 41, 45, 48, 49, 50, 51, 52, 55, 56, 56 (n. 339), 57, 58, 59, 60, 60 (n. 358), 61, 62, 64, 64 (n. 377), 65, 68 (n. 409),

71, 73, 76, 79 (n. 478), 83, 86 (n. 525), 101, 03, 105, 108

Chien River 建水, 73

Chien Stream 建溪, 11 (n. 66)

Chien-an, Princess of 建安, 94

Chien-an 建安 (District), 4, 63

*Chien-chiao t'ai-shih* 檢校太師, 37 (n. 231)

Chien-k'ang Market 建康市, 30

Chien-ning 建寧 (District), 79 (n. 478)

Chien-yang 建陽 (District), 56, 57

Ch'ien 錢, surname of Wu-yüeh 吳越 royal family, 75, 86, 109

Ch'ien Ch'uan-hsiang, 錢傳珦, 34

Ch'ien Hung-i 錢弘億, 75

Ch'ien Liu 錢鏐, 33 (n. 206), 39, 104

*Ch'ien lu* 錢錄, 74 (n. 454)

Ch'ien Lung 乾隆 (reign), 35 (n. 216)

Ch'ien Prefecture 虔州, 77 (n. 467)

Ch'ien Ta 錢達, 53

Ch'ien Yüan-kuan 錢元瓘, 48

*Chih-hui-shih* 指揮使, commander of a guards division, 24 (n. 158)

Ch'ih Prefecture 池州, 77

Chin 金, Lady *née*, 20

Chin 晉 dynasty, *see* Later Chin dynasty

Chin Yün-ming 金雲銘, 119

Chin-an 晉安, 68 (n. 416); *see also* 'Fu Prefecture

Chin-chiang 晉江 (District), 13 (n. 82)

*Chin-ch'i hsien-i'an* 金谿閒談, 89

Chin-ling 金陵 (Southern T'ang 南唐 capital), 30, 61

Chin-t'ang Island 金塘山, 77 (n. 465)

Ch'in 秦 dynasty, 19, 20 (n. 133), 36 (n. 221)

Ch'in Shih Huang-ti 秦始皇帝, 9

Ch'in Tsung-ch'üan 秦宗權, 31

China, conquest of Annamese lands by, 36 (n. 211)

Chinese " gooseberry ", 67

" Chinese olive ", 67

*Ching* 麏 (kind of deer), 69 (n. 421)

Ching 荊 (state of Ching-nan 荊南, 76 (n. 459)

Ching Tsung 景宗 (Emperor of Min), *see* Wang Yen-hsi

Ch'ing-ch'eng Temple 慶城寺, 15

*Ch'ing-i lu* 清異錄, 119

Ch'ing-ko Village 清歌里, 16 (n. 105)

Ch'ing-yüan Army 清源軍, 61 (n. 361); *see also* Ch'üan Prefecture

Ch'ing-yüan Princess 清遠公主, 20, 42 (n. 260)

*Chiu T'ang shu* 舊唐書, 79 (n. 476)

*Chiu Wu Tai shih* 舊五代史, x, 107, 119

*Chiu-kuo chih* 九國志, 119

Chiu-lung Pavilion 九龍殿, 81, 82; *see also* Nine Dragon Pavilion

*Chiu-yü chih* 九域志, 11 (n. 66)

Cho Yen-ming 卓嚴明, 12, 58, 58 (n. 348), 59, 59 (n. 354), 95, 108

Chou 周 (surname), 36 (n. 224)

Chou, Duke of 周公, 52 (n. 316)

Chou 周 dynasty, 17, 106 (n. 638); *see also* Later Chou dynasty

Chou Ang 周昂, xi

*Chou li* 周禮, 43 (n. 263)

Chou Wei-yüeh 周維岳, 18, 26–27

Chou Yen-ch'en 周彥琛, 39 (n. 240); *see also* Wang Yen-ping

Chou-shan Archipelage 舟山羣島, 77 (n. 465)

*Ch'ou-hai t'u-pien* 籌海圖編, 77 (n. 465)

Chrysanthemum, 4

Chu Ch'üan-chung 朱全忠, 76 (n. 463), 88

Chu 朱 family, rulers of Liang 梁, 77; *see also* Chu Ch'üan-chung, Later Liang dynasty

Chu Wen-chin 朱文進, 25, 27, 46, 52, 53–56, 56 (n. 338, 341), 57 (n. 342), 58, 74, 89, 105, 108

*Chu-yeh-t'ing tsa-chi* 竹葉亭雜記, 5

*Ch'u* 楚 (dynasty), 39, 77 (n. 467)

Chuang Tsung 莊宗, Emperor of Later T'ang 後唐, 36

Ch'un-ch'iu 春秋 period, 80 (n. 488)

*Chung-chün-shih* 中軍使, 19

Chung-i Wang-Miao 忠懿王廟, 83; *see also* Patriotic and Estimable Prince

Ch'ung-an 崇安 (Village), 57

Ch'ung-miao pao-sheng chien-lao Pagoda 崇妙保聖堅牢塔, 94

Ch'ung-shun Wang 崇順王, 97, 98, 101

Ch'ü Prefecture 衢州, 77

Ch'üan Prefecture 泉州, 4, 11, 14, 14 (n. 88), 16, 16 (n. 108), 27 (n. 178), 29, 32, 33, 34, 34 (n. 207), 34 (n. 210), 36, 37 (n. 230), 45, 47, 49, 50, 53, 54, 54 (n.

330), 55, 55 (n. 338), 56, 58, 59, 60, 61, 61 (n. 361), 62, 64 (n. 377), 65, 66, 66 (n. 387), 67, 67 (n. 399, 401, 404, 406), 68, 68 (n. 416), 69, 73, 76, 77, 78 (n. 468), 78, 79 (n. 478), 84 (n. 512), 85, 90 (n. 554), 93, 105, 106

*Ch'uan T'ang wen* 全唐文, 90

*Ch'üan Wu Tai shih* 金五代詩, 119, 120

*Ch'uan-chou-fu chih* 泉州府志, 11 (n. 71, 72), 55 (n. 338)

*Ch'üan-huo lu* 泉貨錄, 74 (n. 454)

Chüeh-chü 絕句, verse from, 89

Cicada guaze, 69

Cinnabar, 98 (n. 594), 99 (n. 602), 105

*Cinnamomum camphorum,* 4

Citron, 67

*Citrus medica,* var. *chirocarpus,* 67

*Citrus nobilis,* var. *microcarpa,* 67

Civet, 66 (n. 390)

Clams, 65

Close of Manjusri 文殊院, 92

Cloth, 69; of banana, 67, 69; cotton, 69; hemp, 69; of *pueraria,* 63, 64, 69; silk, 69

Cloudy Terrace Mountain 雲臺山, 16

Coast, trade of Chien Prefecture 建州 with, 73

Cockscomb (flower), 4

Coiling Dragon Mountain 盤龍山, 14

Coins, 74–75

Coir palm, 4

Commander of Galleons 樓船指揮使, 7, 19, 38

Commerce, 65, 66, 75–78 (n. 468); *see also* Sea Voyages

Commissioner for Ceremonies of Patent 冊禮使, 39, 45

Commissiner of Defense 防禦使, 77 (n. 467)

Commissiner of Palace Parks 宮苑使, 94

Commissioner of Police 鎮遏使, 29, 57, 58

Commissioner of Portals 閤門使, 52 (n. 316)

Commissioner of Salt and Iron 鹽鐵使, 51

Commissioner of the Combined Armies 統軍使, 48, 54

*Complete Poetry of the Five Dynasties* 全五代詩, 88, 89

"Comprehensive Culture" 通文 (reign title), 44 (n. 271)

Confucianism, 16, 92, 97 (n. 586); official

cult, 100–101; orthodox literary criticism, 88; orthodox view of Wang Shen-chih 王審知, 70

Conifers, 3

Conscription, 52

Consorts, Imperial, 20 (n. 138), 24 (n. 155)

Constellation Wu 婺宿, 95, 95 (n. 575)

Controller of the Guards of the Six Armies 判六軍諸衛, 43, 43 (n. 263), 50; *see also* Controller of the Six Armies 判六軍, 45 (n. 281), 53, 59

Copper, 63, 65; coins, 74, 75 (n. 456); prohibition of coins, 75

Coral, 81

Cosmetics, 15 (n. 102)

Cotton cloth, 69

Crab apple, 4

Criticism, orthodox literary, 88

Crops, rice, 70

Crystal, decoration in Tzu-wei Palace 紫微宮, 99; screen of, 22 (n. 147)

Crystal Palace 水晶宮, 78 (n. 475), 80 (n. 488); *see also* Shui-ching Palace

Cunninghamia, 4, 10

Currency, 74–75; debasement of, 75

Đai Cồ-Việt 太瞿越, 78 (n. 474)

Death penalty, commutation of, 73; *see also* Torture

Debasement of currency, 75

Deer, 5, 69 (n. 421); as auspicious omen, 106; horn, 66; skins, 69 (n. 421)

Deification, of Emperor, 97; of humans, 14 (n. 88), 101

Department of State, 尙書省, of Min, 39 (n. 244)

"Deputy" 留後, 32, 35, 37, 59

Destiny, of South China, 95 (n. 575); of Wang family's rule, 91; *see also* Physiognomy

Diamond Sutra 金剛般若經, 100 (n. 604)

*Dioscorea batatas,* 4

Diplomacy, 34, 42 (n. 260), 45, 52, 54, 59, 60, 76; *see also* Ambassador, Envoy, Tribute

Dipped Moon Pond 蘸月池, 10

Director of Finances 判三司, 72

Director of the Six Armies 總六軍, 53 (n. 321); *see also* Controller of the Six Armies

Dismemberment, 41; of corpse, 73, 104; *see also* Cannibalism

Divination, with words and graphs, 104, 109; *see also* Auras, Omen, Physiognomy, Prophecy

Diviner, 104, 105

Division Commanders 都指揮使, 55

"Doctoral degree" 進士, 87 (n. 533)

Donatives, to imperial guards, 24, 71, 72

Dragon, imperial symbol on tent, 82; as omen, 97; omen of accession of Wang Yen-chün 王延鈞; in popular lore, 109 (n. 655); of rainbow, 106; sea-deity like, 103; temple to, 99; *see also* Nine Dragon Tent

Dragon Boat, 22 (n. 147)

"Dragon Disclosure" 龍啟 (reign title), 39 (n. 242a), 106

Dragon's Prance, Palace of 龍躍宮, 106

"Dragon Tea", 64, 64 (n. 377), 65, 65 (n. 381)

"Dragon-brain", 4, 66: see also *Lung-nao*, Borneol, *Dryobalanops*

"Dragon's-eye", *see* Longan

"Dragon-tiger" 龍虎 (name of Army), 43 (n. 263)

Dream, as guide to mineral wealth, 105; image prayed to for realization of, 102; poem composed in, 89; as portent, 85; of Wang Shen-chih 王審知, 102

Drinking, *see* Wine-drinking

Drought-resistant rice, 70

Drum Tower, 82, 101

Drums, "Flower-drums", 63; earthquake sounding like, 106

Drunkenness, antidote for, 16; *see also* Wine-drinking

*Dryobalanops camphora*, 4, 66

Dyed silk, 69

Earthquakes, as omens, 106

East Gate 東門, 7, 8

East Lake 東池, 7 (n. 35)

Eastern Military Gate 東武門, 8

Eastern Palace 東宮, 83

Eberhard, W., viii, 109 (n. 655)

*Eburna japonica,* 66 (n. 390)

Eels, shooting of, 14 (n. 90)

Eel Stream 鱔溪, 14 (n. 90)

"Eighteenth maiden lichee" 十八娘荔枝, 67

*Elaphurus* 麋 5, 69 (n. 421)

Elephant, 4, 5, 65

Elixir, Taoist, 71, 99 (n. 602)

Elixir of the Great Returning 大還丹, 99

Embassies, 47, 76; from Silla, 104, from Southern T'ang; to Khitans, 47 (n. 289); *see also* Ambassador, Diplomacy, Envoys, Tribute

Empress, 41, 44, 94; tribute for, 73; *see also* Golden Phoenix, Spring Swallow

Empress Ch'en, *see* Golden Phoenix

Empress Dowager 皇太后, 40, 42

Empress Li 李, *see* Li, Lady *née*, Spring Swallow

"Enduring Spring" Palace, *see* Ch'ang-ch'un Palace

Engineering Commissioner 橋道使, 60

Enveloping Wall 羅城, 6

Envoys, 41, 49, 51, 54, 107; see also Ambassador, Diplomacy, Embassies, Tribute

Erh-shih of Ch'in 秦二世, 19, 20 (n. 133)

*Eriobotrya japonica,* 67

*Essay on the Founding of An-ch'i District in Ch'uan Prefecture* 泉州初建安溪縣記, 5

Estimable Consort 賢妃, 20 (n. 138), 44 (n. 269), 52; *see also* Hsien Fei

Estuary of Fishnets 晉浦, 8

Estuary of White Shrimps 白蝦浦, 8

Eunuchs, vii (n. 2), 20 (n. 139), 42 (n. 260), 43 (n. 267)

Euphemistic title, 37 (n. 227)

Exorcism, 9 (n. 55)

Expenditures, for palace buildings, 83; *see also* P'an Ch'eng-yu, Taxation

Expiation, of sovereign's guilt by subject, 48; *see also* Morality

Fa-yün Temple 法雲寺, 11

Family relationships, morality of, 46

Fan Hui 范暉, 32

Fans, 68

Fealty, to Sovereign, 46 ; *see also* Morality
Fei-chieh Division 飛捷都, 29
Feng-kuo Legate 奉國節度使, 38 (n. 233)
Fennel, 66
Fertility, cult, 101 ; of rice-fields, 70
Festivals, Bacchanalian, 82, 82 (n. 497, 498),
  88 ; Tuan-yang 端陽, 10
*Ficus Wightiana* var. *Japonica* 68
" Field and fallow " taxes, 73
*Fifteen Panegyrics* on the flora of Min 閩中
  草木頌十五首, 4
Fire-arrows, 68
"First-born ", as Taoist title, 98
Fiscal Intendant 國計使, 40, 71, 98
Fish, 65 ; tax on, 73 ; *see also* Sea-food
Five Dynasties 五代, vii–xii, 43 (n. 267),
  44, 47, 63, 70, 76 ; *see also* Later Chin
  dynasty, Later Chou dynasty, Later Liang
  dynasty, Later T'ang dynasty
" Flayer ", 30, 73, 74 ; *see also* Yang Ssu-
  kung
Fleets, 6, 7, 8, 10, 11, 37, 58 ; *see also*
  Naval warfare, Warships
Flower-drums, 69
Flowers, in omen, 108 ; *see also* names of
  individual flowers
Folk songs, 89
Folklore, 102–109 ; *see also* Omen, Spirit
*Fomes japonicus*, 106 ; *see also* Fungus
Foochow fir, 4
Footbinding, early reference, to, 88
Forced labor, 73
Foreign trade, *see* Commerce, Sea voyages,
  Shipping
Francolin 鷓鴣, name of design on tea-
  cups, 86
Frankincense, 66, 66 (n. 384)
Fratricide, justified, 52 ; omen of, 103
Frontier, between Min and Southern Han,
  35
Fruit, 67, 67 (n. 395) ; tax on, 72, 73
Fu 福, Prince of, 40 ; *see also* Wang Chi-
  p'eng
Fu Prefecture 福州, 5, 5 (n. 27), 6, 7, 8,
  9, 10, 11, 11 (n. 66), 12, 14, 28, 29, 29 (n.
  189), 31 (n. 193), 32, 33, 33 (n. 206), 37,
  38, 40, 50, 52, 54, 55, 56, 57, 58, 59,
  60, 61, 62, 64, 64 (n. 377), 65, 66, 66
  (n. 386), 67, 67 (n. 396, 401–2,405–6),
  68, 68 (n. 416), 69, 69 (n. 428–29), 74,
  76, 77, 79 (n. 478), 80, 83, 86, 92, 95,
  101, 107, 109 ; Legate of, 44 (n. 275)
*Fu-chien t'ung-chih* 福建通志, 64, 92, 94, 102,
  114, 119, 120
*Fu-chien wen-hua* 福建文化, 33 (n. 203)
Fu-ch'ing, Princess of 福清公主, 94
Fu-ch'ing 福清 (District), 9, 15 (n. 103), 21
  (n. 147), 82, 101
Fu-i Wang 富義王, 101
Fu-ning 福寧, Metropolitan Prefecture of, 28
Fu-sha 富沙, Prince of, 29, 49 ; *see also* Wang
  Yen-cheng
Fu-ting 福鼎 (District), 102
Fukien, descendants of Min dynasty in
  modern, 60
Fukienese, 5, 48 ; Northern estimate of,
  87 ; a religious people, 90 ; *see also*
  Barbarians
Fungus, purple, 12, 106, 107

Garrison of the South 南鎮軍, 48
Garrotting, 46
Gastropod Peak 螺峯, 99 (n. 603)
" General Lichee " 將軍荔枝, 68
Geography, political, 78 (n. 474)
*Geography, Monograph of* 地理志 (*Han shu*
  漢書), 36 (n. 211)
Ghost, 25 (n. 161) ; of Buddhist priest,
  103 ; of palace girl, 89 ; of Wang Yen-
  chün 王延鈞, 103 ; of Wang Yen-ping 王
  延稟, 21
Ginger, 66
Glass, 68, bowl in grave of Wang Shen-
  chih 王審知 15 ; dishes, 86 ; imported
  vase, 78
*Gleditschia japonica*, 4, 107 (n. 645)
Goddess, Taoist, 95
Gold, 65 ; applique on tent, 82 ; armor of
  deity, 102 ; basin, 107 ; bracelet in grave
  of Wang Shen-chih 王審知 ; dishes of
  imperial guards, 72 ; dust, 65 ; girdles,
  65 ; images of Taoist deities, 71, 99 ;
  lances of guards, 108 ; leaf on palace
  pillars, 81 ; plating on Buddhist images,

92; Sanskrit word for, 94 (n. 574);
supernatural mallet of, 98; vessel, 51,
65; wire on bundles of tea, 86 (n. 525)
Gold Dragon Candles, 86
Golden Millet, image of Buddha of 金粟像,
86
Golden Phoenix 金鳳, 9, 10, 20–22, 21–22
(n. 147), 41, 42, 80, 86–87, 89; see also
Empress
Golden Talisman, Commissioner of 金吾使,
52
Government Councilor 參政事, 43, 100
Governor of Min 知閩國事, 54
Grand Empress Dowager 太皇太后, 44
Grand General of the Yü-lin Army 羽林軍,
61
"Grand Supreme Augustus" 太上皇, 59
(n. 354–55)
Graphs (Chinese characters), divination
based on analysis of, 104; joke based on,
76 (n. 459)
Grave, of Han Wo 韓偓, 84 (n. 512); of
Huang Feng 黃諷, 23; of Huang T'ao 黃
滔, 14, 84 (n. 512); of Liu An-jen 劉安
仁, 84; of Min princess, 67, 84; of
Wang Shen-chih 王審知, 12 (n. 75), 15;
of Wang Yen-cheng 王延政 28; of Yü
Hsing 于兢, 15 (n. 103)
Grave of the Thousand Men 千人塚, 56 (n.
338)
Graves, of followers of Wang Shen-chih
王審知, 15
"Great Benightedness" 大昏 (pseudo-reign
title), 25
Great General of Cavalry 驃騎大將軍, 40
Great Government-General 大都督府, 33
(n. 206)
"Great Offering" 大亨 (name of Army),
43 (n. 264)
"Great Tea" 大茶, 64, 65
Great Yin 大殷, see Yin, Empire of
Gresham's Law, 75
Guard Divisions, 24, 46; see also Ch'en-wei
Division; Fei-chieh Division; Household
Division; Kung-ch'en Division; K'ung-
ho Division; Yüan-tsung Division
Guards, 45 (n. 281), 57, 71, 72, 108; see

also Guard Divisions
Guards of the Six Armies, 43; see also
Controller of Guards of the Six Armies
Guerrilla warfare, 49

Han 漢 dynasty, 36 (n. 221), 68 (n. 417),
81 (n. 491), 82 (n. 497), 98 (n. 594)
Han Hsi-tsai 韓熙載 84, 84 (n. 515)
Han shu 漢書, 36 (n. 221), 68 (n. 417), 95
(n. 575)
Han Wo 韓偓, 3 (n. 7, 8), 4 (n. 10), 22
(n. 147), 34 (n. 207), 84 (n. 512), 85, 88,
95
Han-lin hsüeh-shih 翰林學士, 18
Hang Prefecture 杭州, 78 (n. 468), 96
Hanging, 50
Hao-yüan 浩源 (monk), 106
Harbor, 9, 102, 103; of Lieh 洌, 77
Heaven, imperial sacrifice to, 101; as judge
of kings, 53, 108; as potent over human
events, 91; as sanctioning rule, viii, 96
"Heavenly Imperium" 天霸 (name of
Army), 43 (n. 263)
Heavenly Master, 98, 98 (n. 594, 595)
Heavenly Venerable Ancient Sovereign 天尊
老君, 99; see also Lao-tzu
"Heavenly Virtue" 天德 (reign title), 51
Hegemony, of North China, 61 (n. 365);
see also Five Dynasties
Heir Apparent, appointment of, 82; resi-
dence of, 83
Hemp, sackcloth, 69
Herbs, see Aromatics, Medicines
Hibiscus, 4
Hibiscus mutabilis, 4
Hibiscus syriacus, 4
Hino Kaisaburō 日野開三郎, 63 (n. 373)
"Historical Memoirs" 史記, 36
Historiography, orthodox, 70
Ho Ching-chu 何敬洙, 57
Ho Prefecture 和州, 61
Ho-lung Miao-k'ung 和龍妙空, 96
Ho-lü, King of Wu 吳王闔閭, 80 (n. 488)
Ho-p'u 合浦, 68 (n. 414)
Honey locust, 4
Hopei 河北, 34 (n. 211)
Horn, see Rhinoceros horn

Horse, murder of Wang Yen-hsi 王延羲 while riding, 53 (n. 319), 108; in omen, 108; oracle about "horse year", 105–106; white, 14

Horses, obtained from Khitan, 47 (n. 289)

Hou-kuan 侯官 (District), 8 (n. 47), 11, 12 (n. 75), 15, 23, 28, 35 (n. 216), 80, 85, 99 (n. 603)

*Hou-kuan-hsien hsiang-t'u chih* 侯官縣鄉土志, 60 (n. 359)

*Hou-shan t'an-ts'ung* 後山談叢, 5 (n. 26)

Household Division 親從都, 19; *see also* Yüan-tsung Division

Hsi-yen 西巖 (place), 60 (n. 358)

Hsiang Ssu 項斯, poem of, 99 (n. 602)

Hsieh Pi 謝泌, 90

Hsien Fei 賢妃, title of imperial consort, 20 (n. 138), 24 (n. 155), 27, 42, 95

Hsien of Kuan 管鮮, 52 (n. 316)

Hsin, Prefect of 信州刺史, 40

Hsin Prefecture 信州, 56, 77

Hsing-hua 興化 (District), 79 (n. 478), 84 (n. 512)

Hsing-hua Army 興化軍, 79 (n. 478)

Hsü 徐, adopted surname of Southern T'ang rulers, 60 (n. 355)

Hsü Chih-hao 徐知諤, 41

Hsü Hsüan 徐鉉, 41 (n. 256)

*Hsu Kung tiao-chi wen-chi* 徐公釣磯文集, 89

Hsü Wen-chen 許文稹, 29, 54, 55, 60, 61

Hsü Wen-shen 許文縝, 54 (n. 324)

Hsü Yen 徐彥, 96, 97

Hsü Yin 徐寅, 3 (n. 8), 4 (n. 18), 76 (n. 463), 87 (n. 533), 88, 88 (n. 542), 89, 95, 100 (n. 604)

Hsüan Tsung 玄宗 (Emperor of T'ang 唐), 20 (n. 138), 34 (n. 211)

Hsüan-hsi 玄錫, Taoist title, 97, 97 (n. 587)

*Hsuan-hui* 宣徽, "manifest superbness", 43 (n. 267)

*Hsuan-hui-shih* 宣徽使, 43, 43 (n. 267)

Hsüan-ling 宣陵, 49

Hsüan-miao kuan 玄妙觀, 81 (n. 494)

Hsüeh Chü-cheng 薛居正, x, 107, 107 (n. 646)

Hsüeh Wan-chung 薛萬忠, 48

Hsüeh Wen-chieh, 薛文傑, 18–19, 40, 71, 71 (n. 439), 98, 104

Hu San-hsing 胡三省, 9, 10 (n. 66), 20 (n. 139), 38 (n. 233), 48 (n. 291), 58 (n. 346, 348), 73–74, 76, 97 (n. 586), 107

*Hua-man lu* 畫墁錄, 86 (n. 525)

Huai-an 懷安 (District), 83 (n. 505)

Huai-nan 淮南, 34, 61, 62, 77, 77 (n. 467); *see also* Southern T'ang, Wu (dynasty)

Huai-nan-tzu 淮南子, 97 (n. 587), 99 (n. 602)

Huang 黃, Lady *née*, 18, 40, 42

Huang Ch'ao 黃巢, 31

Huang Ching-chung 黃敬忠, 50, 105

Huang Chün 黃峻, 25, 26, 50

Huang Feng 黃諷, 23

*Huang Hsien-sheng wen-chi* 黃先生文集, 88

Huang Jen-feng 黃仁諷, 29, 57, 58, 59

Huang Na-yü 黃訥裕, 18 (n. 123)

Huang Nieh-p'an 黃涅槃 ("Nirvana"), 96, 96 (n. 582)

Huang Shao-p'o 黃紹頗, 51, 53, 54, 55, 73

Huang T'ao 黃滔, 14, 84 (n. 512), 88, 89, 92

Hui Huang-ti 惠皇帝, 42 (n. 261)

Hui Ti 惠帝, 42 (n. 261)

Hui Tsung 惠宗 (Emperor of Min), 9, 17, 44; *see also* Wang Yen-chün

Hui-leng 慧稜, 85, 93, 95 (n. 577), 96

Hu-nan 湖南, 77 (n. 467); *see also* Ch'u

Hung Prefecture 洪州, 109

I Well 義井, 93

I Shan 懿山, Monk of, 105

I Shan 怡山, 107

I-ts'un 義存 (priest), 95 (n. 577)

"Immaculate Consort" 淑妃, 20 (n. 138); *see also* Shu Fei

Imperial City Commissioner 皇城使, 42

Imperial throne, 44; metaphors for, 98 (n. 594)

Imperial title, Wang Shen-chih's 王審知 rejection of, 70; heavenly support for adoption by Wang Yen-chün 王延鈞, 96, 97; first assumption in Min, 39; assumption by Wang Yen-hsi 王延羲, 50; assumption by Wang Yen-cheng 王延政, 51; *see also* Imperial throne

Imports, 66, 78; *see also* Commerce

Incense, 66 n. 390, 71; *see also* Aromatics

Incest, 21 (n. 144)

"Independent Prince" 自在王, 28

India, 4 (n. 12)

Indonesia, 66, 69 (n. 421), 77; *see also* Sea voyages

Inner Chancellor 內樞密使, 19 (n. 129)

Inscription, on burial tablet, 84; at grave of Hsü Yin 徐夤, 89; mysterious inscription of Wang Pa 王霸, 107; at pagoda, 92; in pagoda of Wang Yen-hsi 王延羲, 94–95

Insurrection, 45, 99, 108; *see also* Rebellion

Intoxication, *see* Wine-drinking

Iron, 69; coins, 74, 75, 75 (n. 456); ease of counterfeiting with, 75; staff, 104

Iron Lion Range 鐵獅嶺, 12

Iron Lion Summit 鐵獅頂, 12

Ivory, 63 (n. 373), 65

Jade, girdle in grave of Wang Shen-chih 王審知, 15

Jao Prefecture 饒州, 61 (n. 362), 77

Jasmine, 66

*Jasminum sambac,* 66

Jasper, dishes, 86

Jehol, 34 (n. 211)

Jen 任, Lady *née*, 12

*Jih-nan* 日南, *see* Champa

Joke, chauvinistic, 76 (n. 459)

Junipers, at dream temple, 85

Kai-chu 蓋竹 (place), 56

K'ai Yüan Temple 開元寺, 92, 92 (n. 560)

K'ai-feng 開封, 41 (n. 254), 65, 70, 76

"K'ai-Min Wangs" 開閩王, 60

*K'ai-yüan t'ung-pao* 開元通寶, 74

Kanaka-cakra-rāja Buddha 金輪王佛, 94, 94 (n. 573)

*Kan-lu t'ang* 甘露堂, 83

K'ang Tsung 康宗 (Emperor of Min), 47; *see also* Wang Chi-p'eng

*K'ang-hsi tzu-tien* 康熙字典, 25 (n. 163)

Kao-t'ing Mountain 高亭山, 83

Kao-t'ing Palace 高亭宮, 83

*Karma,* 91

Keeper of the Seal [門下] 侍中, 33, 55

Khitans 契丹, 44 (n. 271), 47 (n. 289), 61 (n. 365); Emperor of, 41 (n. 254)

Kiangsi 江西, *see* Chiang-hsi

King (title), 17, 28; of Great Min, 36; of Min, 45, 45 (n. 277), 46, 46 (n. 284), 49, 55, 76; of Min-yüeh 閩越, 36; tokens of, 106; Wang family destined to be, 91; word for, 107 (n. 644)

King Wu-chu of Min-yüeh 閩越王無諸, *see* Wu-chu

Kingdom, 36, 46

Kingship, magical essence of, 104; *see also* Imperial title

*Ko* 葛, *see* Pueraria

Korea, 44 (n. 271)

Koryŏ 高麗, 44 (n. 271)

Ku-shih 固始, 13, 14, 31

Ku-t'ien 古田 (District), 54

*Kuan-ch'a-shih* 觀察使, 32 (n. 196)

Kuang Prefecture 光州, 13, 31, 58

Kuang Prefecture 廣州, *see* Canton

*Kuang-chi yüan* 廣濟院, 56 (n. 338)

Kuang-shan 光山, 13; *see also* Kuang Prefecture

*Kuang-wei chen-yüan chiang-chün* 光威振遠將軍, 101

Kuei Fei 貴妃, title of Imperial consort, 20 (n. 138)

Kuei Shou-ming 歸守明, 21, 42

Kuei-hua 歸化 (District), 79 (n. 478)

Kumquat, 67

Kung Ch'eng-shu 龔澄樞, 20 (n. 139)

Kung-ch'en Division 拱宸都, 24, 43 (n. 264), 52 (n. 318), 53

K'ung-ho Division 控鶴都, 24, 52 (n. 318)

Kuo Chung-shu 郭忠恕, viii

Kuo Yü-lin 郭毓麟, 33 (n. 203)

*Kuo-chi-shih* 國計使, 19

Kuwabara Jitsuzō 桑原隲藏, 41 (n. 254)

Kwangsi 廣西, *see* Southern Han

Kwangtung 廣東, 4, 66 (n. 392), 67, 84; *see also* Southern Han

Kweichou 貴州, 66, 68 (n. 416)

*Lagerstroemia indica,* 81 (n. 491)

Lai Prefecture 萊州, 76, 77

Landscape Aromatic 山水香, 98 (n. 594)

Lang-yeh, Prince of 瑯邪王, 33, 37, 84, 92

*Lang-yeh-chun-wang Wang Shen-chih shen-tao pei* 瑯琊郡王王審知神道碑, 15 (n. 100)

Lao-tzu 老子, image of, 71, 99

Later Chin 後晉 dynasty, 24, 41 (n. 256), 44, 44 (n. 271), 45, 45 (n. 277, 278), 46 (n. 284), 47, 48, 49, 54, 55, 58, 58 (n. 349), 59, 61, 61 (n. 365), 62, 64, 76, 107

Later Chou 後周 dynasty, 29, 62, 76

Later Liang 後梁 dynasty, vii, 16, 33, 33 (n. 206), 34, 34 (n. 211), 35, 71, 74, 76, 76 (n. 463), 77, 77 (n. 467), 100

Later T'ang 後唐 dynasty, 20 (n. 133), 24 (n. 158), 35, 35 (n. 214), 36, 37, 38, 38 (n. 233), 39, 39 (n. 244, 246), 40, 41 (n. 256), 42, 44, 101

Lead, coins, 74, 75 ; as meaning of " black tin ", 97 (n. 587)

Leather boots, 69

Legate 節度使 (title), vii, 28, 29, 32, 33, 34, 36, 37, 37 (n. 232), 38 (n. 233), 42, 44, 44 (n. 275), 46, 49, 50, 54, 60 (n. 355), 61 (n. 361), 62, 92

Legitimacy, of imperial rule, viii, i70 ; *see also* Confucianism, Imperial title

Lessing, F. D., 94 (n. 574)

Letters of appointment, 51

Li 李, Lady *née* (daughter of Li Chen 李眞, consort of Wang Yen-hsi 王延義), 27, 52–53, 94

Li 李, Lady *née* (daughter of Li Min 李敏, first wife of Wang Chi-p'eng 王繼鵬), 44

Li 李, Lady *née* (sister of Li Fang 李倣, consort of Wang Chi-p'eng 王繼鵬), *see* Spring Swallow

Li 李, surname of Southern T'ang 南唐 rulers, 60 (n. 355)

Li Chen 李眞, 27, 47, 52, 95

Li Chien-ch'eng 李建成 (brother of T'ang T'ai Tsung 唐太宗), 52 (n. 316)

Li Chun 李準, 26 (n. 172)

Li Fang 李倣, 8, 21, 22, (n. 147), 42, 43

Li Hung-i 李弘義, *see* Li Jen-ta

Li Hung-ta 李弘達, *see* Li Jen-ta

Li Jen-ta 李仁達, 8, 12, 13, 27, 29, 57–60, 59–60 (n. 355), 61, 62, 95, 108

Li Jen-yü 李仁遇, 51

Li Ju-yün 李儒贇, *see* Li Jen-ta

Li K'o-yin 李可殷, 21, 42, 82

Li Kuang-chun 李光準, 26, 51, 56,

Li Min 李敏, 39, 39 (n. 244), 44, 50, 51

Li Shih-chen 李時珍, 4, 66 (n. 390), 68 (n. 415), 97 (n. 587)

Li ta 李達, *see* Li Jen-ta

Li T'ing-o 李廷鍔, 55

Li Yen-hao 李延皓, 43

Li Yüan-chi 李元吉 (brother of T'ang T'ai Tsung 唐太宗), 52 (n. 316)

Liang, Lady of State of 梁國夫人, 44 ; *see also* Li 李, Lady *née* (daughter of Li Min)

Liang 梁 dynasty, 107 (n. 646) ; *see also* Later Liang dynasty

Liao Yen-jo 廖彦若, 32

Lichee, 3, 67, 67 (n. 407), 68

Lieh, Harbor of 洌港, 77, 77 (n. 465)

Lien Chung-yü 連重遇, 25, 27, 29, 46, 47, 52, 53, 56, 56 (n. 341), 80, 89, 108

Lien-chiang 連江 (District), 65

Lin En 林恩, 47

Lin Hsing 林興, 45, 47, 96, 98, 99, 108

Lin Hsing-tsou 林省鄒, 45 (n. 278), 93

Lin Jen-han 林仁翰, 56, 56 (n. 341), 57

Lin Shou-liang 林守亮, 50, 55

Lin T'ung-ying 林同穎, 94 (n. 572)

Lin Yen-yü 林延禺, 42 (n. 260)

Lin-ching kuan 臨津館, 33 (n. 206)

Lin-hai Commandery 臨海郡, 45 (n. 277)

Ling-hsiu Mountain 靈秀山, 28

Lingnan 嶺南, *see* Kwangtung

Lip rouge, 66 (n. 385, 390) ; *see also* Cosmetics

Literati, 45, 83, 87, 88 ; *see also* Confucianism, Scholars

Literature, 87–89 ; *see also* Poems

Liu An-jen 劉安仁, 84

Liu Chen-ling 柳眞齡, 104

Liu Hsin 劉信, 77 (n. 467)

Liu Hsing-ch'üan 劉行全, 101 ; *see also* Ch'ung-shun Wang

Liu I 劉乙, 24, 45 (n. 78)

Liu Shan-fu 劉山甫, 89, 103

Liu Ts'ung-hsiao 留從效, 11, 54, 54 (n. 330), 55, 55 (n. 333), 56 (n. 338), 61–62, (61 n. 361), 76, 96, 105

Liu Yen 劉巖, 20, 34, 34 (n. 209), 35

Liu Yin 劉隱, 33 (n. 206)

Liu Yung 柳邕, 36

*Liu-hou* 留後, 32 (n. 197)

Lo Feng 螺峯 (Mountain), 99, 99 (n. 603)

*lo-ch'eng* 羅城, 6, 80

*Lo-chung chi-i* 洛中紀異, 47 (n. 289)

Lo-han Temple 羅漢寺, 85

*Lo-yang ch'ieh-lan chi* 洛陽伽藍記, 11 (n. 72)

Long River 長江, 77 ; *see also* Yangtze River

Longan 龍眼, 67

Loquat, 67

Lotus, 4

Lotus Flower Peak 蓮華峯, 12 (n. 75), 15, 28

Lotus Sutra 法華經, 100 (n. 604), 103

Lou Ts'ung-hsiao 婁從敩, 54 (n. 330) ; *see also* Liu Ts'ung-hsiao

Loyalty, to emperor, 60, 103 ; to T'ang dynasty, 15 ; *see also* Morality

Lu, Grand Lady of 魯國太夫人, 40

Lu Chin 盧進, 54

Lu Prefecture 廬州, 77

Lu Sun 盧損, 24, 45, 45 (n. 278)

Lump-tea 團茶, 65, 65 (n. 381), 86 (n. 525)

*Lun yü* 論語, 24 (n. 158)

Lung-ch'i 龍溪 (District), 83

Lung-hsing Temple 龍興寺, 85

Lung-jen 隆仁 (Village), 82 (n. 502)

*Lung-nao* 龍腦, 4, 16

Lung-yao Mountain 龍腰山, 99 (n. 603)

Lung-yüeh Palace 龍躍宮, 81

Luxury goods, 65, 68, 78


Ma Ling 馬令, xi, 84

Ma Yin 馬殷, 39

Mad Monk of Chien Prefecture, 108–109

Madder, for dying silk, 69

Magical, staff, 104 ; swords, 103–104 ; *see also* Shamans, Spirit

Magnolia, 4

Manchuria, 47 (n. 289)

Manichaean Temple, 102

Manjusri, 12 ; Close of 文殊院, 92 ; Terrace of 文殊臺, 12

Marines, 11, 51, 61 ; *see also* Naval Warfare

Market of Wu-chu 無諸市, 9

Marriage, alliance by, 52 ; royal, 34, 84

Maspero, G., 78 (n. 474)

Master Kuei 歸郎, 21

Medicines, 63, 64, 66, 68, 68 (n. 415, 416)

Memorial, from Min to Chin 晉, 45

Memorial Transmission Officer 進奏官, 47

*Men-hsia shih-chung* 門下侍中, 33 (n. 205a)

Merchants, 65, 76 (n. 459) ; foreign, 78 ; tax on, 72 ; travel in China, 76 ; *see also* Commerce, Sea voyages

Metaphors, for imperial throne, 98 (n. 594)

Metaphysical beliefs, in tenth century Fukien, 91

Miao-ying Ta-shih 妙應大師, 96

Military heroes, deification of, 101

Min, August of Great, 50 ; cause of downfall, 74 ; destined rise of, 107 ; Empire of Great, 39 ; end of dynasty, 60 ; final partition, 62 ; founding of, 53 ; Governor of, 54 ; guardian stars of, 95 (n. 575) ; name on coins, 74 ; Prince of, 33 ; reestablished by Wang Yen-cheng 王延政 ; *see also* King of Min, Prince of Min

Min 閩 (District), 8 (n. 47), 9, 12, 83, 93, 100

Min River 閩江, 6, 7, 10, 38

*Min tu chi* 閩都記, 6 (n. 29, 31), 7, 9, 15 (n. 102), 81 (n. 492)

*Min-chiang chu-shui pien* 閩江諸水編, 7 (n. 37)

Min-ch'ing 閩清 (District), 101

Min-chung Commandery 閩中郡, 36 (n. 211)

*Min-hou hsien-chih* 閩侯縣志, 43 (n. 263), 85 (n. 519), 92 (n. 561), 107 (n. 646)

*Min-hsien hsiang-t'u chih* 閩縣鄉土志, 7 (n. 37), 60 (n. 359)

Min-yüeh 閩越, 36, 36 (n. 221), 92 (n. 558), 101

Minerals, *see* Amber, Cinnabar, Copper, Gold, Iron, Jade, Lead, Salt, Silver, Stone

Ming 明 dynasty, 14, 77 (n. 465), 98 (n. 594)

*Ming i-t'ung chih* 明一統志 9 (n. 54)

Ming Prefecture 明州, 77, 77 (n. 465), 78 (n. 468)

Ming Tsung 明宗 (Emperor of Later T'ang

後唐), 20 (n. 133), 36
Ming Wei Pavilion 明威殿, 81
Minister of State 尚書令, 39, 39 (n. 244), 51
Mirror, inscribed, 84; as Taoist symbol, 97 (n. 587)
Miyasaki Ichisada 宮崎市定, 79 (n. 452a)
Mo-hsiao Peak 摩霄峯, 102
*Mo-ni* 摩尼, Sanskrit " pearl ", 102 (n. 616)
*Mogera wogura,* 68
Mole skins, 68
Mollusc, operculum as source of aromatic, 66, 66 (n. 390)
Monk of the Shattered Stone 碎石僧, 104
Monkey, 4
Monopolies (salt and iron), 15; *see also* Commissioner of Salt and Iron, Iron, Salt
Moon, Goddess of, 95
Morality, traditional, 45 (n. 278), 46, 59, 70, 92; *see also* Virtue
*Moschus chinloo,* 5
Mound, burial, 84; *see also* Graves
Mountain, of the, Five Terraces 五臺山, 12; of Grand Tranquillity 太平山, 17; of the Horse-herds 馬牧山, 7; of the Jade Maiden 玉女山 12; of Kings' Graves, 王墓山, 28; sacred, 9; spirits, 109 (n. 655)
Mountains of the King of Yüeh 越王山, 7 (n. 41)
Mourning, 42 (n. 260)
Murder, see Assassination
*Musa coccinea,* 67 (n. 396)
Music, 22 (n. 147), 86–87; in Taoist temples, 99
Musk-deer, 5, 69 (n. 421)
Mussels, 65
*Myrica rubra,* 4

Nageśvara Buddha 龍自在佛, 95
Name, of Min princess given to lichee, 67; of ruling family as omen, 75, 109
Names, personal, changes of, 39, 42, 60 (n. 355), 61, 61 (n. 363–65), 62, 62 (n. 368); variant writings of, 58 (n. 348), 63 (n. 373)
Nan Prefecture 南州, 62 (n. 366); *see also* Chang Prefecture
*Nan T'ang shu* 南唐書, xi, 84, 120
Nan-an 南安 (District), 14, 16 (n. 105), 18, 32, 83, 84, 85
*Nan-chiao* 南郊 sacrifice, 101
Nan-chien Prefecture 南劍州, 64 (n. 377), 66, 67 (n. 403), 69 (n. 427), 79 (n. 474)
*Nan-chou i-wu chih* 南州異物志, 66 (n. 390)
Nan-p'ing, Prince of 南平王, 33 (n. 206)
Nan-t'ai 南臺 (District), 33 (n. 206)
Nan-t'ai River 南臺江, 7
Nan-yüeh 南越, 36 (n. 211); *see also* Annam
Nanmu 楠 [木] (wood), 81
" National Patriarch " 國翁, 23, 43 (n. 267)
Naval warfare, 7, 38, 61, 68 (n. 417); *see also* Commander of Galleons, Fleets, Warships
*Nephelium longana,* 67
New Year's, Day, 41; Night, 82
Nine Dragon Pavilion 九龍殿, 26, 82, 108; *see also* Nine Dragon Tent
Nine Dragon Tent, 21, 42, 82
Ning-hua 寧化 (District), 63
Ningpo 寧波, 77 (n. 465); *see also* Ming Prefecture
" Nirvana " 涅槃, name of priest, 96
" Noble Consort " 貴妃, 20 (n. 138)
North Gate, 6, 8
Northern Capital, see Chien Prefecture; *see also* Southern Capital
Northern Palace, 25, 46, 82, 108
Northern Park 北苑, 64
Northern Temple 北廟, 97
Nutmeg, 66

Oath, of allegiance, 28; of brotherhood sealed in blood, 103; to build pagoda, 92
Observator 觀察使, 32 (n. 196), 87
Ocean-going ships, 68; *see also* Ships
Ochre robe (of investiture), 45
Offices, sale of, 72, 73
Oil, for ships' bottoms, 67
Omen, of death of Wang Yen-ping 土處景, 103; of death, 104; dragon, 97; invasion of Wu-yüeh 吳越, 86; of rise, duration and fall of Min Empire, 105–109

Oolong tea, 64

Oracles, 45, 99; *see also* Prophecy

Orchid, 4

Ou-yang Hsiu 歐陽修, x, 107 (n. 646)

Overland travel, within China, 76, 77

" Overseer of All Military Affairs in the Southern Capital " 都督南都內外諸軍事, 57

" Ox-drink ", 26

Oysters, 65

Pacification Commissioner of Chiang-hsi 江西安撫使, 56

*Paeonia albiflora*, 3

*Paeonia moutan*, 3

Pagoda, of Wang Shen-chih 王審知, 92; of Wang Yen-hsi 王延義, 50 (n. 301), 94–95, 114

Pagoda tree, 3

Pagodas, 90

Paikche, 44 (n. 271)

Painting, viii; skill of singing girls from North China, 87; on Buddhist images, 93

Palace Commissioner 宮使, 20, 20 (n. 139)

Palace of the Dragon's Prance 龍躍宮, 106; *see also* Dragon Disclosure

Palace of Enduring Spring 長春宮, 22 (n. 147); *see also* Ch'ang-ch'un Palace, Southern Palace

Palace of Precious August, Commissioner to 寶皇宮使, 98; *see also* Pao-huang Palace, Precious August

Palace of Purple Sublety 紫微宮, 81 (n. 491)

Palace officials, 43 (n. 267)

Palace Parks, Commissioner of, 宮苑使, 94

Palaces, 80–81, 83

P'an Ch'eng-yu 潘承祐, 29, 50, 51, 52, 73, 83

P'an Shih-k'uei 潘師逵, 48, 49

Pao Hung-shih 包洪實, 51

Pao Ssu-jun 鮑思潤, 53

Pao-en ting-kuang to-pao Pagoda 報恩定光多寶塔, 92

*Pao-hua Yüan* 寶華院, 86

Pao-huang Palace 寶皇宮, 81, 96–97, 99, 106, 107; *see also* Precious August

Pao-kuo Close 報國院, 67

Paper, glossy, 69

" Parched aromatic " 煎香, 66

Partition, of Min, 62

Patent of investiture, 45

" Patriotic and Estimable Prince " 忠懿王, 35

Paulownia, 3

Pavilion of the Great Bacchanal 大酺殿, 21, 88; *see also* Ta-p'u Pavilion

Pavi lions, 81–82

Peach, 3

Peach Forest, 3 (n. 7); Village 桃林里, 106

Peach-branch Lake 桃枝湖, 101

Pearls, 68, 68 (n. 414), 81

Peasants, disaffection of, 60 (n. 358)

*Pei shih* 北史, 43 (n. 267)

P'ei Chieh 裴傑, 39

Pelliot, P., 102 (n. 616)

*Pen-ts'ao yen-i* 本草衍義, 66 (n. 390)

P'eng 蓬, Islands of, 95

Peony 牡丹, 3; herbaceous 芍藥, 3

Pepper, 66

" Perpetual Accord " 永和 (reign title), 41

" Perpetual Eminence " 永隆 (reign title) 25

Persecution, of Buddhism, 92

Personal names, taboo on, 62 (n. 366); *see also* Names

Phoenix Mountain 鳳凰山, 64

Phoenix Pond Mountain 鳳池山, 12

" Phoenix Tea " 鳳茶 64 (n. 377), 65, 65 (n. 381)

Physiognomy, physiognomizing, 14, 14 (n. 91), 95, 104, 105

Pien Hao 邊鎬, 56, 60

Pien Prefecture 汴州, 24 (n. 158)

Pilon, Ch., viii

Pine-nuts, 67

*P'ing-chou k'o-t'an* 萍洲可談, 78 (n. 468)

P'ing-lu Legate 平盧節度使, 34

Pistachio, 99

Plague, in Southern T'ang 南唐, 54

Pleasure boats, 10, 22 (n. 147), 87

Plum, 3; red, 3

Po Chü-i 白居易, 89

*Po-chu-pu* 白苧布, 69

Po-lung Temple 白龍寺, 99

Poems, of Golden Phoenix 金鳳, 22 (n. 147), 89; of Han Wo 韓偓, 3 (n. 8), 4 (n. 10), 88; of Hsü Yin 徐寅, 3 (n. 8, 9), 4 (n. 18), 89, 100 (n. 604); of Liu I 劉乙, 24 (n. 157); of Su Shih 蘇軾, 104; of Wang Chi-p'eng 王繼鵬, 44, 89

Poet, the Priest Hui-leng 慧稜 as, 85

Poets, ix, 88–89; see also Poems

Poisoning, 50

Police, see Commissioner of Police

Politics, role of omens on, 109; see also Omens

Poll tax, 72, 74

Pongee, 69

Population, of Fukien, 79

Pork, tax on, 72

Porphyra tenera, 67 (n. 398)

Portrait, of Wang Shen-chih 王審知, 15; self-portraits of singing girls, 86

Ports, 77, 78 (n. 468); see also Harbor, Sea voyages, Shipping

Posthumous titles, 42, 101

Pottery, Buddhist images, 93; kiln near Fu Prefecture 福州, 86; tea-cups, 86

Prabhūta-ratna Buddha 多寶佛, 94

Precious August 寶皇 (Taoist divinity), 71, 97, 99; see also Pao-huang Palace

Priests, grants of rice-fields to, 70

Prime Marshal of Cavalry 兵馬元帥, 50

Prince 王, of Ch'ang-lo 長樂, 50; of Chien 建 43; of Fan-yang 郢陽, 28; of Fu 福, 40; of Fu-sha 富沙, 29, 49; of Kuang-shan 光山, 28; of Lang-yeh 瑯邪, 33, 37, 84, 92; of Lin-hai Commander 臨海郡, 45 (n. 277); of Lu 漉, 44; of Min 閩, 33, 33 (n. 206), 34, 35, 37, 45 (n. 277), 50, 94; of Nan-p'ing 南平, 33 (n. 206); of Wu-yüeh 吳越, 33 (n. 206), 34; "Patriotic and Estimable" 忠懿, 35, 35 (n. 216); "Radiantly Martial" 昭武, 36

Private armies, 45; see also Bodyguards

Privy, as asylum, 25

Prophecy, 40, 97, 104, 107; see also Omens

Prose, 89

P'u an 普安 (District), 68 (n. 416)

P'u-ch'eng 浦城 (District), 40

P'u-t'ien 莆田 (District), 79 (n. 478), 88, 89

P'u-yang Huang Yü-shih chi 莆陽黃御史集, 88

Pueraria 葛, 63, 63 (n. 373), 64, 69

Pun, 44; as omen, 109; see also Graphs, Names

Purple, as Taoist Color, 98 (n. 594); as auspicious color, see Fungus; see also Tzu-wei Palace

Pyrus spectabilis, 4

Python bile, 68

Pythons, 68 (n. 416)

Quince, 67

"Radiantly Martial Prince" 昭武王, 36

"Radiantly Martial Emperor" 昭武皇帝, 53

"Radiantly Martial Filial Emperor", 昭武孝皇帝, 39

Rainbow, meaning of in omen, 108 (n. 647); portentious dragon of, 106, 108

Ramie, 69, 69 (n. 427)

Rattan, 68

Rebellion, 19, 35, 40, 44, 46, 55, 61, 71; accusation of, 48, 98; see also Insurrection

Recorder of Military and State Business 錄軍國事, 51

Red, color of auspicious serpent, 108; color of "rainbow-dragon", 106; symbol of blood, 107 (n. 641)

Red Range 赤嶺, 57, 58 (n. 346)

Refugees, from T'ang 唐, 13, 83, 85, 87; see also Literati

Regent 監國, 42

Regicide, 19; justification of, 27; see also Assassination

Remonstrator 諫議大夫, 23, 25–26, 48 (n. 290), 53

Retired Emperors, 59 (n. 354)

Reign titles 年號, 25, 36, 39, 41, 44, 44 (n. 271), 46, 46 (n. 284), 54, 55 (n. 337), 58, 58 (n. 349), 59, 82, 85 (n. 521)

Rhinoceros horn, 63 (n. 373), 65

Rice, 69, 70; double harvest of, 90; prayers for, 101; supernatural damage to crop, 106; tax on, 73

Ritual, cannibalistic, 41 (n. 254), 60 (n.

356)

River, *see* Min River

Robe of investiture, 45, 53

Rose, 3, 4, 4 (n. 10)

Rotours, des, 32 (n. 196)

Rouge Mountain 胭脂山, 15 (n. 102)

*Rubia cordifolia*, 69

Sackcloth, 69

Sacred mountain, terrace as, 9 ; Eastern 東嶽, 81

Sacrifice, to Heaven, 101 ; to sea spirits, 103

Safflower, 66

*Salanx microdon*, 65

*Salix babylonica*, 3

Salt, 63, 65, 73

*Samsara*, 91

*San Ch'in chi* 三秦記, 81 (n. 491)

*San-shan chih* 三山志, 94 (n. 573)

Sandal, 66 (n. 390) ; *see also* Sandalwood

Sandalwood, 3, 81 ; *see also* Sandal

*Santalum album*, 3

Scholars, refugee, 13, 15, 83, 85, 87 ; *see also* Literati

Schools, established in 8th century, 87

Screen, of crystal, 22 (n. 147) ; of pearl, 81

Scriptures, *see* Sutras

Sculpture, 12, 12 (n. 78), 85, 86, 91, 92, 93 ; gold images of deities, 71, 99

Sea Gate 海門, 9

Sea route, to Shantung 山東, 76–77 ; *see also* Commerce, Sea voyages

Sea spirits, 103

Sea voyages, 34, 71, 76, 77 ; *see also* Commerce

Sea-food, 63, 65

Seal, of prefectural government, 55

Secretary of State 中書令, 33 (n. 206), 37, 39 (n. 245), 49, 50

"Secretary's Temple" 侍郎廟, 18 (n. 126)

Seers of Auras 望氣者, 108 ; *see also* Diviner, Omen

Serpent, omen of kingship, 108 ; in popular lore, 109 (n. 655)

Sha 沙 (District), 4 (n. 10), 79 (n. 478), 93 (n. 568)

Shakyamuni (Buddha), 92, 95

Shamans, 41 (n. 255), 45, 47, 96–99, 108

Shan-hua Gate, 善化門, 7

Shang 商, dynastic title as substitute for Yin 殷, 28 (n. 182)

Shang 尚, Lady *née*, 27, 52, 95

Shang Pao-yin 尚保殷, 52

Shang-kuan 上官, Lady *née*, concubine of Wang Yen-hsi 王延羲, 82, 108

Shang-lan 上藍 (monk), 109, 109 (n. 654)

*Shang-lin fu* 上林賦, 67

Shantung 山東, 34 (n. 211), 76

Shao-wu 邵武, 56, 79 (n. 478), 84 ; Army, 79 (n. 478)

Shark-skins, 68

Shellfish, 65

Shen 沈 (surname), taboo on in Fukien, 51 (n. 307)

Shen-kuang Temple 神光寺, 95

Sheng Mountain 昇山, 101

Sheng T'ao 盛韜, 41 (n. 255), 96, 98

*Shih chi* 史記, 82 (n. 497)

Shih Ssu-ming 史思明, 79 (n. 482)

Shih Tsung 世宗 (Emperor of Later Chou 後周), 29, 62, 76

*Shih-kuo ch'un-ch'iu* 十国春秋, xi, xii, 119

Shipbuilding, 68, 78 ; *see also* Sea voyages

Shipping, hazards to, 9, 103 ; *see also* Commerce

Ships, 67, 68 (n. 417) ; of "Southern Outlanders", 78

Shou Prefecture 壽州, 77

Shou-ning 壽寧 (District), 28

Shrine of Prefect Wang 王刺史祠, 14 (n. 88)

Shu 蜀 (dynasty), ix, 87

Shu Fei 淑妃 (title of Imperial consort), 20, 23–24, 24 (n. 155)

Shu Prefecture 舒州, 77

*Shu-i chi* 述異記, 80 (n. 488)

*Shu-mi-shih* 樞密使, 43 (n. 267) ; *see also* Chancellor

Shui-ching Palace 水晶宮, 80, 80 (n. 488), 82 ; *see also* Crystal Palace

Shun-ch'ang, Princess of 順昌公主, 94

Shun-ch'ang 順昌 Village, 18, 49

Sickness, as sent by gods, 98

Silla 新羅, 44 (n. 271), 103, 104

Silk cloth, 69; worn by imperial guards, 71

Silver, 63, 63 (n. 373); girdles of guards, 71; wine cups of, 26 (n. 170), 84

"Silver fish" 銀魚, 65

Singing, 86–87

Singing girls, of Han Hsi-tsai 韓熙載, 84; of Wang Yen-pin 王延彬, 87

"Single-eyed Dragon" 獨眼龍, 18

Six Armies 六軍, 43 (n. 263)

Sixty, prophesied length of Yen-chün's 延鈞 rule, 97

Slaves, female, 28

Smelted Cinnabar Well 鍊丹井, 107

Smoke, omen of, 108

Snowy Peak 雪峯, 10, 12, 95, 95 (n. 577)

Son of Heaven, 17, 43 (n. 263), 97; fealty to, 46

*Sophora japonica*, 3

*Sou shen chi* 搜神記, 4

South China, destiny of in stars, 95 (n. 575)

South China Sea, 77

South Gate 南門, 8

South Lake 南池, 10

South-facing, reference to Emperor, 109

Southeast Asia, 65

Southern Capital 南都, 29, 57, 58; see also Fu Prefecture

Southern Han 南漢, 5, 20, 20 (n. 139), 34, 34 (n. 209), 35, 42 (n. 260), 68 (n. 414), 78, 78 (n. 474), 84

"Southern Outlanders" 蠻, 78

Southern Palace 南宮, 80, 82, 108; see also Ch'ang-ch'un Palace

Southern T'ang 南唐, xi, 7, 8, 16, 22, 28, 29, 29 (n. 189), 30, 41 (n. 256), 49, 49 (n. 293), 52, 54, 56, 57, 57 (n. 342, 344), 58, 59, 60, 60 (n. 355), 61, 61 (n. 365), 62, 74, 76, 84, 87, 108

Sparrow, as symbol of life of Wang Yen-pin 王延彬, 106

Spices, *see* Aromatics

Spies, 35, 44, 48, 76

Spirit, evil, 17, 103; in an iron staff, 104; in a sword, 104-105; mountain, 109 (n. 655); see also Dragon, Ghost, Omen

Spring Swallow 春燕, 21, 22 (n. 147), 42, 43, 44, 81, 99 (n. 602)

Spring Warbler 春鶯, 26

*Ssu-k'ung* 司空, 14, 47

Ssu-ma Ch'ien 司馬遷, 36

Ssu-ma Hsiang-ju 司馬相如, 67

Ssu-ma Kuang 司馬光, xi, 47 (n. 289), 74, 107 (n. 646)

*Ssu-pu-hsiang* 四不像, 5

Staff, magical, 104

"Stalactite tea" 石乳茶, 64

Steles, 85; see also Inscription, Tablet

Sterculia Range 梧桐嶺, 8

Stipends, to army, 55; see also Donatives

Stone, pagoda of Wang Yen-hsi, 94 (n. 573); smoke from, 108

Strategist, 56, 57; see also Wang Hsün, Yang Ssu-kung

Stream of Mulberries of Lustration 楔桑溪, 9, 22 (n. 147)

Su Shih 蘇軾, 104

Suburb, Altar to Heaven in, 101

Sugar, refined, 69

Sugar cane, 67

Sui 隋 dynasty, 20 (n. 138)

Sung 宋 dynasty, viii, 14 (n. 88), 16, 28, 55 (n. 333), 62, 64, 68 (n. 413), 78 (n. 473), 79, 79 (n. 478), 83, 84, 90, 91, 93; historiography, 70; sea-ports of, 78 (n. 468); topography, 6

*Sung History* 宋史, 63, 65, 70, 120

*Sung Kao-seng chuan* 宋高僧傳, 96

*Sung shih* 宋史, see *Sung History*

Superior Army Commissioner 上軍使, 40

Supernatural, *see* Dragon, Ghost, Omen, Spirit, Taoism

Su-t'ien Village 蘇田里, 15, (n. 103)

Sutras, 91, 100 (n. 604); collections, 93, 93 (n. 567)

Sweet flag, 1

Sweet Pear Harbor 甘棠港, 9

Sword, magic, 103–104

*Synchronismes Chinois*, 57 (n. 342)

Ta-liang 大梁, 47, 107; see also K'ai-feng

Ta-lo 大羅, Taoist Heaven, 97

Ta-ming Palace 大明宮, 81

Ta-p'u Pavilion 大酺殿, 81, 82; see also

Pavilion of the Great Bacchanal

Ta-tse Temple 大澤寺, 101

Ta-yün Temple 大雲寺, 92 (n. 560)

Tablet of Virtuous Government 德政碑, 15 (n. 99), 35 (n. 216)

Taboo, on father's name, 62 (n. 366); on gathering a vegetable, 67 (n. 398)

Taboo Rock 禁石, 67 (n. 398)

T'ai Prefecture 台州, 77

T'ai Tsu 太祖 (of Min), 39, 53; see also Wang Shen-chih

T'ai Tsung 太宗 (of T'ang 唐), 39 (n. 244), 52 (n. 316)

T'ai Tsung 太宗 (spurious title of Wang Yen-chün 王延鈞 of Min), 42 (n. 261)

T'ai-mu Mountain 太姥山, 102

T'ai-p'ing hsing-kuo Temple 太平興國寺, 93

T'ai-p'ing huan-yu chi 太平寰宇記, 63 (n. 377)

T'ai-shan miao 泰山廟, 81

T'ai-tzu t'ai-fu 太子太傅, 47

Talisman, Taoist, 95, 97

Tamarisk, 4

Tamarix chinensis, 4

T'an Ch'üan-po 譚全播, 77 (n. 467)

T'an Prefecture 鐔州, 51, 60, 60 (n. 358)

T'an Tzu-hsiao 譚紫霄, 98, 98 (n. 594), 99 (n. 602)

T'ang 唐, as surname, 16

T'ang 唐 dynasty (618–907), vii, 15, 16, 18 (n. 119), 20 (n. 138), 24 (n. 158), 32, 33, 34 (n. 211), 39 (n. 244), 43 (n. 267), 70, 74, 77, 78 (n. 474), 79, 79 (n. 476, 477, 478), 82 (n. 498), 83, 87, 87 (n. 533), 88, 92, 94; see also Later T'ang dynasty, Southern T'ang

T'ang History 唐書, 69; see also T'ang shu

T'ang shu 唐書, vii (n. 1), 43 (n. 267), 65, 79 (n. 476), 87, 88, 120

Tao 道, and Wang Yen-chün 王延鈞, 97

T'ao Hung-ching 陶弘景, 68 (n. 416)

T'ao Ku 陶穀, 67

T'ao Yüeh 陶岳, 35 (n. 218), 107

Taoism, Taoist, 12, 23, 35, 39, 47, 102 (n. 616), 81 (n. 491), 91, 93, 96–100; allusions in Buddhist inscription, 95; crane

as symbol in, 24 (n. 158); immortals, 66 (n. 393), 95, 97; recluse as ancestor of Wang 王 family, 107; rice-fields granted to temples, 70; support of by Wang Chi-p'eng 王繼鵬, 71; see also Ch'en Shou-yüan, Hsü Yen, Lin Hsing, Sheng T'ao, T'an Tzu-hsiao

Tax, on Commerce, 64; see also Tribute

Taxation, 58 (n. 346), 60 (n. 358), 70–74, 94; see also Expenditures, Yang Ssu-kung

Tchang, M., 57 (n. 342)

Te Fei 德妃, title of Imperial consort, 20 (n. 138)

Te-hua 德化 (District), 79 (n. 478)

Tea, 63, 63 (n. 373), 64, 64 (n. 377), 86 (n. 525)

Tea Mountain 茶山, 10

"Tea tasters" 試茶家, 86

"Tea-grease" 茶膏, 86 (n. 525)

Temple, names for Manichaean, 102 (n. 616); of the Five Hundred Arhats 五百羅漢寺, 85 (n. 519); of the Great Prince West of the River 水西大王廟, 14 (n. 88); to King Wu-chu 無諸, 101; of the Noble and Devoted Prince 英烈王廟, 18; of Precious August 寶皇宮, see Paohuang Palace; see also Ancestral Temple

Ten Kingdoms 十國, ix–xii, 87

Teng Prefecture 登州, 76, 77

Tenth century, vii–xii, 33 (n. 205a)

Terrace of the Three Clear Ones 三清臺, 99

Textiles, see Cloth

"Third Gentleman of the White Horse" 白馬三郎, 14

Three Clear Ones 三清臺, 99 (n. 600, 602)

"Three Dragons" 三龍, 13

Ti-tsang t'ung-wen Temple 地藏通文寺, 85

Tiao-lung River 釣龍江, 7 (n. 37)

T'ien-ch'i Village 玷琦里, 100

T'ien-men-tung 天門冬, 67

T'ien-te t'ung-pao 天德通寶, 74

Tiger, 5

Tiger, Compendium 虎薈, 5

Timber, 67 (n. 395)

Tin, 97 (n. 587)

T'ing Prefecture 汀州, 12, 14, 29, 35, 46,

49, 50, 51, 54, 55, 56, 60, 61, 62, 64 (n. 377), 66, 68, 69, 79 (n. 480), 84

Titles, official, sale of, 72 ; posthumous, 37 (n. 227), 39 ; *see also* Imperial title

" Titular Minister " 同中書門下平章事, 27, 33, 36, 47, 50, 53, 55, 57, 60 (n. 355), 94, 95

T'o-chuang 陁莊 (place), 46

Toba Emperors, 43 (n. 267)

Tokiwa Daijō 常盤大定, 15 (n. 99), 92 (n. 558), 93 (n. 567), 94 (n. 573), 95 (n. 577)

Tombs, 84 ; *see also* Grave

Topography, 6, 76

Tortoise, auspicious, 107 ; carapaces, 68 ; shell, 68

Torture, instruments, of, 17, 19, 40, 71

Trade, *see* Commerce

Travel, *see* Overland travel, Sea voyages

Traveling Palace of the Eastern Sacred Mountain 東嶽行宮, 81

" Treasure-beckoning Secretary " 招寶侍郎, 78

Trees, in omen, 108–109 ; *see also* names of individual trees

Tribute, 34, 35 (n. 214), 39, 45, 47, 59, 63, 63 (n. 373), 64 (n. 377), 65, 66, 67 (n. 398), 68, 68 (n. 416, 417), 69 (n. 421, 425, 431–33), 71, 73, 76, 77

True-ones of the Grotto, First-born of the 洞眞先生, 98

*Tsai-hsiang* 宰相, 27 (n. 175)

Ts'ai Chung-hsing 蔡仲興, 76

Ts'ai Hsiang 蔡襄, 64, 67, 74 (n. 452)

Ts'ai Prefecture 蔡州, 31

Ts'ai Shou-meng 蔡守蒙, 72

Tsang Hsün 臧循, 56, 76

*Ts'e-fu yuan-kuei* 冊府元龜, on tribute missions, 63 (n. 373)

Tse-t'ien 則天, T'ang 唐 empress, 24 (n. 158)

*Tso chuan* 左傳, 44 (n. 269)

Tsu Ch'üan-en 祖全恩, 57

Ts'ui 崔, Lady *née*, 17, 103

Ts'ui Tao-jung 崔道融, 89

*Tu* 都 " division (of imperial guards) ", 24 (n. 158)

Tu Chin 杜進, 55

Tu Han-ch'eng 杜漢崇, 48

Tu of Ts'ai 蔡度, 52 (n. 316)

Tuan-yang 端陽 festival, 10

Tung 董, Lady *née*, 13 (n. 80a)

Tung Ssu-an 董思安, 54, 55, 58, 60, 62, 62 (n. 366)

Tung-ch'ing Gate 東青門, 9

Tung-hua Palace 東華宮, 81, 83

*T'ung chung-shu men-hsia p'ing-chang-shih* 同中書門下平章事, 27 (n. 175)

T'ung-an, Princess of 同安公主, 95

*T'ung*-bark fans 桐皮扇子, 68, (n. 418)

Tzu-ch'en Gate 紫宸門, 8, 9

*Tzu-ch'eng* 子城, 6, 11

*Tzu-chih t'ung-chien* 資治通鑑, xi, 120

*Tzu-ts'ai* 紫菜, 67 (n. 398)

Tzu-wei Palace 紫微宮, 81 ; a Taoist edifice, 99

Under-Secretary of State 中書舍人, 45 (n. 278)

Upright Unity, First-born of 正一先生, 98, 98 (n. 594)

" Vase aromatic " 瓶香, 66 (n. 384)

Vegetables, 67 ; tax on, 72, 73

Vice-Keeper of the Seal 門下侍郎, 39, 57

Vice-Legate 節度副使, 94

Vice-Minister of State for the Left 尙書左僕射, 39

Vice-Minister of State for the Right 尙書右僕射, 39

Vice-Secretary of State 中書侍郎, 39, 47, 51

Vietnam 越南, *see* Annam

Virtue, as criterion of right to own magic staff, 104 ; as index of rule, 53 ; as motivating divine aid, 103 ; *see also* Morality

" Virtuous Consort " 德妃, 20 (n. 138)

Wall, of Wang Yen-cheng 王延政, near T'ing Prefecture 汀州, 84

Wan Chen 萬震, 66 (n. 390)

Wan-an 萬安 (town), 21 (n. 147)

Wan-sui Temple 萬歲寺, 86

Wang 王, Lady *née*, 94

Wang Ch'ang 王昶, *see* Wang Chi-p'eng

Wang Ch'ao 王潮, 13, 14, 31–33, 92, 101, 103, 104, 105, 106, 107, 107 (n. 646), 109 (n. 654)

Wang Chi-ch'ang 王繼昌, 29, 57, 58, 59 (n. 352)

Wang Chi-ch'eng 王繼成, 55, 55 (n. 335), 61

Wang Chi-ch'ien 王繼濟, 94

Wang Chi-ch'iung 王繼瓊, 83

Wang Chi-hsiung 王繼雄, 7, 38

Wang Chi-hsün 王繼勳, 28, 55, 55 (n. 334, 335), 61, 89, 96

Wang Chi-jou 王繼柔, 26

Wang Chi-kung 王繼恭, x, 44, 44 (n. 275), 45, 45 (n. 277), 46, 47

Wang Chi-lun 王繼倫, 38

Wang Chi-lung 王繼隆, 23

Wang Chi-p'eng 王繼鵬, 8, 21, 22–25, 26, 39, 40, 42–46, 47, 48, 71, 72, 80, 80 (n. 484), 81, 83, 85, 91, 93, 97, 98, 98 (n. 594), 99 (n. 604), 100, 103, 104, 107, 108

Wang Chi-sheng 王繼昇, 38

Wang Chi-t'ao 王繼韜, 21, 42

Wang Chi-t'u 王繼圖, 19

Wang Chi-yeh 王繼業, 46, 49, 50

Wang Chi'-yen 王繼嚴, 43, 45, 50

Wang Chi-yung 王繼㽞, 45

Wang Chi-yü 王繼裕, 45 (n. 281); see also Wang Chi-yen

Wang Chi-yüan 王繼源, 94

Wang Chien 王建 (in Korea), 44 (n. 271)

Wang Chien 王建 (in Shu), ix

Wang Chien-feng 王建封, 60

Wang Chung-shum 王忠順, 54, 55, 58, 60

Wang Hsi 王曦, see Wang Yen-hsi

Wang Hsiang 王想, 13 (n. 83)

Wang Hsü 王緒, 31, 32, 101, 103

Wang Jen 王恁, 13 (n. 80a)

Wang Jen-ta 王仁達, 7, 19–20, 38

Wang Lin 王璘, see Wang Yen-chün

Wang Pa 王霸, 107, 107 (n. 646)

Wang Shen-chih 王審知, 6, 9, 10, 11, 12, 12 (n. 75), 13, 14–16, 17, 18, 24, 25, 27, 28, 29, 31, 32, 33–35, 33 (n. 203, 206), 36, 37, 39, 39 (n. 244), 51 (n. 307), 53, 58 (n. 347a), 67 (n. 398), 70, 71, 74, 76, 78, 78 (n. 470), 82, 83, 84, 84 (n. 515), 85, 85 (n. 519), 87, 88, 91, 92, 95 (n. 577), 100, 101, 102, 103, 103 (n. 623), 104, 105, 106

Wang Shen-kuei 王審郎, 13, 16, 31, 33, 34, 34 (n. 210), 60 (n. 359), 83

Wang T'an 王倓, 25, 87 (n. 533), 103, 104

Wang Ya-ch'eng 王亞澄, 27, 50, 53, 94

Wang Yen-cheng 王延政, 7, 8, 10, 11, 26, 28–29, 39, 48, 49, 50, 51, 52, 53, 54, 55, 55 (n. 334), 56, 57, 57 (n. 342), 58, 59, 60, 73, 74, 75, 83, 84, 95, 101, 105

Wang Yen-chün 王延政, 6, 9, 10, 11, 16, 17–21, 23, 24, 34, 35 (n. 218), 36, 37–42, 39 (n. 244), 42 (n. 260), 44, 71, 74, 78, 80, 81, 82, 83, 84, 85, 86, 91, 93, 94, 96–98, 101, 103, 106

Wang Yen-feng 王延豐, 33 (n. 201)

Wang Yen-han 王延翰, 6, 8, 10, 16–17, 35–37, 71, 83, 103

Wang Yen-hsi 王延羲, 7, 10, 18 (n. 121), 23, 25–27, 28, 29, 46–53, 46 (n. 284), 58, 72, 73, 75, 76, 82, 83, 86 (n. 525), 89, 93–95, 100, 103, 104, 105, 106, 108

Wang Yen-hsi 王延喜 (of T'ing Prefecture 汀州), 49, 53

Wang Yen-hsing 王延興, 33 (n. 201)

Wang Yen-hsiu 王延休, 33 (n. 201)

Wang Yen-hung 王延虹, 33 (n. 201)

Wang Yen-i 王延義, mistake for Wang Yen-hsi 王延羲, 53 (n. 319)

Wang Yen-mei 王延美, 35

Wang Yen-pin 王延彬, 11, 16, 34, 34 (n. 210), 35, 78, 87, 89, 92–93, 106

Wang Yen-ping 王延稟, 6, 7, 9, 10, 11, 16, 18, 19, 21, 36, 37, 37 (n. 232), 38, 39, 49 (n. 293), 103

Wang Yen-ssu 王延嗣, 16, 92

Wang Yen-tsung 王延宗, 40

Wang Yen-wang 王延望, 45, 99, 108

Wang Yen-wu 王延武, 45, 99, 108

Wang Yü 王于, 119

Warehouse Commissioner 如京使, 40

Warfare, 34 (n. 207), 50, 56 (338)

Warships, 7, 11, 38; see also Commander of Galleons, Fleets

Watchtower, 82

Water lily, 4

Water-peppers, 10

Wax insect, 69

Wax myrtle, 4

"Wax tea" 蠟茶, 64 (n. 377)

Wei 危 family, of Shao-wu 邵武, 84

Wei Ts'ung-liang 魏從朗, 52 (n. 318)

Wei Ying-ch'i 魏應麒, ix, 90–91

"Weight-carriers" 耐重兒, 86 (n. 525)

Wei-wu Army 威武軍, 28, 32, 33, 35, 44, 46, 49, 50, 54, 59, 62, 80, 92

Wei-yang Palace 未央宮, 81 (n. 491)

Well, Smelted Cinnabar 鍊丹井, 107; of I 義井, 93

Wen Prefecture 溫州, 77

Wen Ti 文帝 (Han 漢 emperor), 82 (n. 497)

Wen-chü 文炬 (priest), 96

Wen-ming Pavilion 文明殿, 81

Wen-te Pavilion 文德殿, 81

Weng Ch'eng-tsan 翁承贊, 33 (n. 206), 88

West Gate 西門, 6, 7, 8, 38

West Lake 西池, 7 (n. 35), 9, 10, 80, 81 (n. 490)

Western Asia, 66

White, as evil-omened, 106 (n. 638); deer, 106; dragon, 99; mourning, 42 (n. 260); portentous smoke, 108; sparrow, 106; tortoise, 107

Willow, 3

Wine, as narcotic, 46; special bowel for, 26

Wine-cups, 26 (n. 170)

Wine-drinking, 16, 21, 23, 24, 26–27, 52, 53 (n. 319), 54, 82

"Winter-melon slices", name of wine-cups, 26 (n. 170)

Wizards, see Shamans

Women, dismissal of from palace, 27, 74; procurement of, 17, 27 (n. 178), 36, 73; see also Singing Girls, Slaves, female

Woods, aromatic, 71; see also Aromatics

Wooden pagoda, of T'ang 唐, 94 (n. 573)

Wu 吳, Ancient kingdom of, 80 (n. 488)

Wu 吳 (dynasty), 18 (n. 122), 34, 40, 41, 41 (n. 256), 49, 52, 71, 77, 77 (n. 467), 84 (n. 515)

Wu Ch'eng-i 吳成義, 54, 56, 58

Wu Hsing-chen 吳行貞, 48, 49

Wu Hsü 吳勗, 19 (n. 129), 39, 98

Wu Jen-ch'en 吳任臣, x, xi

Wu Kuang 吳光, 40, 71

Wu Tai ch'un-ch'iu 五代春秋, 46 (n. 283), 53 (n. 219)

Wu Tai wen-hsueh 五代文學, 87 (n. 533)

Wu Tai shih 五代史, x, 57 (n. 342)

Wu Tai shih-pu 五代史補, 35 (n. 218), 107, 107 (n. 646), 109 (n. 654)

Wu Tai shih-hua 五代詩話, 88, (n. 535)

Wu Tsung 武宗 (T'ang 唐 Emperor), 92

Wu-an 吳安, Prince of, 102

Wu-chu 無諸 (King of Min-yüeh 閩越), 9, 36 (n. 221), 101 (n. 609)

Wu-hou ching-kuang t'a 無垢淨光塔, 94

Wu-i 无逸 (name of monk), 94 (n. 572)

Wu-i Mountains 武夷山, 64, 100

Wu-kuo ku-shih 五國故事, 28 (n. 182), 71 (n. 440), 120

Wu-lien-tzu 五斂子, 67 (n. 405)

Wu-ning Hou 武寧侯, 101

Wu-shih Mountain 烏石山, 85, 101

Wu-yüeh 吳越, 5 (n. 27), 7 (n. 40), 8, 25, 33 (n. 206), 34, 38, 39, 40, 41, 43, 48, 49, 52, 56, 59, 60, 61, 62, 75, 77, 77 (n. 467), 86, 104

Yam, 4

Yang 楊, surname of Wu 吳 royal family, 109

Yang 楊 family, rulers of Wu 吳, 77; see also Wu

Yang Hsing-mi 楊行密, 41

Yang I 楊沂, 87 (n. 533)

Yang I-feng 楊沂豐, 50

Yang Jen-ch'uan 仰仁詮, 48, 49

Yang Kuei-fei 楊貴妃, 20

Yang Lung-yen 楊隆演, 34

Yang Meng 楊濛, 41

Yang Prefecture 楊州, 34

Yang Ssu-kung 楊思恭, 30, 51, 57, 58, 58 (n. 346), 60 (n. 358), 73

Yang the Flayer, see Flayer, Yang Ssu-kung

Yang Wo 楊渥, 34

Yang Yin-shen 楊蔭深, 87 (n. 533), 89

Yang-chou 揚州, 95 (n. 575)

Yung-t'ao 羊桃, 67 (n. 405)

Yangtze River 揚子江, 5, 62, 70

Yao Feng 姚鳳, 57

Yeh Ch'iao 葉翹, 22, 43, 44, 48, 89, 100

Yellow, color of auspicious dragon, 106 (n. 639)

Yellow Point 黃崎, 9, 102, 103

Yellowbank Mountain 黃岸山, 23

Yen-p'ing 延平 (town), 16, 49 (n. 297), 51, 60 (n. 358), 64 (n. 377), 73, 79 (n. 478), 105

Yin 殷, Empire of, 28, 55, 56, 101; declared, 51; name changed to Min, 57; name of on coin, 75 (n. 457); see also Wang Yen-cheng

Yin Chu 尹洙, 46 (n. 283)

Ying-t'ien Gate 應天門, 8, 9

Yu-ch'i 尤溪 (District), 34 (n. 207), 50, 51 (n. 307), 54, 55, 63, 79 (n. 478)

Yu-hsien 游仙 (Distaict), 79 (n. 478)

Yu-k'ou 尤口, 50, 51, 51 (n. 307), 52, 105

Yung Lung 永隆 (reign title), 25 (n. 163)

Yung Prefecture 鏞, 56; created, 51

Yung-an Army 永安軍, 61; see also Chien Prefecture

Yung-ch'un 永春 (District), 85

Yung-lung t'ung-pao 永隆通寶, 75

Yung-p'ing 永平 (town), 49

Yung-t'ai 永泰 (town), 44

Yü 余, Lady née, 94

Yü Ching 于兢, 15 (n. 99)

Yü Hsiung 虞雄, 15 (n. 103)

Yü T'ing-ying 儵廷英, 27 (n. 178), 73

Yüan 元 dynasty, 81

Yuan-ho chun-hsien chih 元和郡縣志, 79 (n. 476, 477)

Yüan-miao Kuan 元妙觀, 81, 81 (n. 494)

Yüan-shih t'ien-tsun t'ai-shang lao-chun 元始天尊太上老君, 41; see also Lao-tzu

Yüan-tsung Division, Commander of 元從都指揮使, 58, 58 (n. 347a); see also Li Jen-ta, Household Division

Yü-shan Chiao-jen chi 玉山樵人集, 88

Yü-ti chi-sheng 輿地紀勝, 5, 81, 84, 120

Yüeh 粵, ancient South China, in astrology, 95 (n. 575); Great Yüeh 大越, 34 (n. 209); Lady of the State of 越國夫人, 94

Yüeh-chleng 月城, 6

Yüeh-chün 月君, Lady, 100 (n. 604)

Yün-t'ai shih-chung 雲臺侍中, 16

Zen 禪 priests, 93, 65–96; see also Hui-leng

# Date  Due

| MAY 31 86 | | | |
|---|---|---|---|
| | | | |
| | | | |
| | | | |
| | | | |
| | | | |
| | | | |
| | | | |
| | | | |
| | | | |
| | | | |
| | | | |
| | | | |
| | | | |
| | | | |
| | | | |